WASTELAND

BOOK 04

DOG TRIBE

WASTELAND

BOOK 04

DOG TRIBE

WRITTEN BY ANTONY JOHNSTON
DRAWN BY CHRISTOPHER MITTEN

COVER ART BY BEN TEMPLESMITH

LETTERED BY DOUGLAS E. SHERWOOD
EDITED BY JAMES LUCAS JONES
DESIGNED BY ANTONY JOHNSTON
CREATED BY JOHNSTON & MITTEN

AN ONI PRESS PUBLICATION

PUBLISHER JOE NOZEMACK
EDITOR IN CHIEF JAMES LUCAS JONES
MANAGING EDITOR RANDAL C. JARRELL
MARKETING DIRECTOR CORY CASONI
ART DIRECTOR KEITH WOOD
ASSISTANT EDITOR JILL BEATON
PRODUCTION ASSISTANT DOUGLAS E. SHERWOOD

Oni Press, Inc.
1305 SE Martin Luther King Jr. Blvd, Suite A
Portland, OR 97214
USA
www.onipress.com

www.thebigwet.com

Previously published as issues #21-24 of the Oni Press comic series *Wasteland*.

FIRST EDITION: JUNE 2009
ISBN: 978-1-934964-17-0
1 3 5 7 9 10 8 6 4 2

ONE HUNDRED YEARS AFTER THE BIG WET.
SOMEWHERE IN AMERICA...

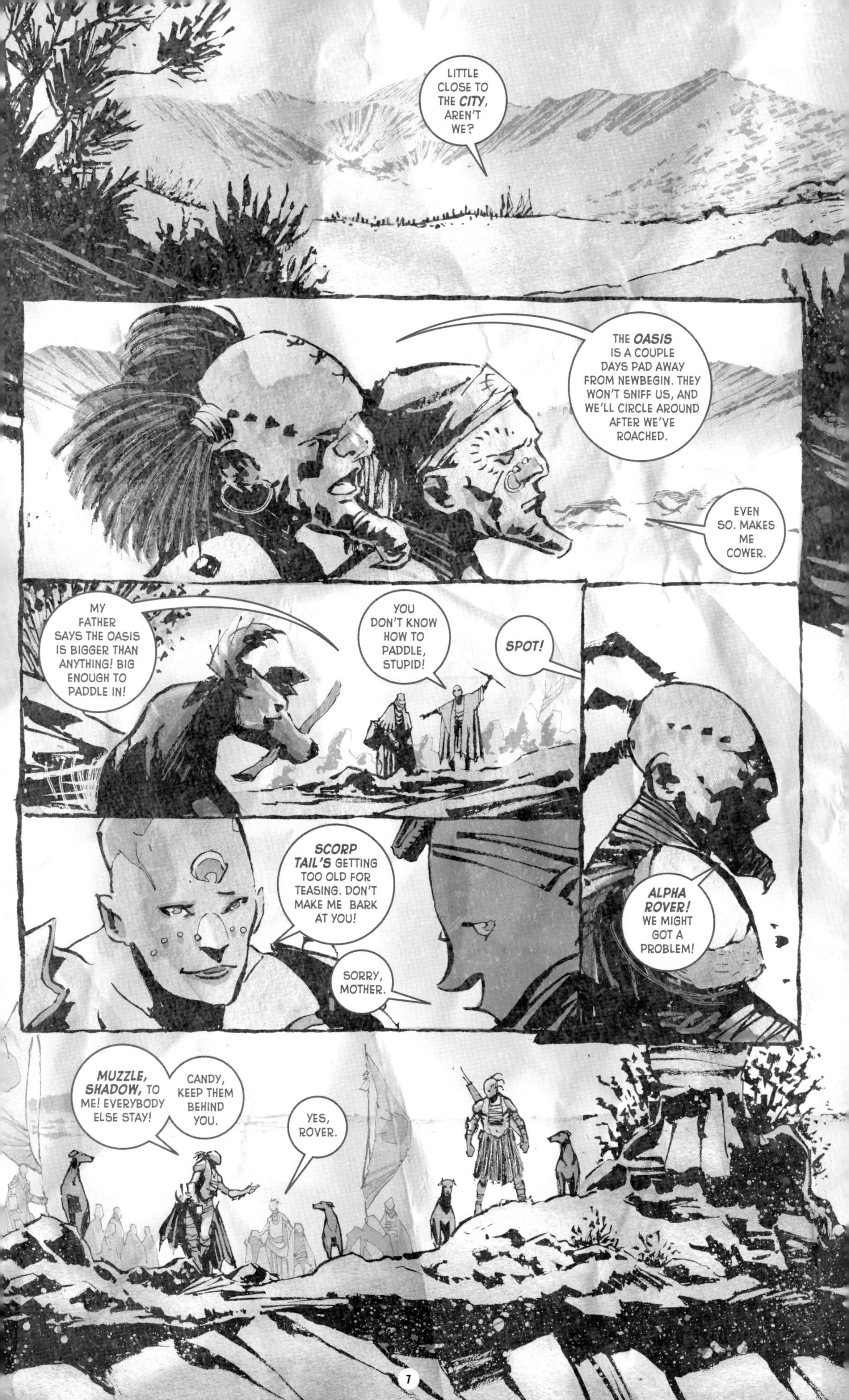
LITTLE CLOSE TO THE CITY, AREN'T WE?
THE OASIS IS A COUPLE DAYS PAD AWAY FROM NEWBEGIN. THEY WON'T SNIFF US, AND WE'LL CIRCLE AROUND AFTER WE'VE ROACHED.
EVEN SO. MAKES ME COWER.
MY FATHER SAYS THE OASIS IS BIGGER THAN ANYTHING! BIG ENOUGH TO PADDLE IN!
YOU DON'T KNOW HOW TO PADDLE, STUPID!
SPOT!
SCORP TAIL'S GETTING TOO OLD FOR TEASING. DON'T MAKE ME BARK AT YOU!
SORRY, MOTHER.
ALPHA ROVER! WE MIGHT GOT A PROBLEM!
MUZZLE, SHADOW, TO ME! EVERYBODY ELSE STAY!
CANDY, KEEP THEM BEHIND YOU.
YES, ROVER.

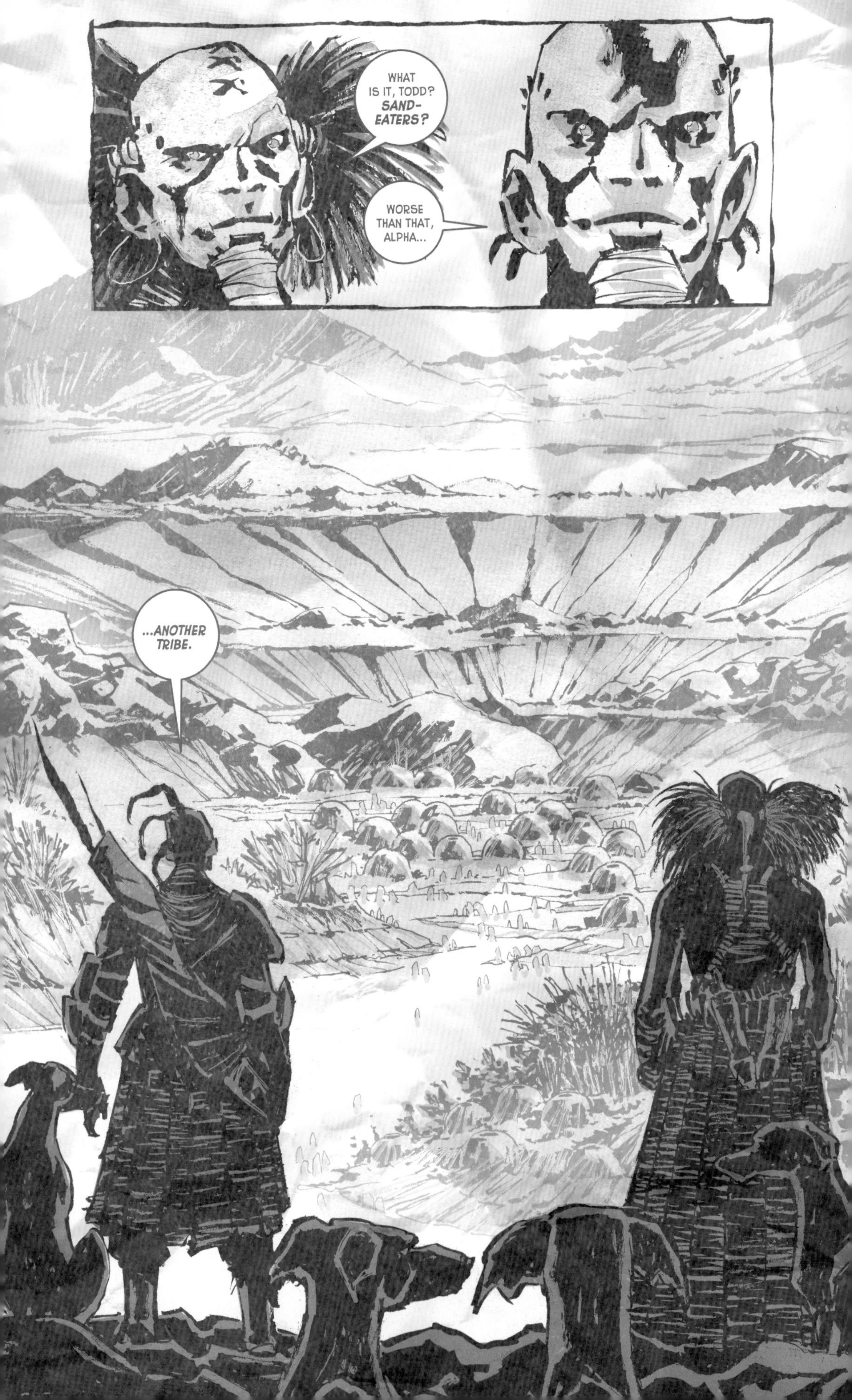

WHAT IS IT, TODD? SANDEATERS?
WORSE THAN THAT, ALPHA...
...ANOTHER TRIBE.

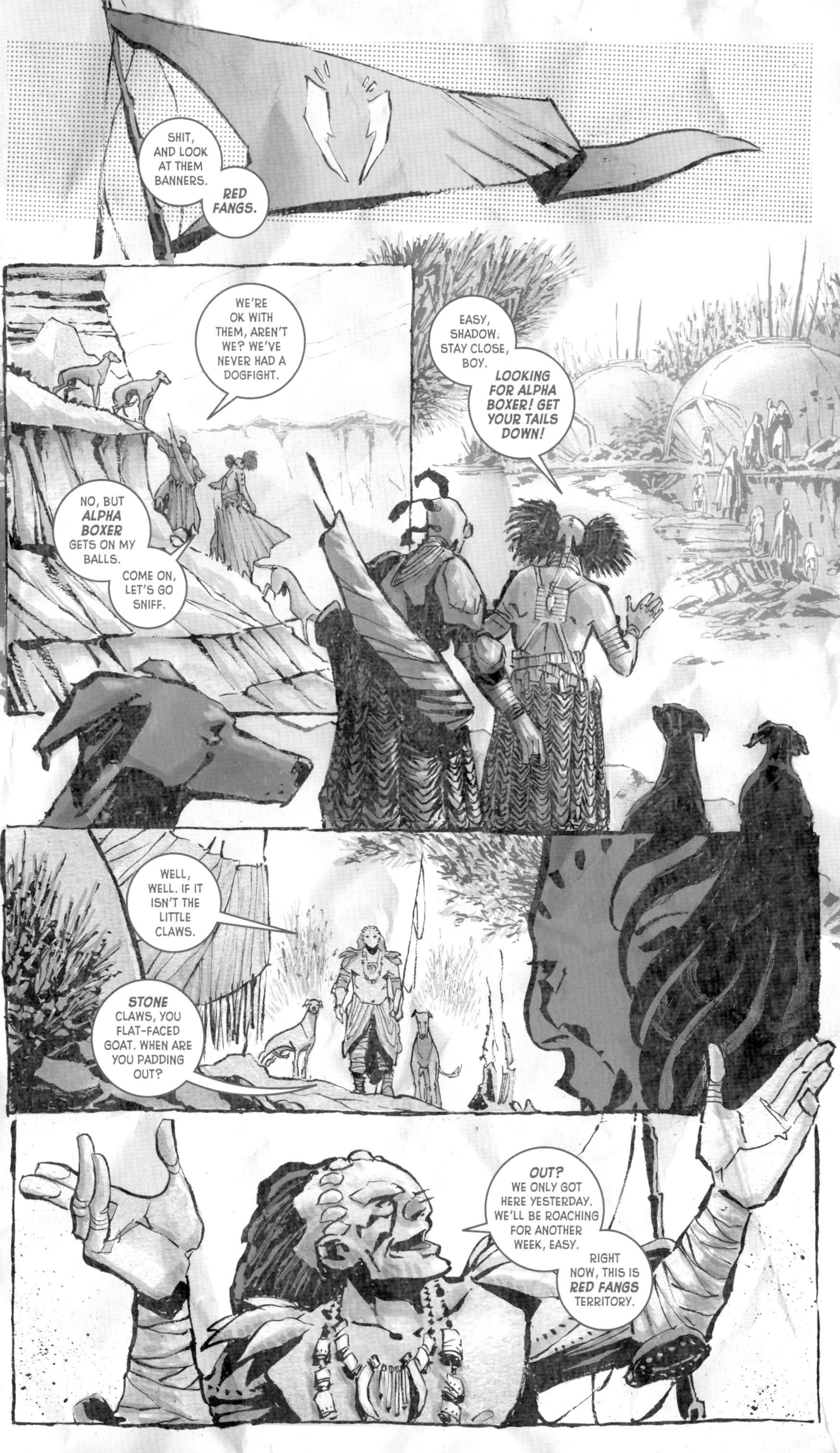
SHIT, AND LOOK AT THEM BANNERS.
RED FANGS.
WE'RE OK WITH THEM, AREN'T WE? WE'VE NEVER HAD A DOGFIGHT.
NO, BUT ALPHA BOXER GETS ON MY BALLS.
COME ON, LET'S GO SNIFF.
EASY, SHADOW. STAY CLOSE, BOY.
LOOKING FOR ALPHA BOXER! GET YOUR TAILS DOWN!
WELL, WELL. IF IT ISN'T THE LITTLE CLAWS.
STONE CLAWS, YOU FLAT-FACED GOAT. WHEN ARE YOU PADDING OUT?
OUT? WE ONLY GOT HERE YESTERDAY. WE'LL BE ROACHING FOR ANOTHER WEEK, EASY.
RIGHT NOW, THIS IS RED FANGS TERRITORY.

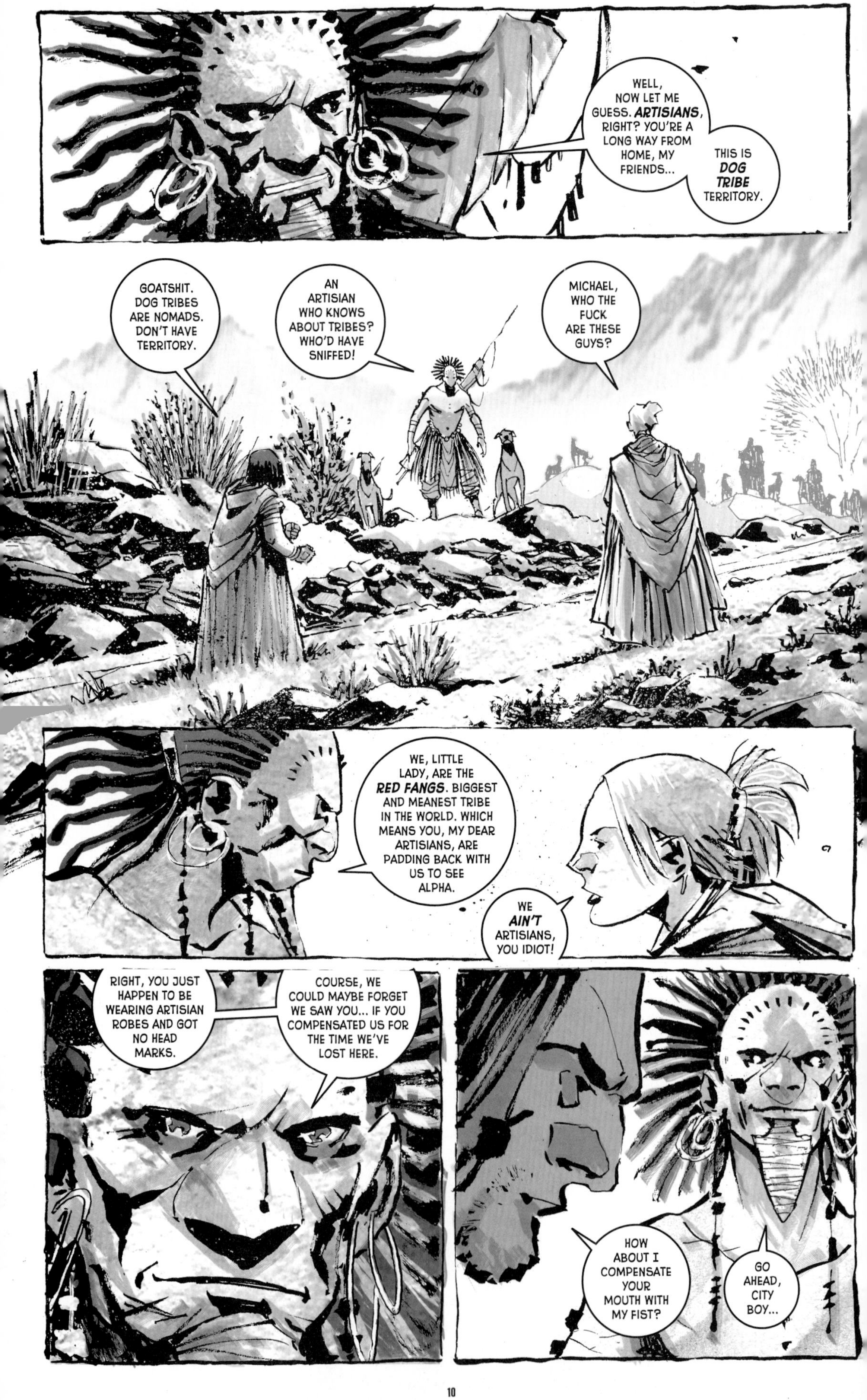

WELL, NOW LET ME GUESS. ARTISIANS, RIGHT? YOU'RE A LONG WAY FROM HOME, MY FRIENDS...
THIS IS DOG TRIBE TERRITORY.
GOATSHIT. DOG TRIBES ARE NOMADS. DON'T HAVE TERRITORY.
AN ARTISIAN WHO KNOWS ABOUT TRIBES? WHO'D HAVE SNIFFED!
MICHAEL, WHO THE FUCK ARE THESE GUYS?
WE, LITTLE LADY, ARE THE RED FANGS. BIGGEST AND MEANEST TRIBE IN THE WORLD. WHICH MEANS YOU, MY DEAR ARTISIANS, ARE PADDING BACK WITH US TO SEE ALPHA.
WE AIN'T ARTISIANS, YOU IDIOT!
RIGHT, YOU JUST HAPPEN TO BE WEARING ARTISIAN ROBES AND GOT NO HEAD MARKS.
COURSE, WE COULD MAYBE FORGET WE SAW YOU... IF YOU COMPENSATED US FOR THE TIME WE'VE LOST HERE.
HOW ABOUT I COMPENSATE YOUR MOUTH WITH MY FIST?
GO AHEAD, CITY BOY...

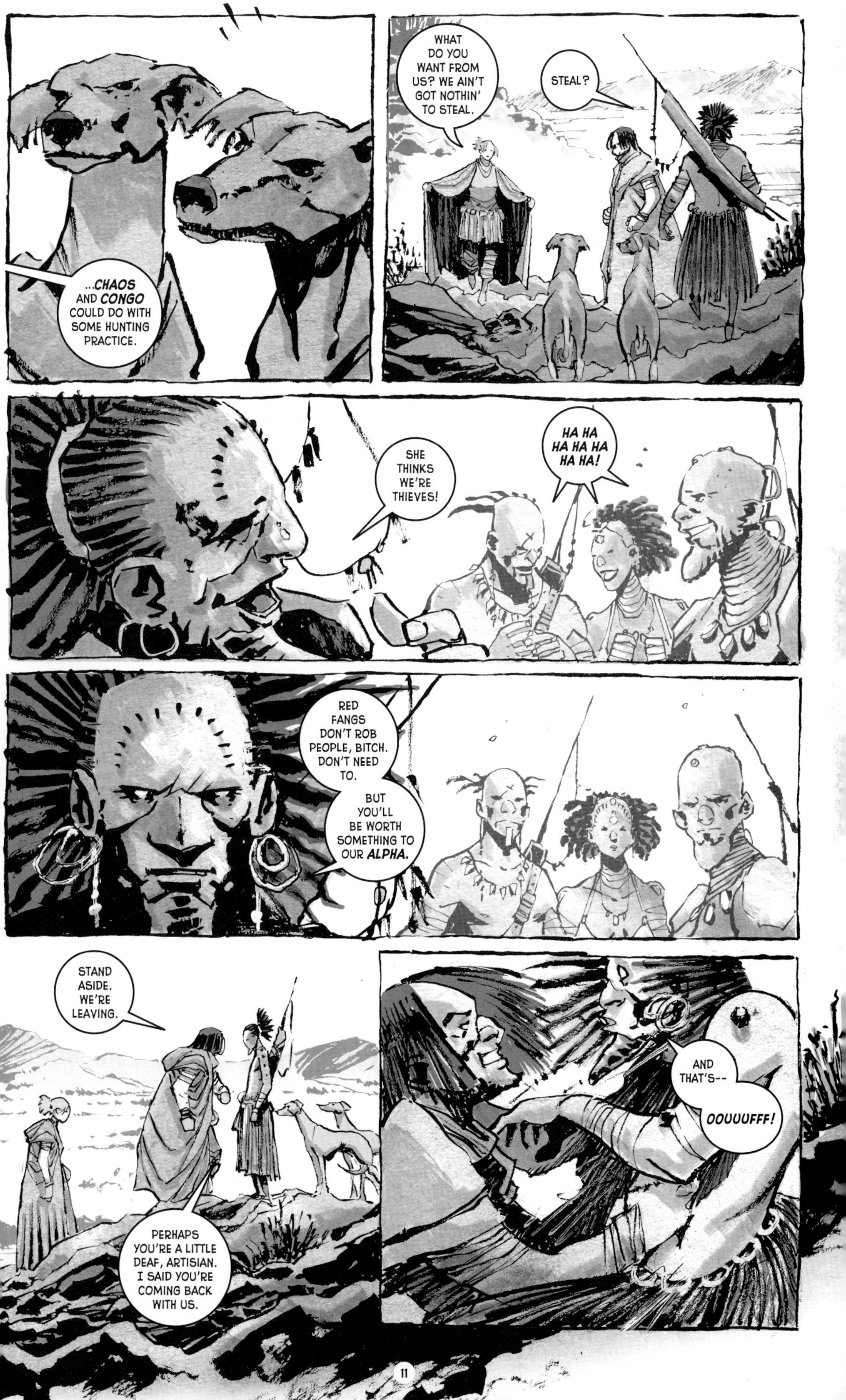
...CHAOS AND CONGO COULD DO WITH SOME HUNTING PRACTICE.
WHAT DO YOU WANT FROM US? WE AIN'T GOT NOTHIN' TO STEAL.
STEAL?
SHE THINKS WE'RE THIEVES!
HA HA HA HA HA HA HA!
RED FANGS DON'T ROB PEOPLE, BITCH. DON'T NEED TO.
BUT YOU'LL BE WORTH SOMETHING TO OUR ALPHA.
STAND ASIDE. WE'RE LEAVING.
PERHAPS YOU'RE A LITTLE DEAF, ARTISIAN. I SAID YOU'RE COMING BACK WITH US.
AND THAT'S--
OOUUUFFF!

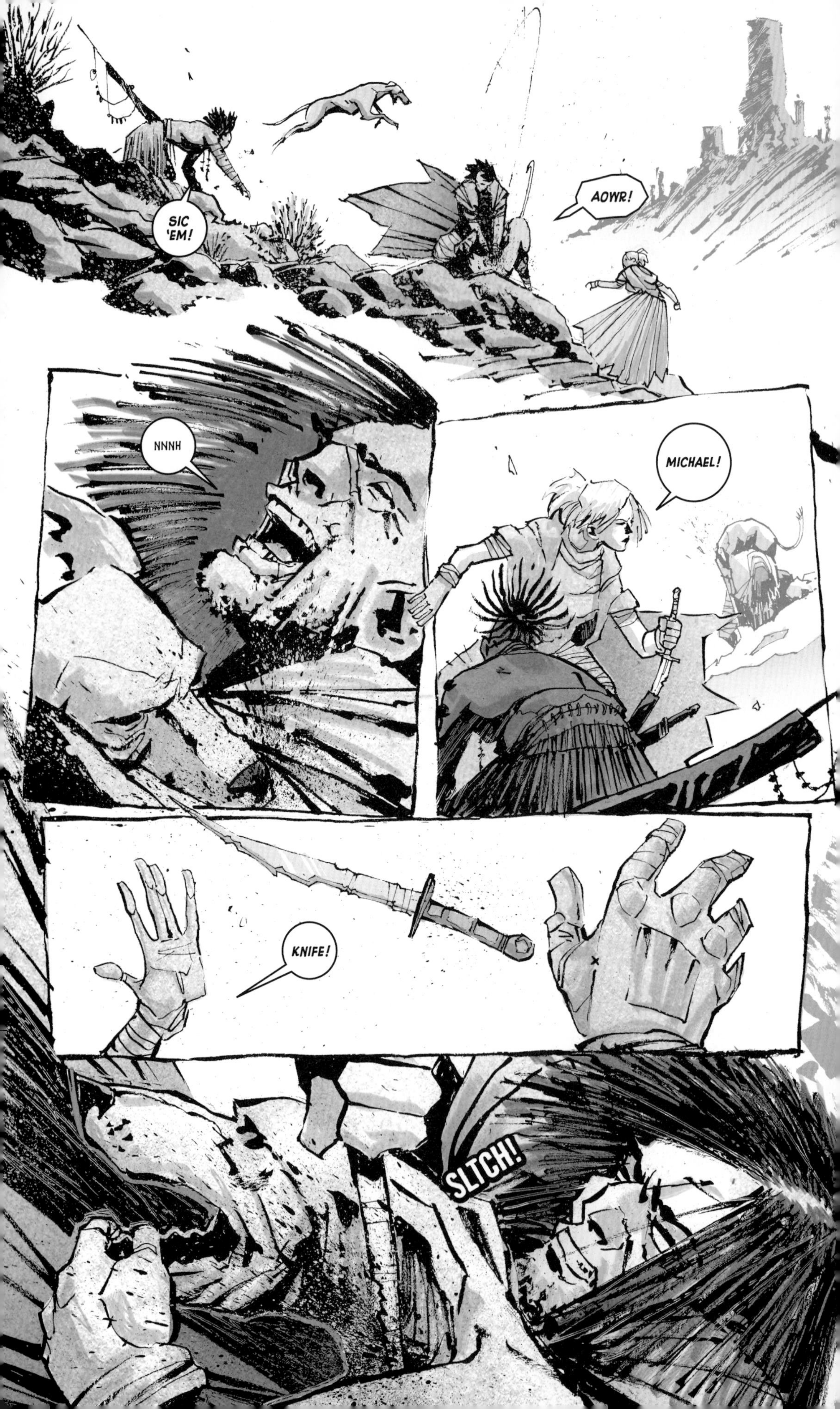
SIC 'EM!
AOWR!
NNNH
MICHAEL!
KNIFE!
SLTCH!

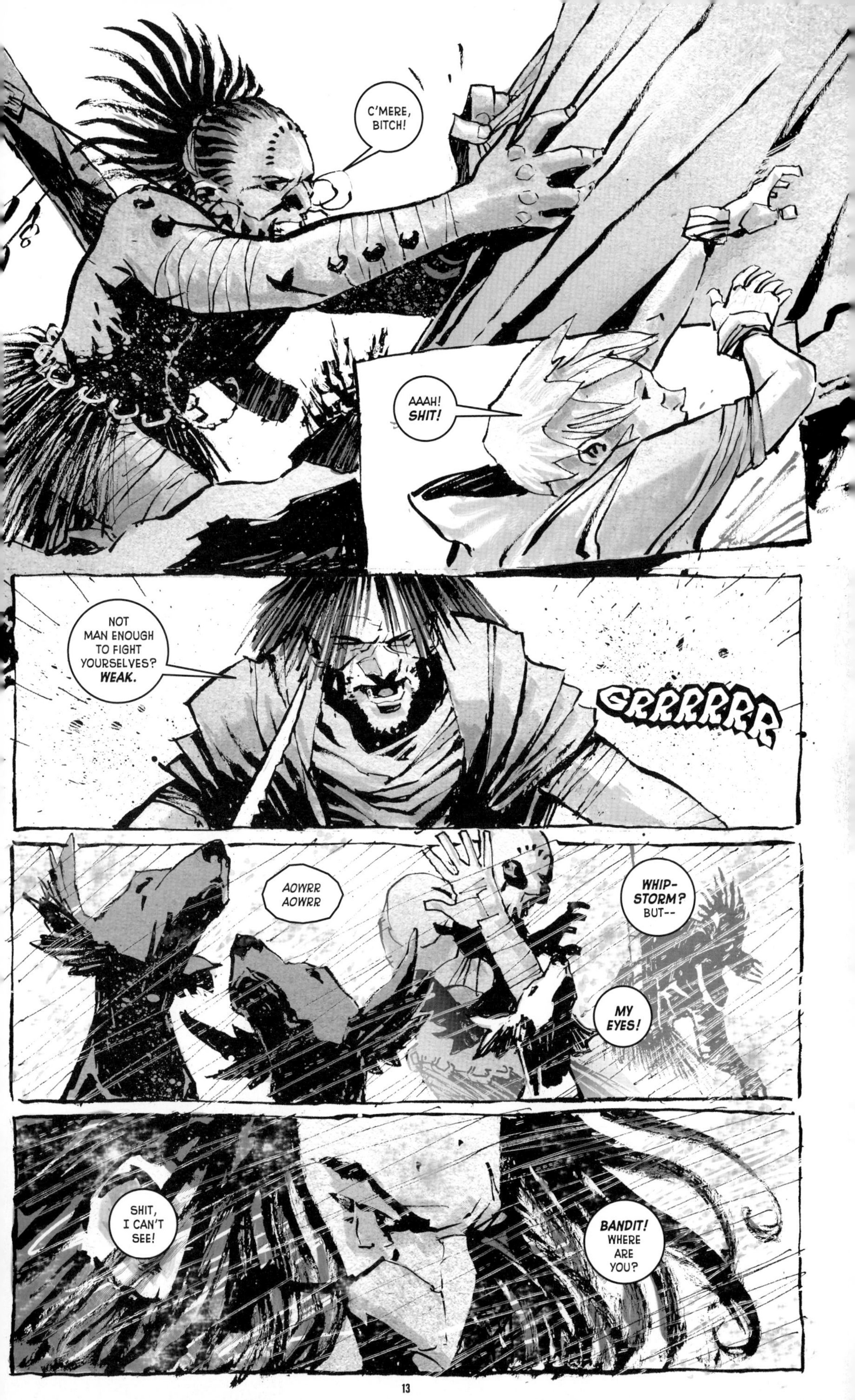

C'MERE, BITCH!
AAAH! SHIT!
NOT MAN ENOUGH TO FIGHT YOURSELVES? WEAK.
GRRRRRR
AOWRR AOWRR
WHIP-STORM? BUT--
MY EYES!
SHIT, I CAN'T SEE!
BANDIT! WHERE ARE YOU?

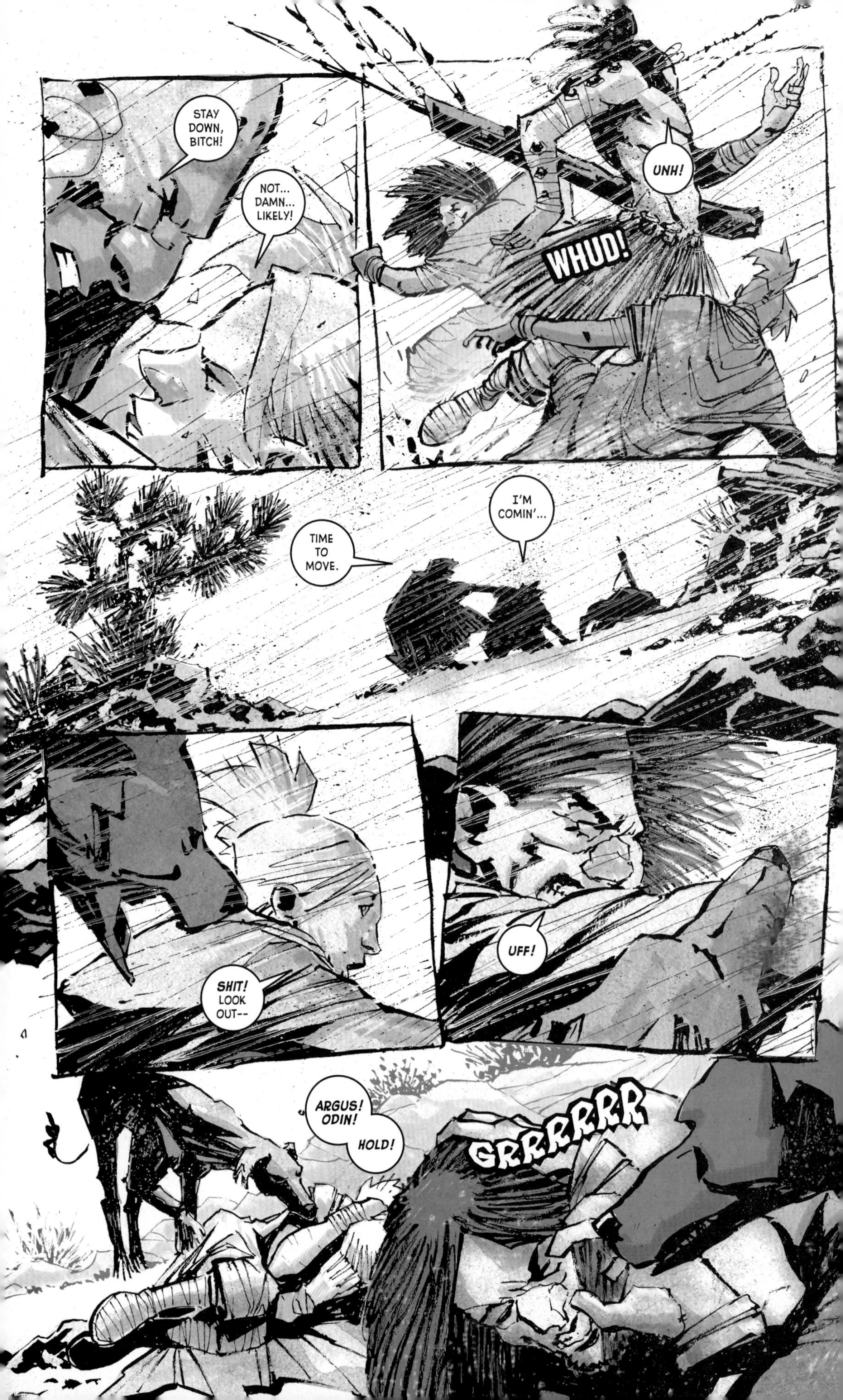
STAY DOWN, BITCH!
NOT... DAMN... LIKELY!
UNH!
WHUD!
TIME TO MOVE.
I'M COMIN'...
SHIT! LOOK OUT--
UFF!
ARGUS! ODIN!
HOLD!
GRRRRRR

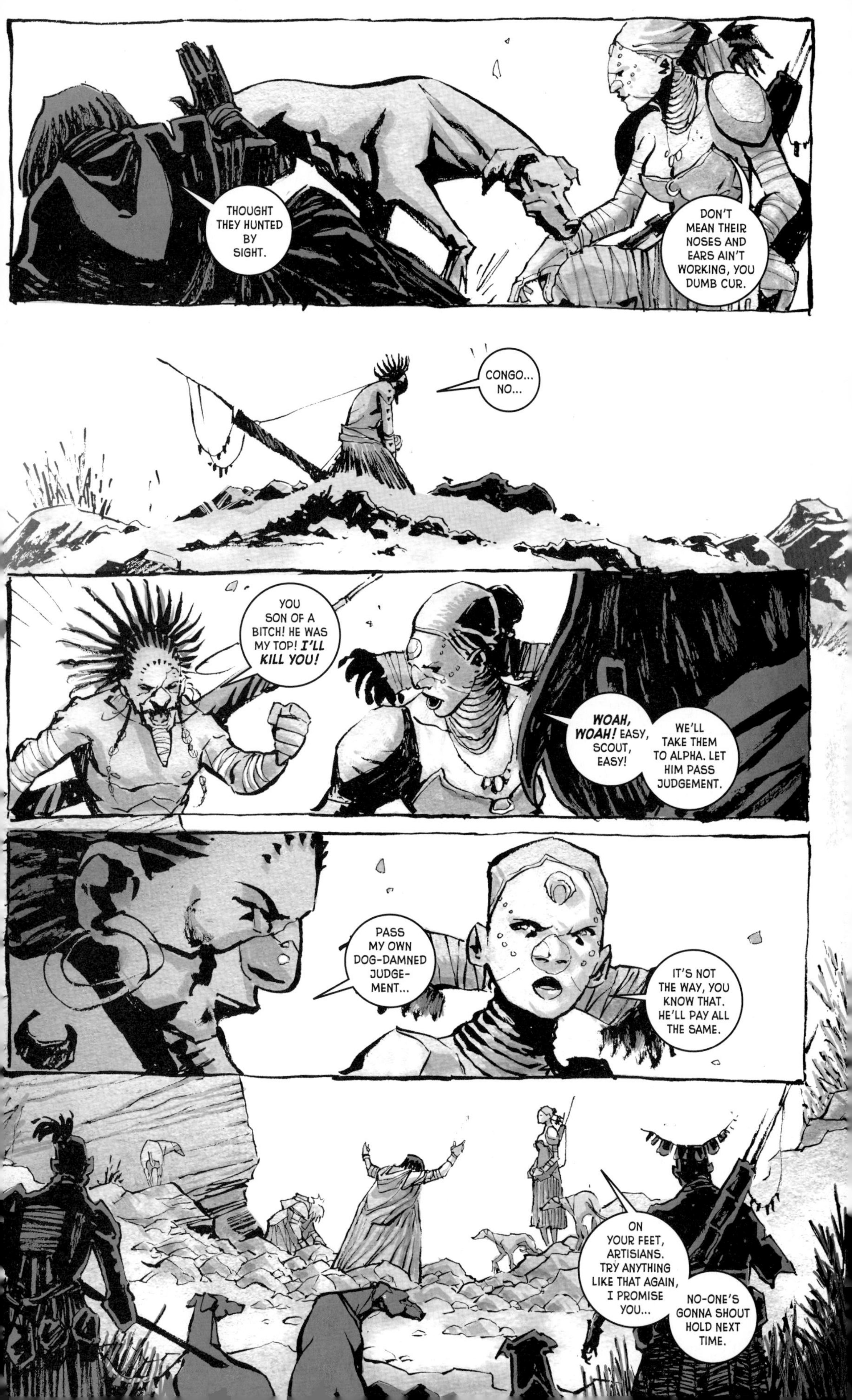
THOUGHT THEY HUNTED BY SIGHT.
DON'T MEAN THEIR NOSES AND EARS AIN'T WORKING, YOU DUMB CUR.
CONGO... NO...
YOU SON OF A BITCH! HE WAS MY TOP! ***I'LL KILL YOU!***
WOAH, WOAH! EASY, SCOUT, EASY!
WE'LL TAKE THEM TO ALPHA. LET HIM PASS JUDGEMENT.
PASS MY OWN DOG-DAMNED JUDGEMENT...
IT'S NOT THE WAY, YOU KNOW THAT. HE'LL PAY ALL THE SAME.
ON YOUR FEET, ARTISIANS. TRY ANYTHING LIKE THAT AGAIN, I PROMISE YOU...
NO-ONE'S GONNA SHOUT HOLD NEXT TIME.

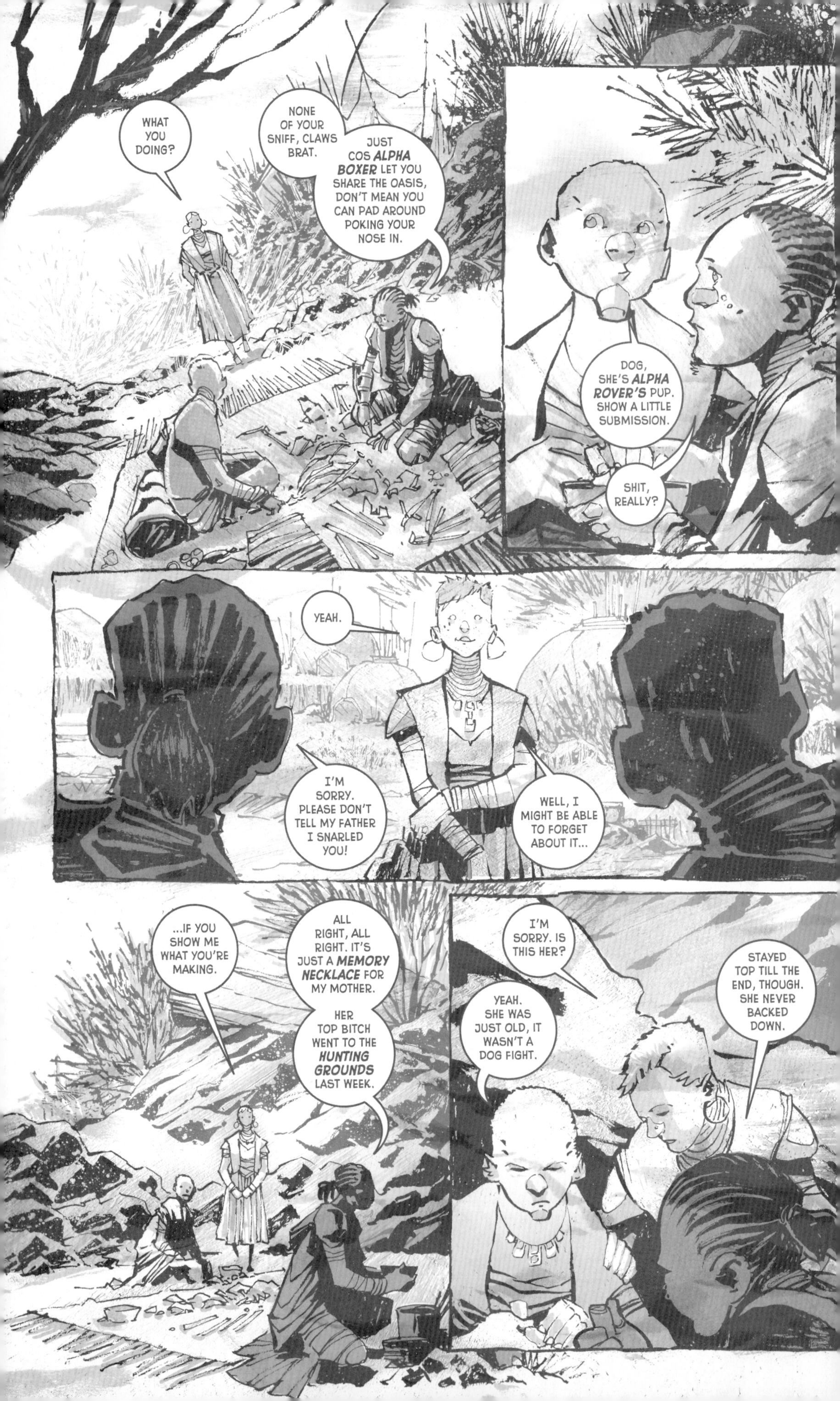
WHAT YOU DOING?
NONE OF YOUR SNIFF, CLAWS BRAT.
JUST COS ALPHA BOXER LET YOU SHARE THE OASIS, DON'T MEAN YOU CAN PAD AROUND POKING YOUR NOSE IN.
DOG, SHE'S ALPHA ROVER'S PUP. SHOW A LITTLE SUBMISSION.
SHIT, REALLY?
YEAH.
I'M SORRY. PLEASE DON'T TELL MY FATHER I SNARLED YOU!
WELL, I MIGHT BE ABLE TO FORGET ABOUT IT...
...IF YOU SHOW ME WHAT YOU'RE MAKING.
ALL RIGHT, ALL RIGHT. IT'S JUST A MEMORY NECKLACE FOR MY MOTHER.
HER TOP BITCH WENT TO THE HUNTING GROUNDS LAST WEEK.
I'M SORRY. IS THIS HER?
YEAH. SHE WAS JUST OLD, IT WASN'T A DOG FIGHT.
STAYED TOP TILL THE END, THOUGH. SHE NEVER BACKED DOWN.

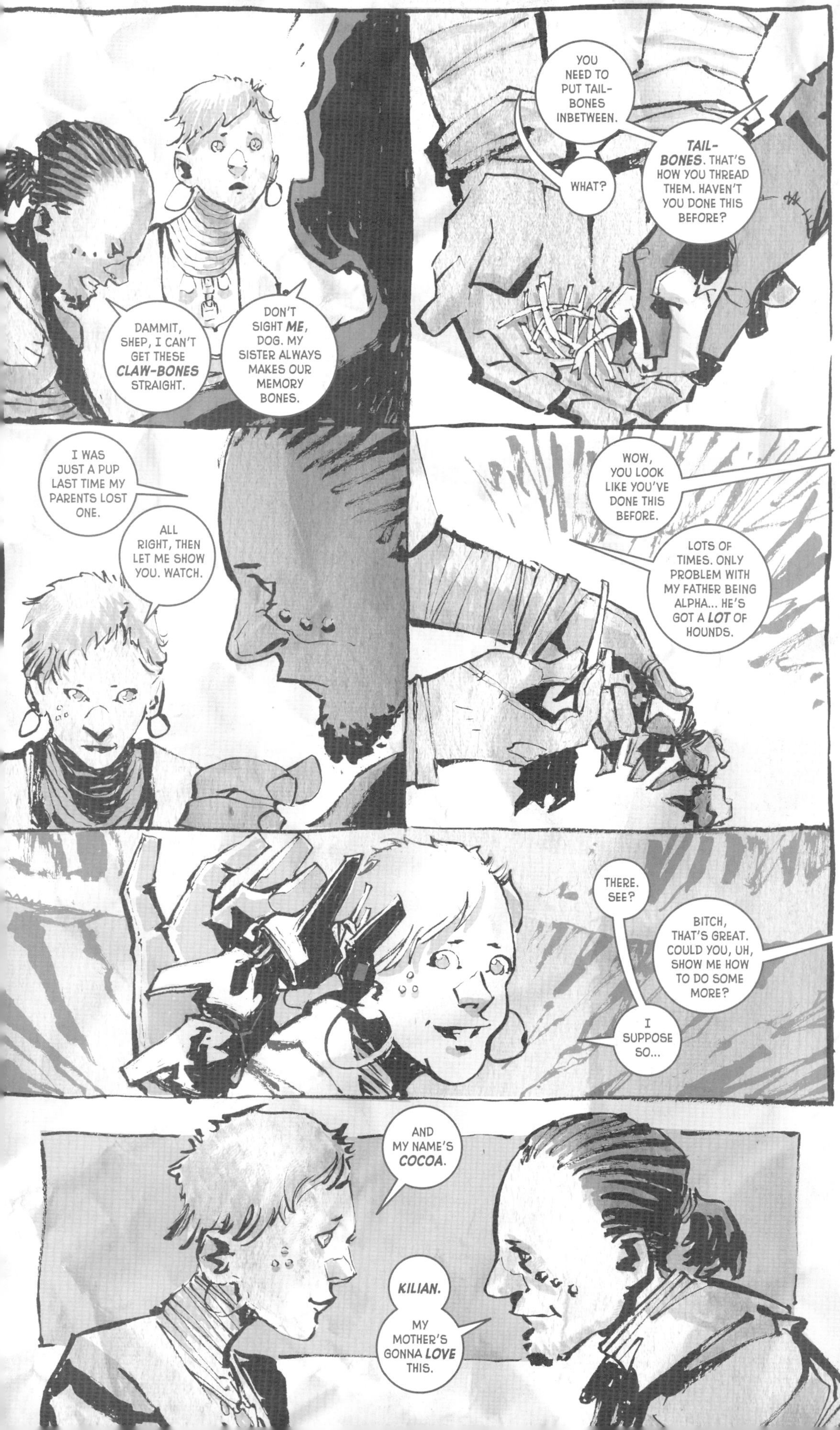
DAMMIT, SHEP, I CAN'T GET THESE CLAW-BONES STRAIGHT.
DON'T SIGHT ME, DOG. MY SISTER ALWAYS MAKES OUR MEMORY BONES.
YOU NEED TO PUT TAIL-BONES INBETWEEN.
WHAT?
TAIL-BONES. THAT'S HOW YOU THREAD THEM. HAVEN'T YOU DONE THIS BEFORE?
I WAS JUST A PUP LAST TIME MY PARENTS LOST ONE.
ALL RIGHT, THEN LET ME SHOW YOU. WATCH.
WOW, YOU LOOK LIKE YOU'VE DONE THIS BEFORE.
LOTS OF TIMES. ONLY PROBLEM WITH MY FATHER BEING ALPHA... HE'S GOT A LOT OF HOUNDS.
THERE. SEE?
BITCH, THAT'S GREAT. COULD YOU, UH, SHOW ME HOW TO DO SOME MORE?
I SUPPOSE SO...
AND MY NAME'S COCOA.
KILIAN.
MY MOTHER'S GONNA LOVE THIS.

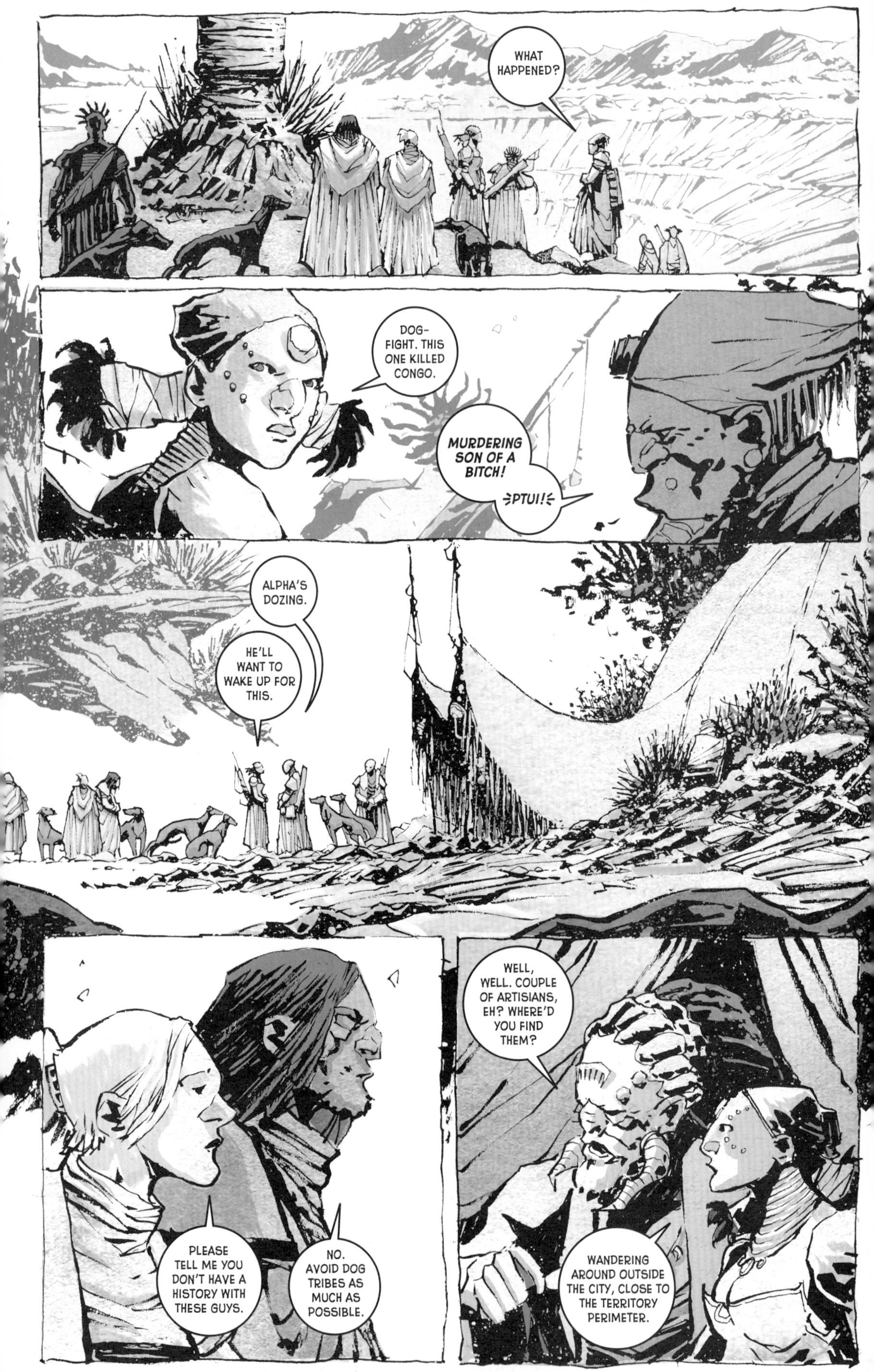
WHAT HAPPENED?
DOG-FIGHT. THIS ONE KILLED CONGO.
MURDERING SON OF A BITCH!
PTUI!
ALPHA'S DOZING.
HE'LL WANT TO WAKE UP FOR THIS.
PLEASE TELL ME YOU DON'T HAVE A HISTORY WITH THESE GUYS.
NO. AVOID DOG TRIBES AS MUCH AS POSSIBLE.
WELL, WELL. COUPLE OF ARTISIANS, EH? WHERE'D YOU FIND THEM?
WANDERING AROUND OUTSIDE THE CITY, CLOSE TO THE TERRITORY PERIMETER.

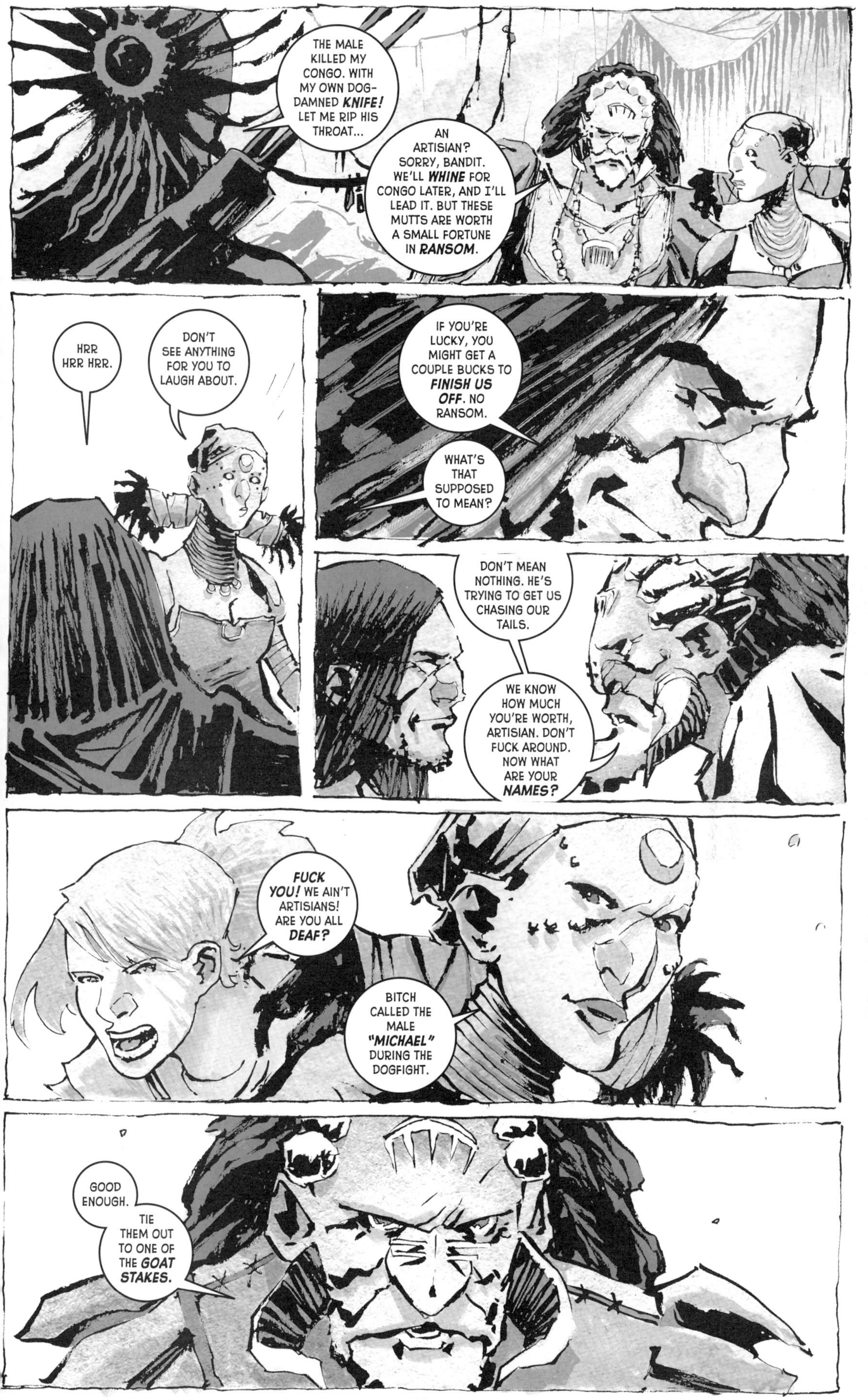
THE MALE KILLED MY CONGO. WITH MY OWN DOG-DAMNED KNIFE! LET ME RIP HIS THROAT...
AN ARTISIAN? SORRY, BANDIT. WE'LL WHINE FOR CONGO LATER, AND I'LL LEAD IT. BUT THESE MUTTS ARE WORTH A SMALL FORTUNE IN RANSOM.
HRR HRR HRR.
DON'T SEE ANYTHING FOR YOU TO LAUGH ABOUT.
IF YOU'RE LUCKY, YOU MIGHT GET A COUPLE BUCKS TO FINISH US OFF. NO RANSOM.
WHAT'S THAT SUPPOSED TO MEAN?
DON'T MEAN NOTHING. HE'S TRYING TO GET US CHASING OUR TAILS.
WE KNOW HOW MUCH YOU'RE WORTH, ARTISIAN. DON'T FUCK AROUND. NOW WHAT ARE YOUR NAMES?
FUCK YOU! WE AIN'T ARTISIANS! ARE YOU ALL DEAF?
BITCH CALLED THE MALE "MICHAEL" DURING THE DOGFIGHT.
GOOD ENOUGH.
TIE THEM OUT TO ONE OF THE GOAT STAKES.

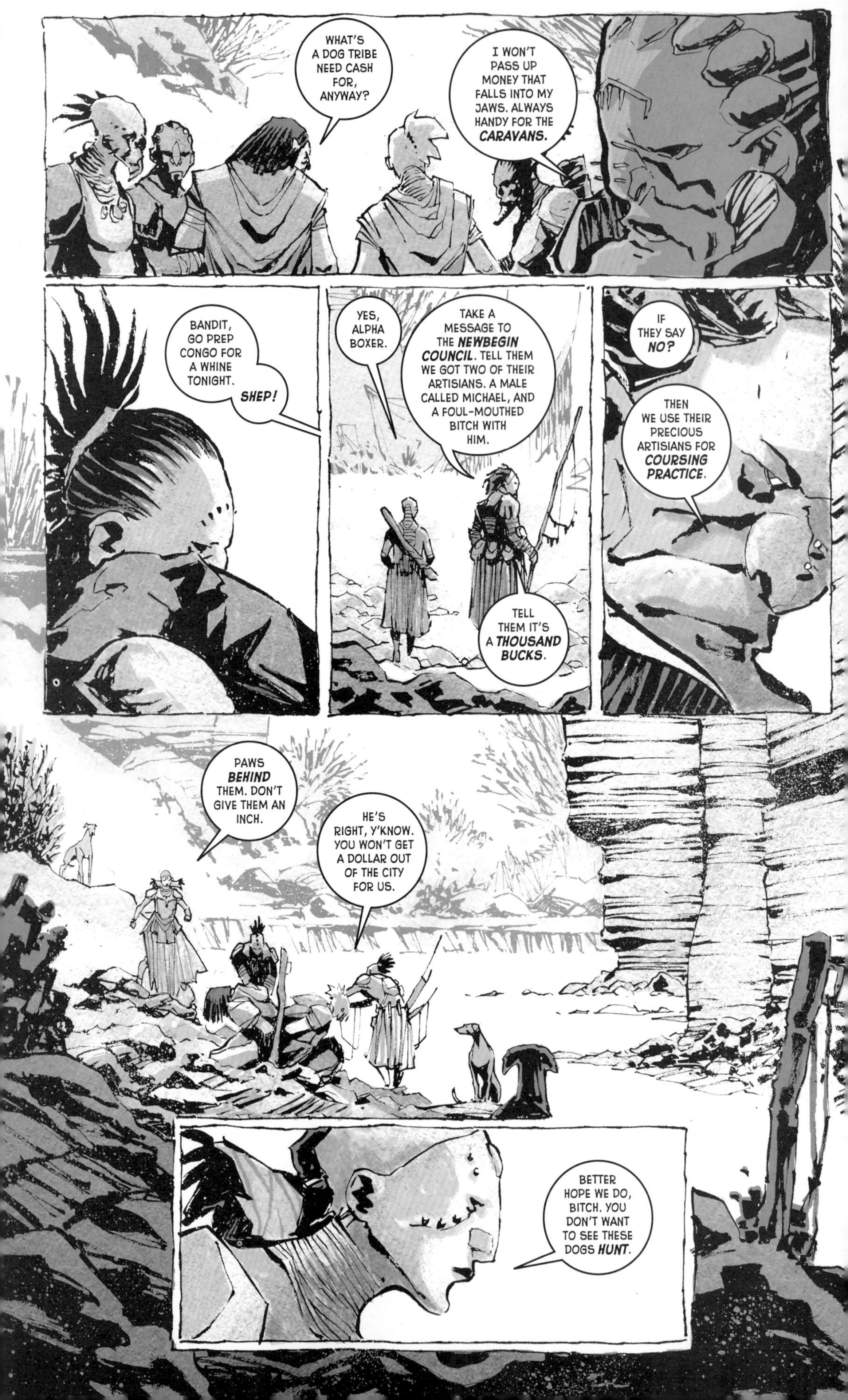
WHAT'S A DOG TRIBE NEED CASH FOR, ANYWAY?
I WON'T PASS UP MONEY THAT FALLS INTO MY JAWS. ALWAYS HANDY FOR THE CARAVANS.
BANDIT, GO PREP CONGO FOR A WHINE TONIGHT. SHEP!
YES, ALPHA BOXER.
TAKE A MESSAGE TO THE NEWBEGIN COUNCIL. TELL THEM WE GOT TWO OF THEIR ARTISIANS. A MALE CALLED MICHAEL, AND A FOUL-MOUTHED BITCH WITH HIM.
TELL THEM IT'S A THOUSAND BUCKS.
IF THEY SAY NO?
THEN WE USE THEIR PRECIOUS ARTISIANS FOR COURSING PRACTICE.
PAWS BEHIND THEM. DON'T GIVE THEM AN INCH.
HE'S RIGHT, Y'KNOW. YOU WON'T GET A DOLLAR OUT OF THE CITY FOR US.
BETTER HOPE WE DO, BITCH. YOU DON'T WANT TO SEE THESE DOGS HUNT.

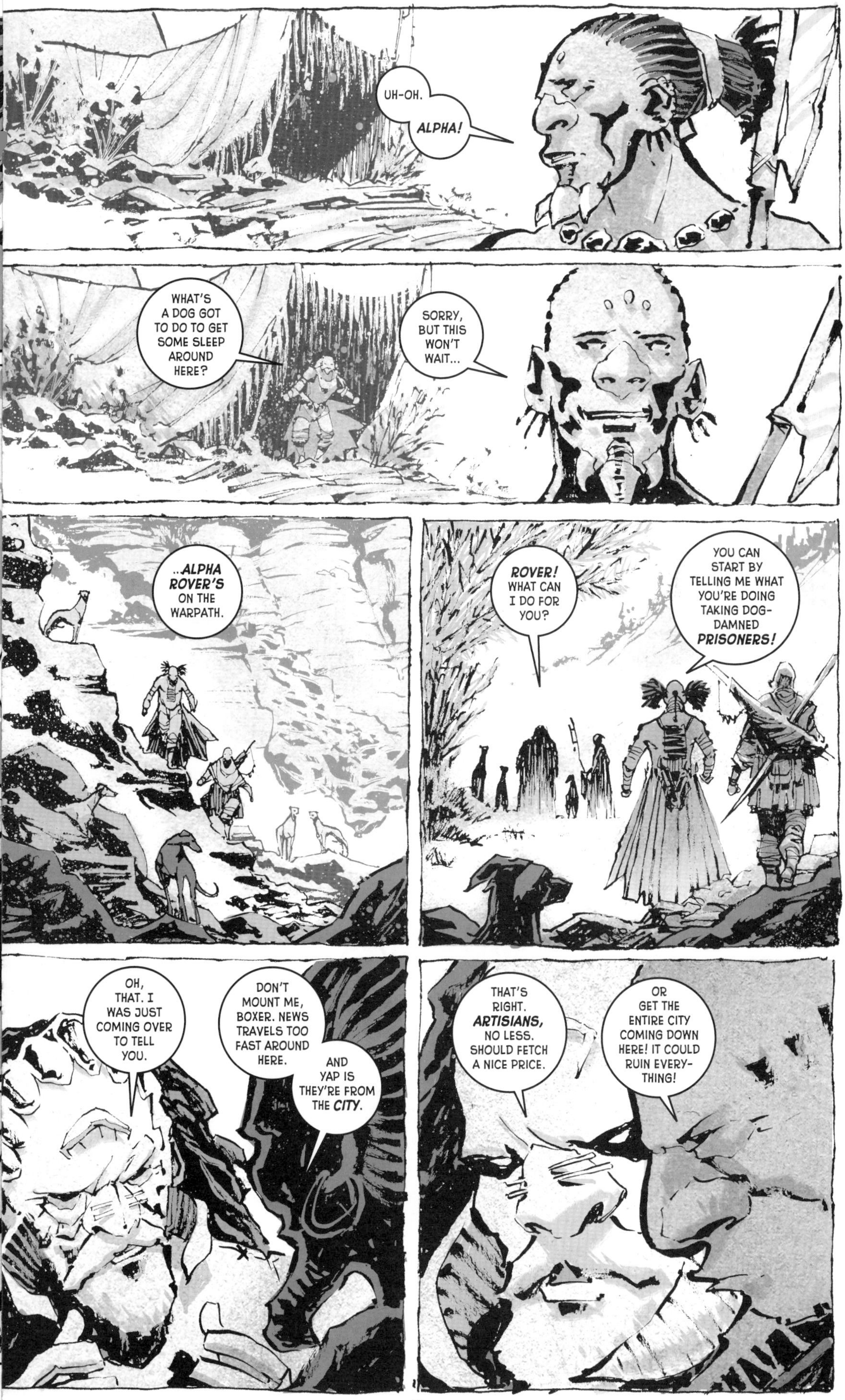
UH-OH.
ALPHA!
WHAT'S A DOG GOT TO DO TO GET SOME SLEEP AROUND HERE?
SORRY, BUT THIS WON'T WAIT...
..ALPHA ROVER'S ON THE WARPATH.
ROVER! WHAT CAN I DO FOR YOU?
YOU CAN START BY TELLING ME WHAT YOU'RE DOING TAKING DOG-DAMNED PRISONERS!
OH, THAT. I WAS JUST COMING OVER TO TELL YOU.
DON'T MOUNT ME, BOXER. NEWS TRAVELS TOO FAST AROUND HERE.
AND YAP IS THEY'RE FROM THE CITY.
THAT'S RIGHT. ARTISIANS, NO LESS. SHOULD FETCH A NICE PRICE.
OR GET THE ENTIRE CITY COMING DOWN HERE! IT COULD RUIN EVERY-THING!

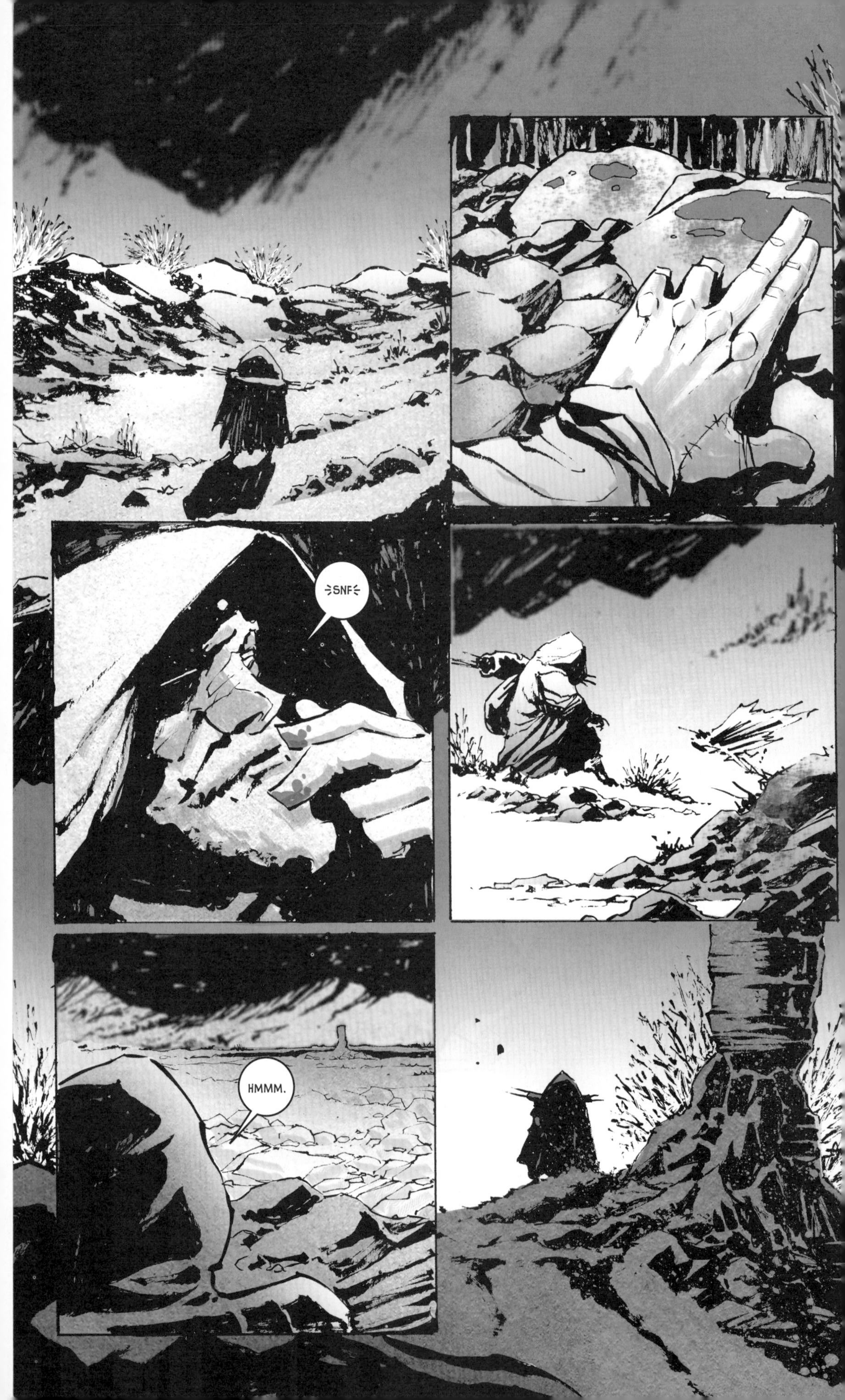
SNF
HMMM.

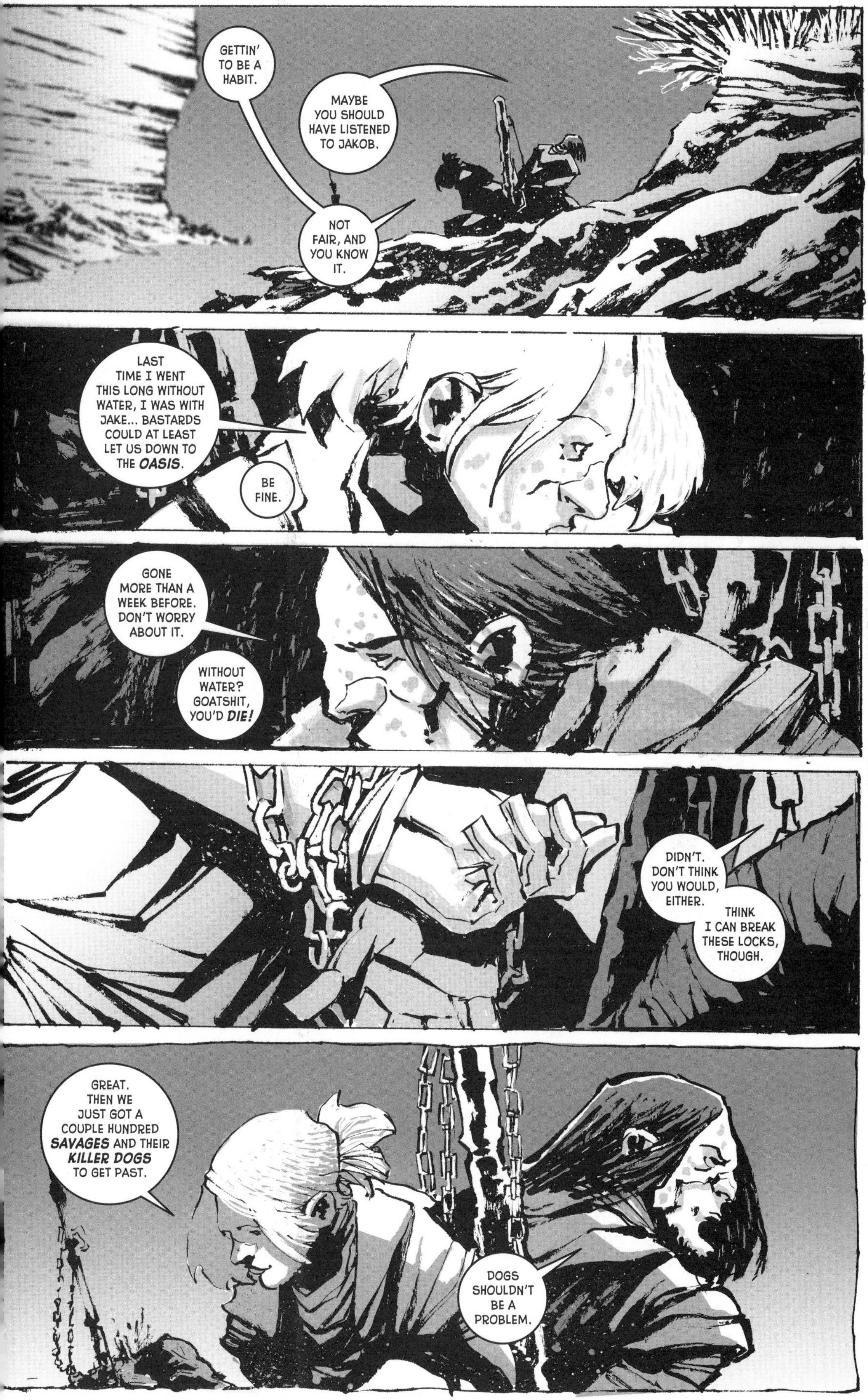
GETTIN' TO BE A HABIT.
MAYBE YOU SHOULD HAVE LISTENED TO JAKOB.
NOT FAIR, AND YOU KNOW IT.
LAST TIME I WENT THIS LONG WITHOUT WATER, I WAS WITH JAKE... BASTARDS COULD AT LEAST LET US DOWN TO THE OASIS.
BE FINE.
GONE MORE THAN A WEEK BEFORE. DON'T WORRY ABOUT IT.
WITHOUT WATER? GOATSHIT, YOU'D DIE!
DIDN'T. DON'T THINK YOU WOULD, EITHER.
THINK I CAN BREAK THESE LOCKS, THOUGH.
GREAT. THEN WE JUST GOT A COUPLE HUNDRED SAVAGES AND THEIR KILLER DOGS TO GET PAST.
DOGS SHOULDN'T BE A PROBLEM.

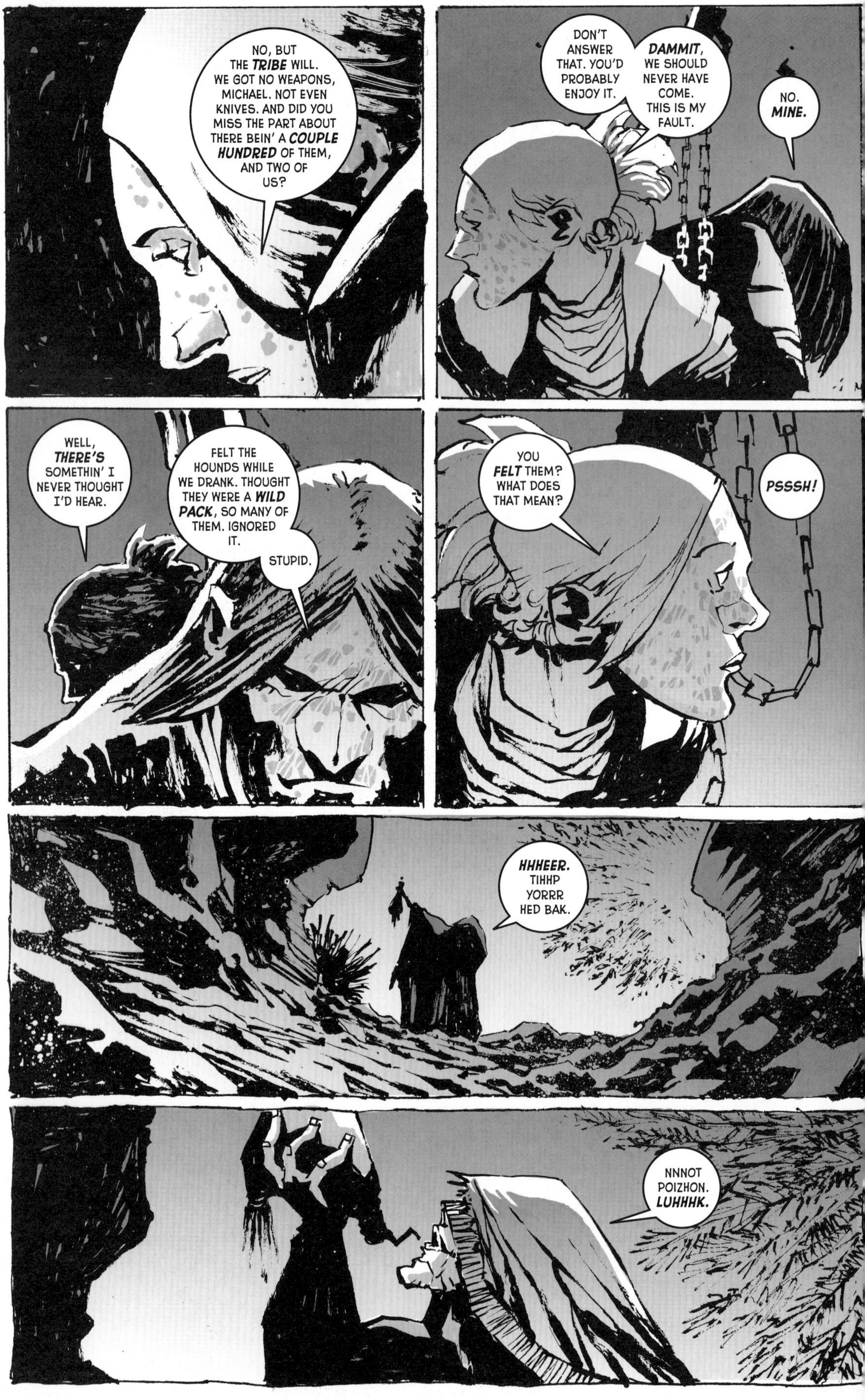
NO, BUT THE TRIBE WILL. WE GOT NO WEAPONS, MICHAEL. NOT EVEN KNIVES. AND DID YOU MISS THE PART ABOUT THERE BEIN' A COUPLE HUNDRED OF THEM, AND TWO OF US?
DON'T ANSWER THAT. YOU'D PROBABLY ENJOY IT.
DAMMIT, WE SHOULD NEVER HAVE COME. THIS IS MY FAULT.
NO. MINE.
WELL, THERE'S SOMETHIN' I NEVER THOUGHT I'D HEAR.
FELT THE HOUNDS WHILE WE DRANK. THOUGHT THEY WERE A WILD PACK, SO MANY OF THEM. IGNORED IT.
STUPID.
YOU FELT THEM? WHAT DOES THAT MEAN?
PSSSH!
HHHEER. TIHHP YORRR HED BAK.
NNNOT POIZHON. LUHHHK.

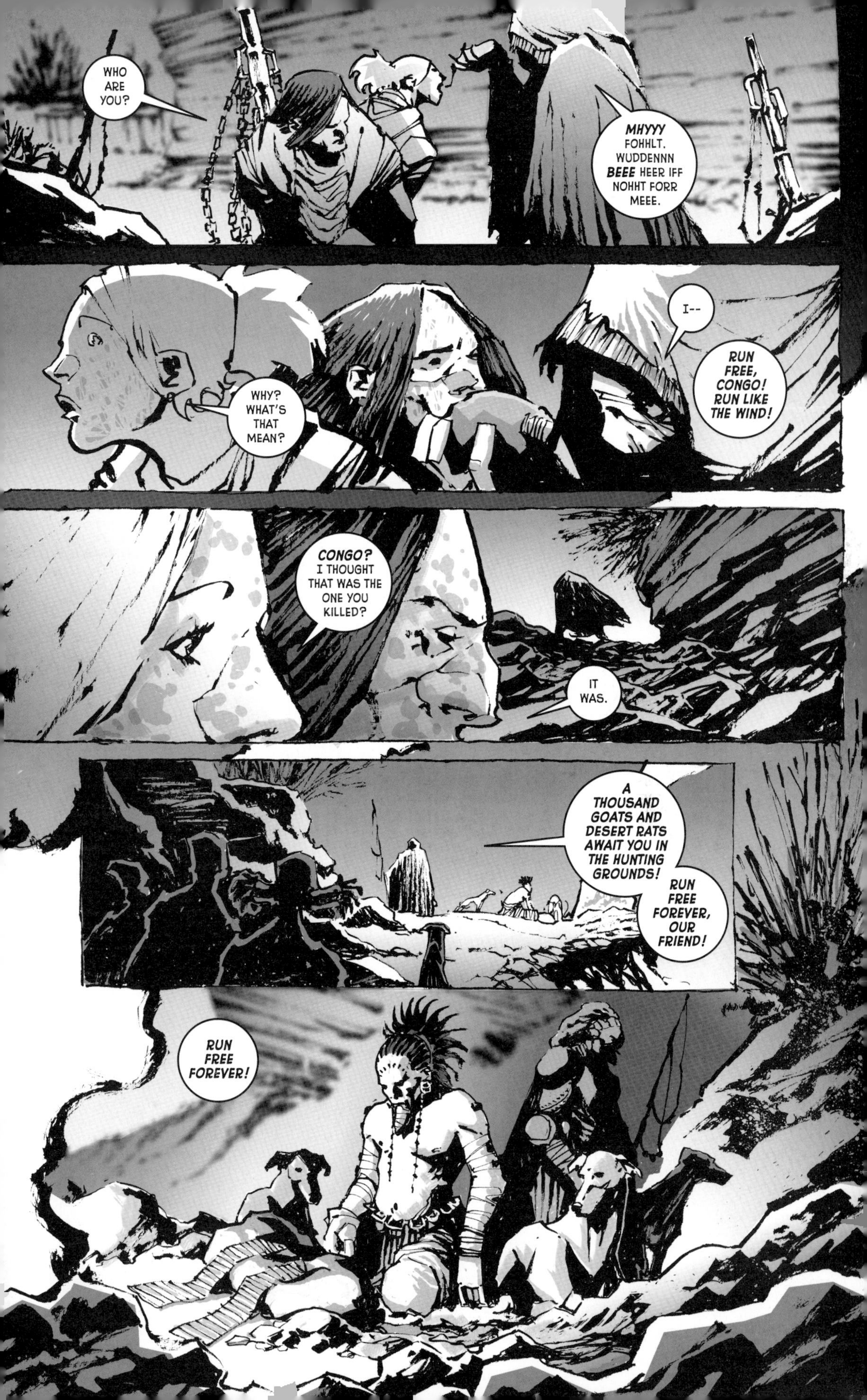
WHO ARE YOU?
MHYYY FOHHLT. WUDDENNN BEEE HEER IFF NOHHT FORR MEEE.
I--
RUN FREE, CONGO! RUN LIKE THE WIND!
WHY? WHAT'S THAT MEAN?
CONGO? I THOUGHT THAT WAS THE ONE YOU KILLED?
IT WAS.
A THOUSAND GOATS AND DESERT RATS AWAIT YOU IN THE HUNTING GROUNDS!
RUN FREE FOREVER, OUR FRIEND!
RUN FREE FOREVER!

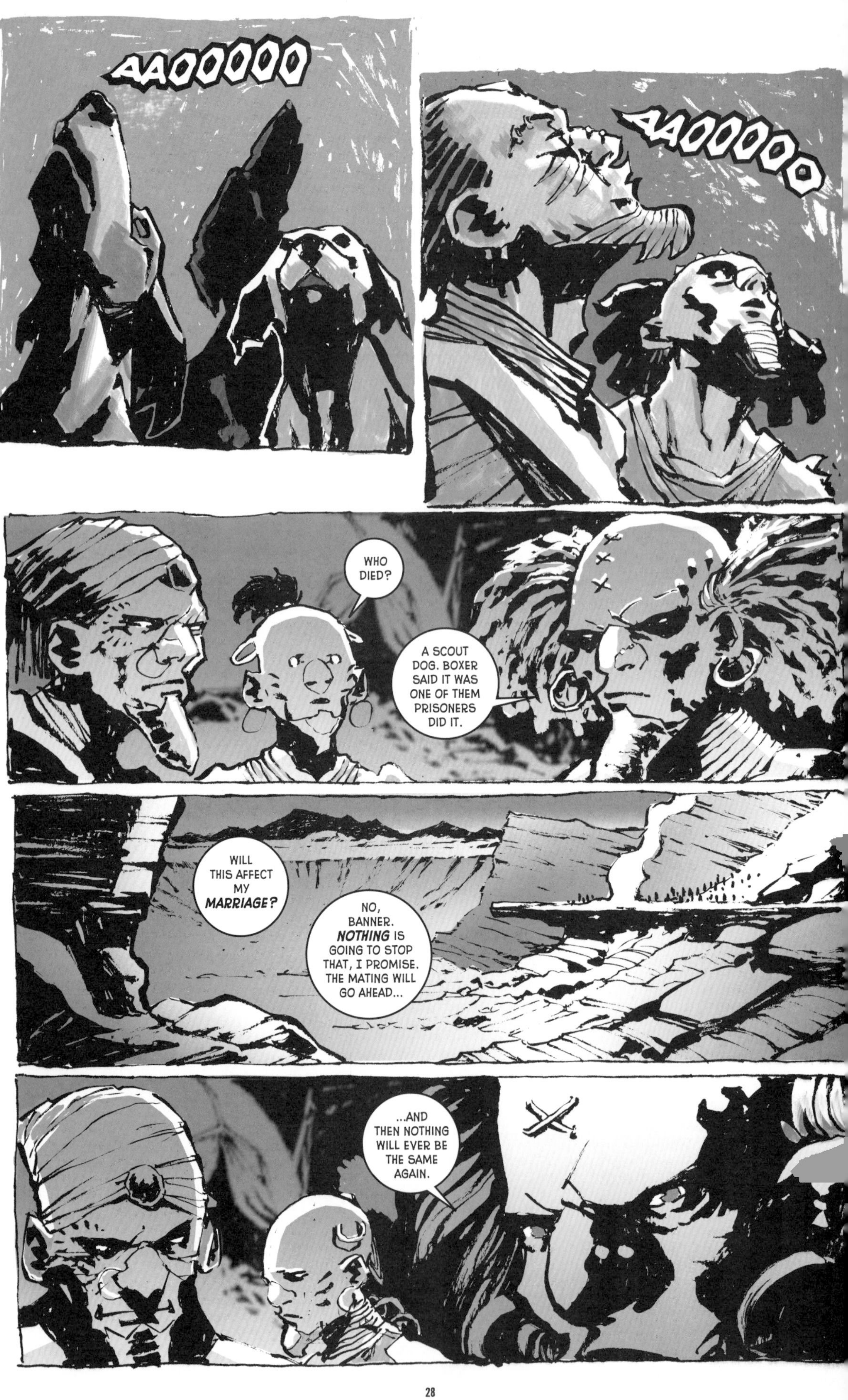
AAOOOOO
AAOOOOOO
WHO DIED?
A SCOUT DOG. BOXER SAID IT WAS ONE OF THEM PRISONERS DID IT.
WILL THIS AFFECT MY ***MARRIAGE?***
NO, BANNER. ***NOTHING*** IS GOING TO STOP THAT, I PROMISE. THE MATING WILL GO AHEAD...
...AND THEN NOTHING WILL EVER BE THE SAME AGAIN.

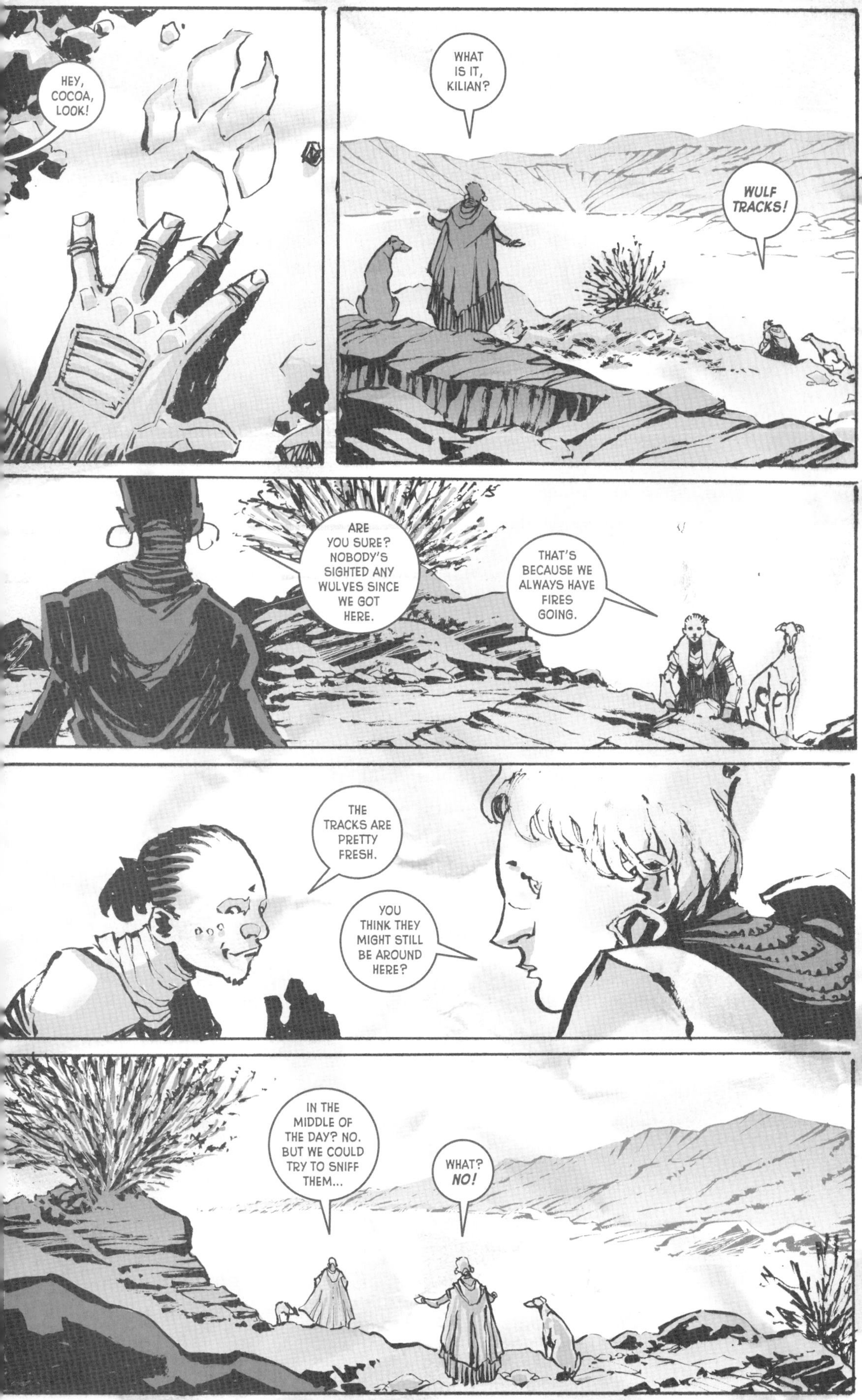
HEY, COCOA, LOOK!
WHAT IS IT, KILIAN?
WULF TRACKS!
ARE YOU SURE? NOBODY'S SIGHTED ANY WULVES SINCE WE GOT HERE.
THAT'S BECAUSE WE ALWAYS HAVE FIRES GOING.
THE TRACKS ARE PRETTY FRESH.
YOU THINK THEY MIGHT STILL BE AROUND HERE?
IN THE MIDDLE OF THE DAY? NO. BUT WE COULD TRY TO SNIFF THEM...
WHAT? NO!

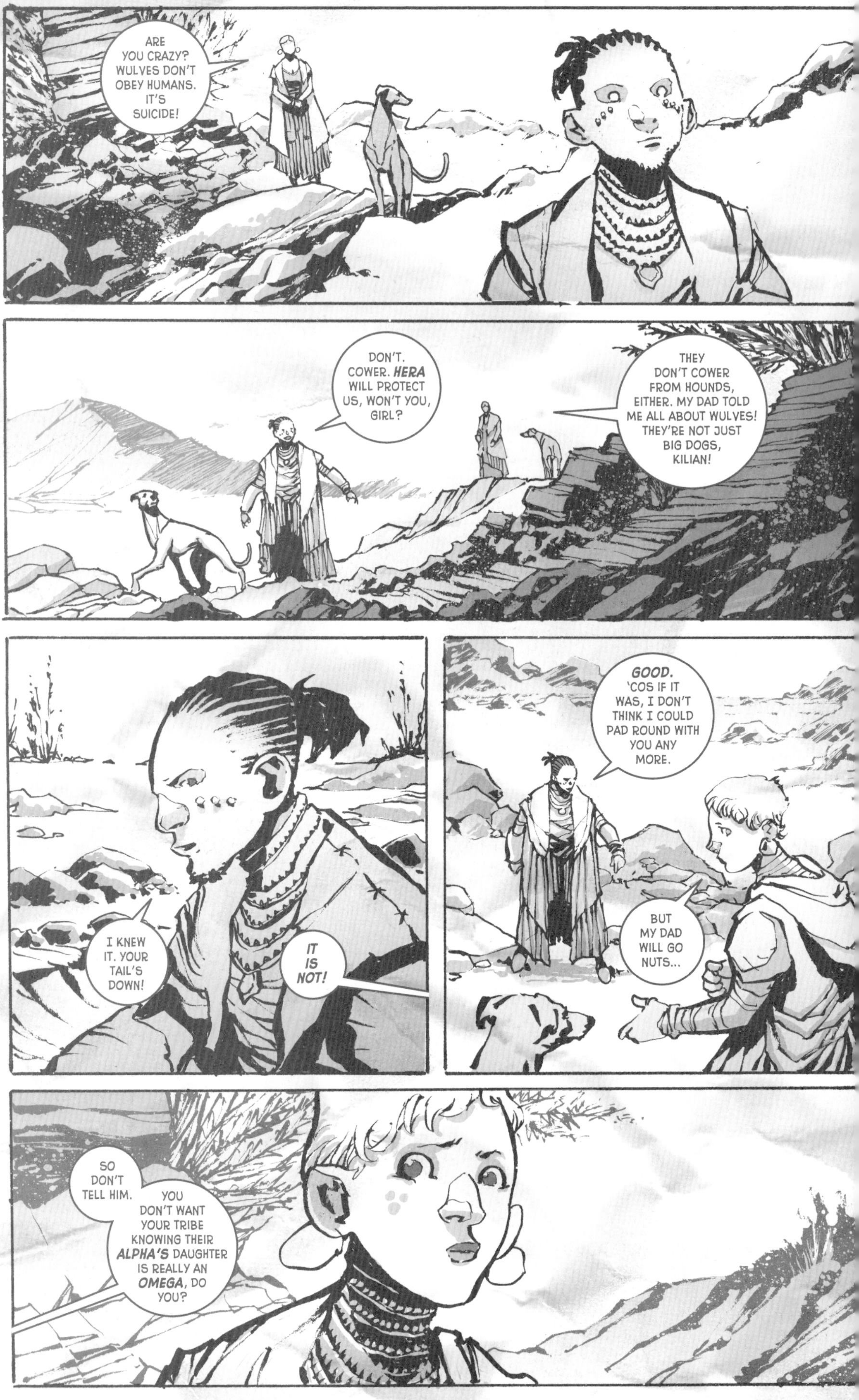
ARE YOU CRAZY? WULVES DON'T OBEY HUMANS. IT'S SUICIDE!
DON'T. COWER. HERA WILL PROTECT US, WON'T YOU, GIRL?
THEY DON'T COWER FROM HOUNDS, EITHER. MY DAD TOLD ME ALL ABOUT WULVES! THEY'RE NOT JUST BIG DOGS, KILIAN!
I KNEW IT. YOUR TAIL'S DOWN!
IT IS NOT!
GOOD. 'COS IF IT WAS, I DON'T THINK I COULD PAD ROUND WITH YOU ANY MORE.
BUT MY DAD WILL GO NUTS...
SO DON'T TELL HIM.
YOU DON'T WANT YOUR TRIBE KNOWING THEIR ALPHA'S DAUGHTER IS REALLY AN OMEGA, DO YOU?

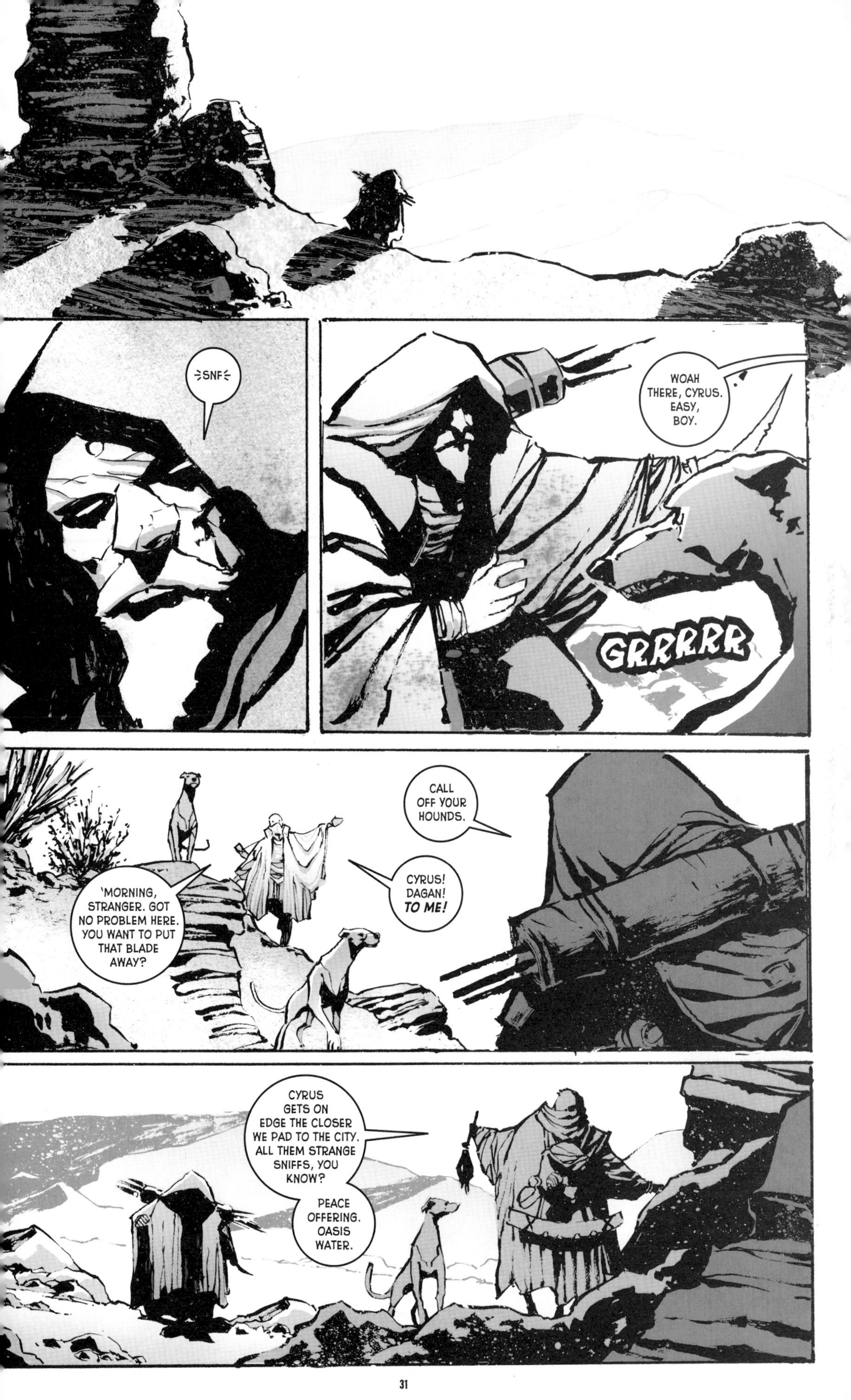

SNF
WOAH THERE, CYRUS. EASY, BOY.
GRRRRR
CALL OFF YOUR HOUNDS.
CYRUS! DAGAN! TO ME!
'MORNING, STRANGER. GOT NO PROBLEM HERE. YOU WANT TO PUT THAT BLADE AWAY?
CYRUS GETS ON EDGE THE CLOSER WE PAD TO THE CITY. ALL THEM STRANGE SNIFFS, YOU KNOW?
PEACE OFFERING. OASIS WATER.

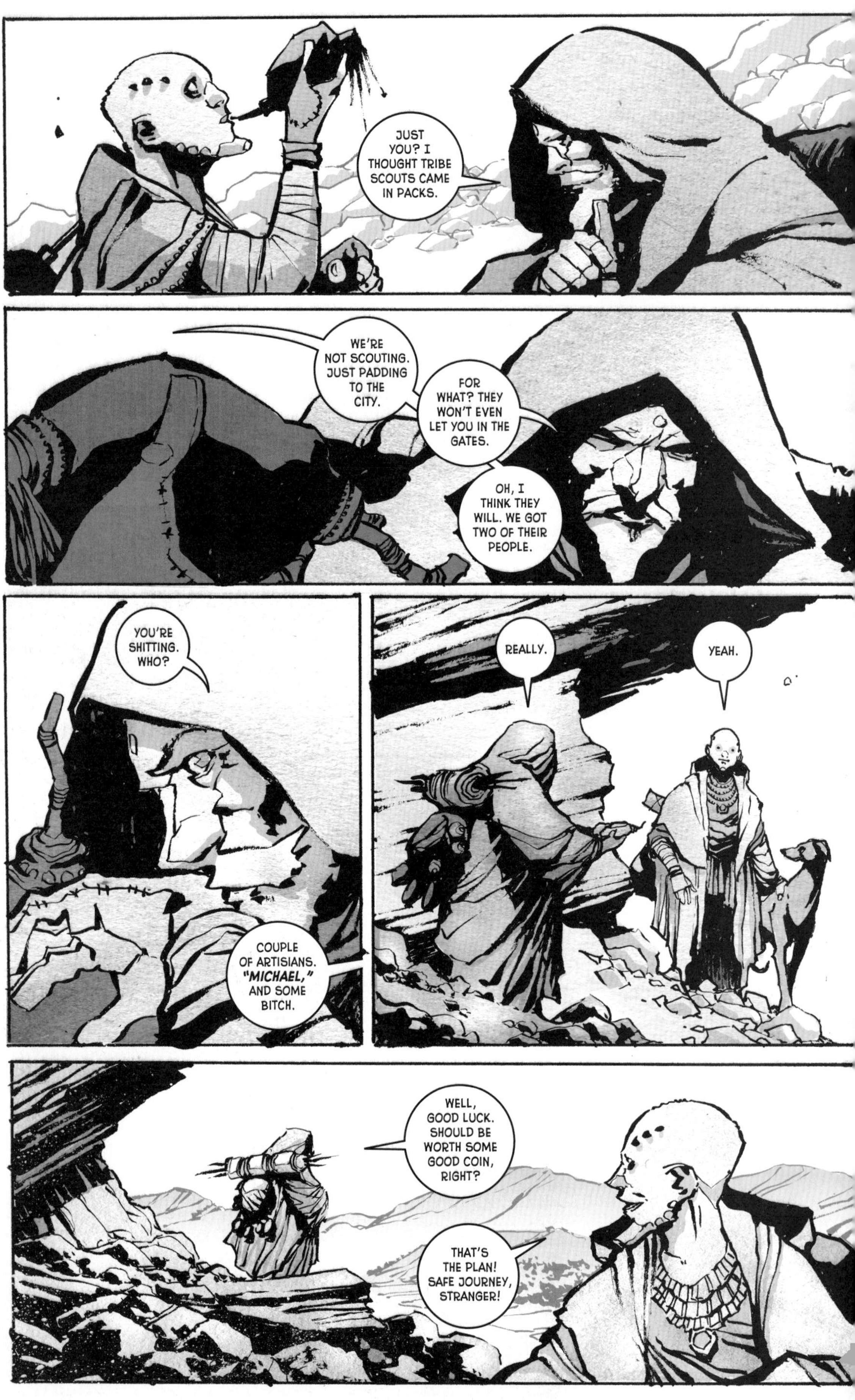
JUST YOU? I THOUGHT TRIBE SCOUTS CAME IN PACKS.
WE'RE NOT SCOUTING. JUST PADDING TO THE CITY.
FOR WHAT? THEY WON'T EVEN LET YOU IN THE GATES.
OH, I THINK THEY WILL. WE GOT TWO OF THEIR PEOPLE.
YOU'RE SHITTING. WHO?
COUPLE OF ARTISIANS. "MICHAEL," AND SOME BITCH.
REALLY.
YEAH.
WELL, GOOD LUCK. SHOULD BE WORTH SOME GOOD COIN, RIGHT?
THAT'S THE PLAN! SAFE JOURNEY, STRANGER!

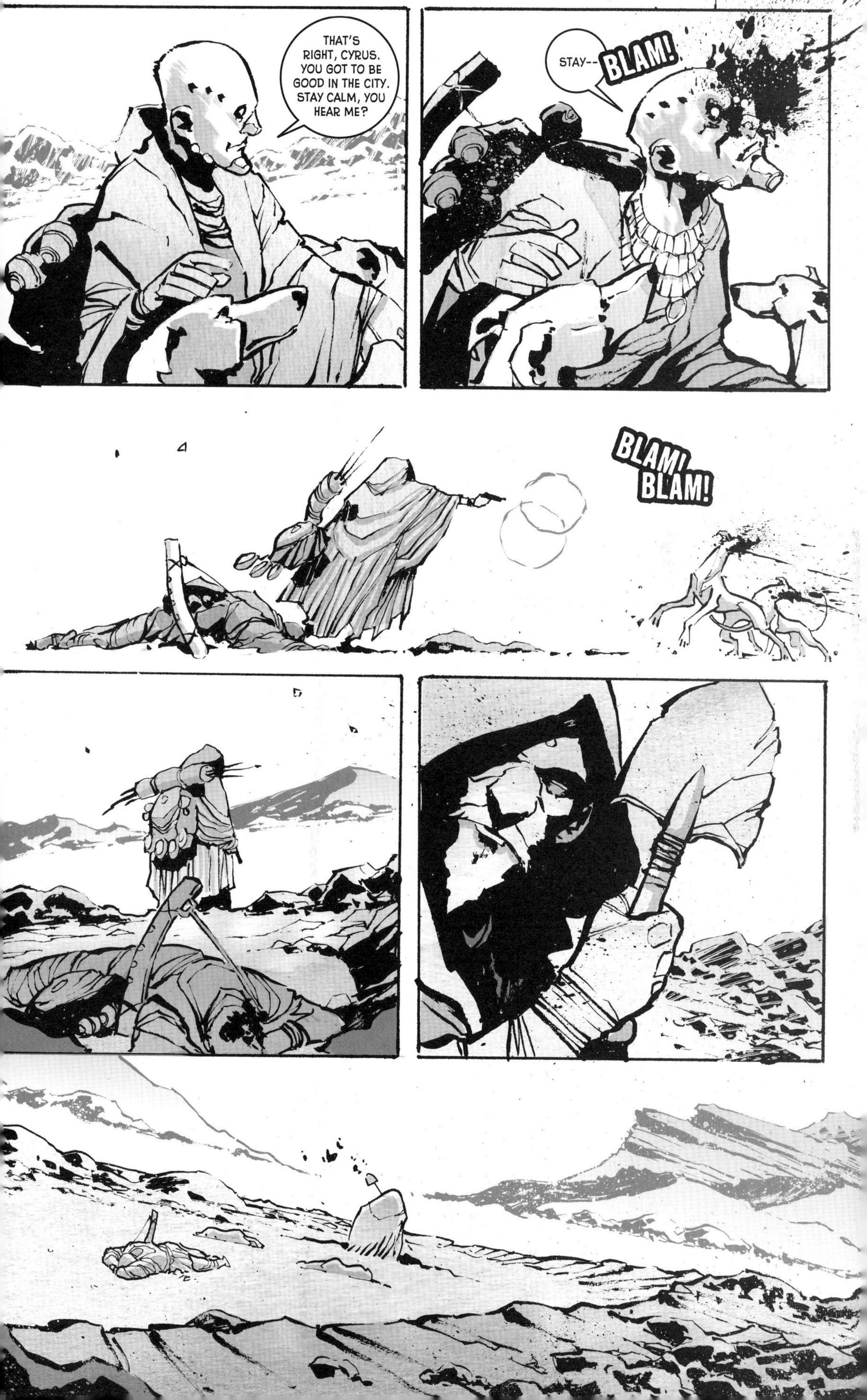
THAT'S RIGHT, CYRUS. YOU GOT TO BE GOOD IN THE CITY. STAY CALM, YOU HEAR ME?
STAY--
BLAM!
BLAM! BLAM!

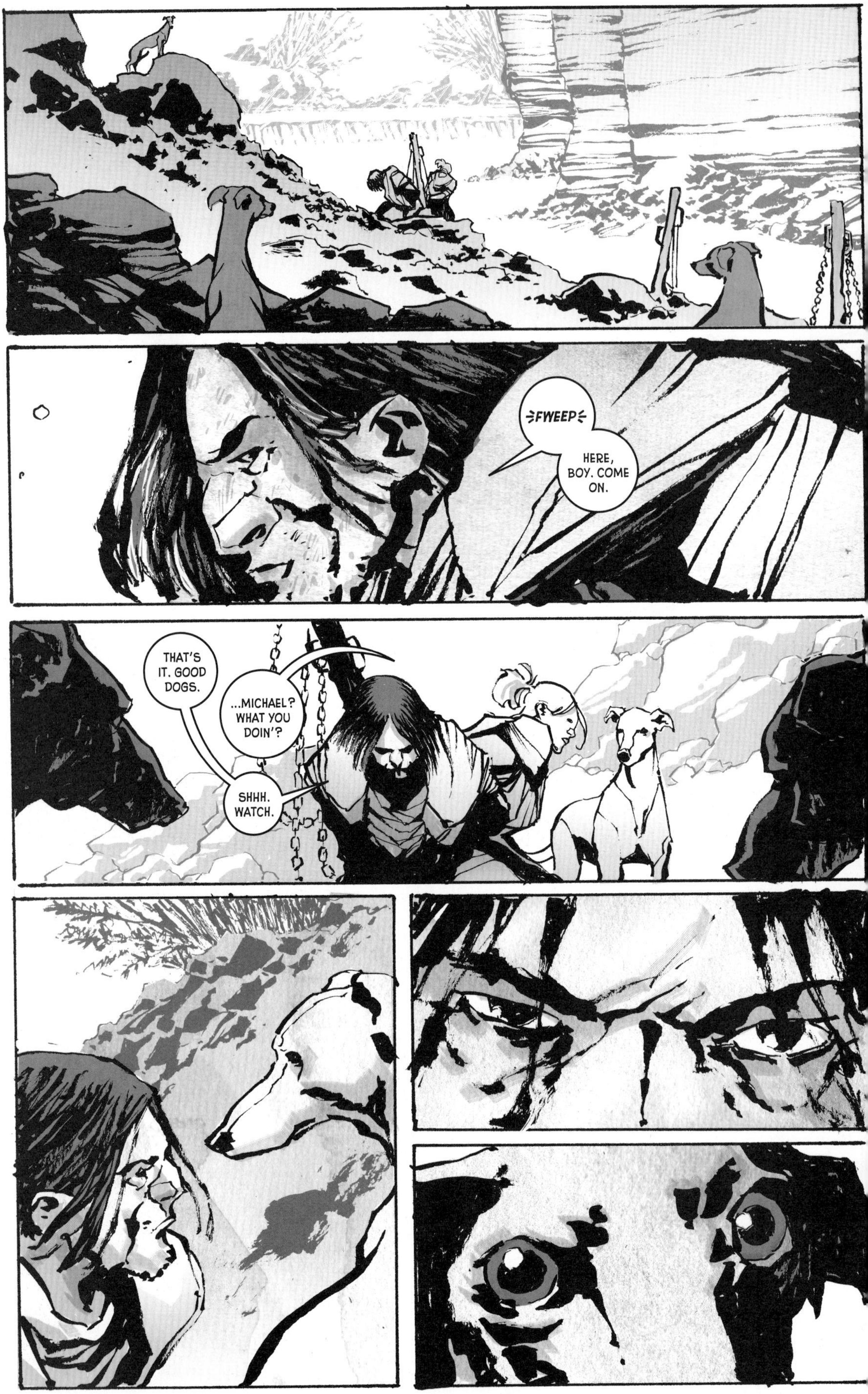
FWEEP
HERE, BOY. COME ON.
THAT'S IT. GOOD DOGS.
...MICHAEL? WHAT YOU DOIN'?
SHHH. WATCH.

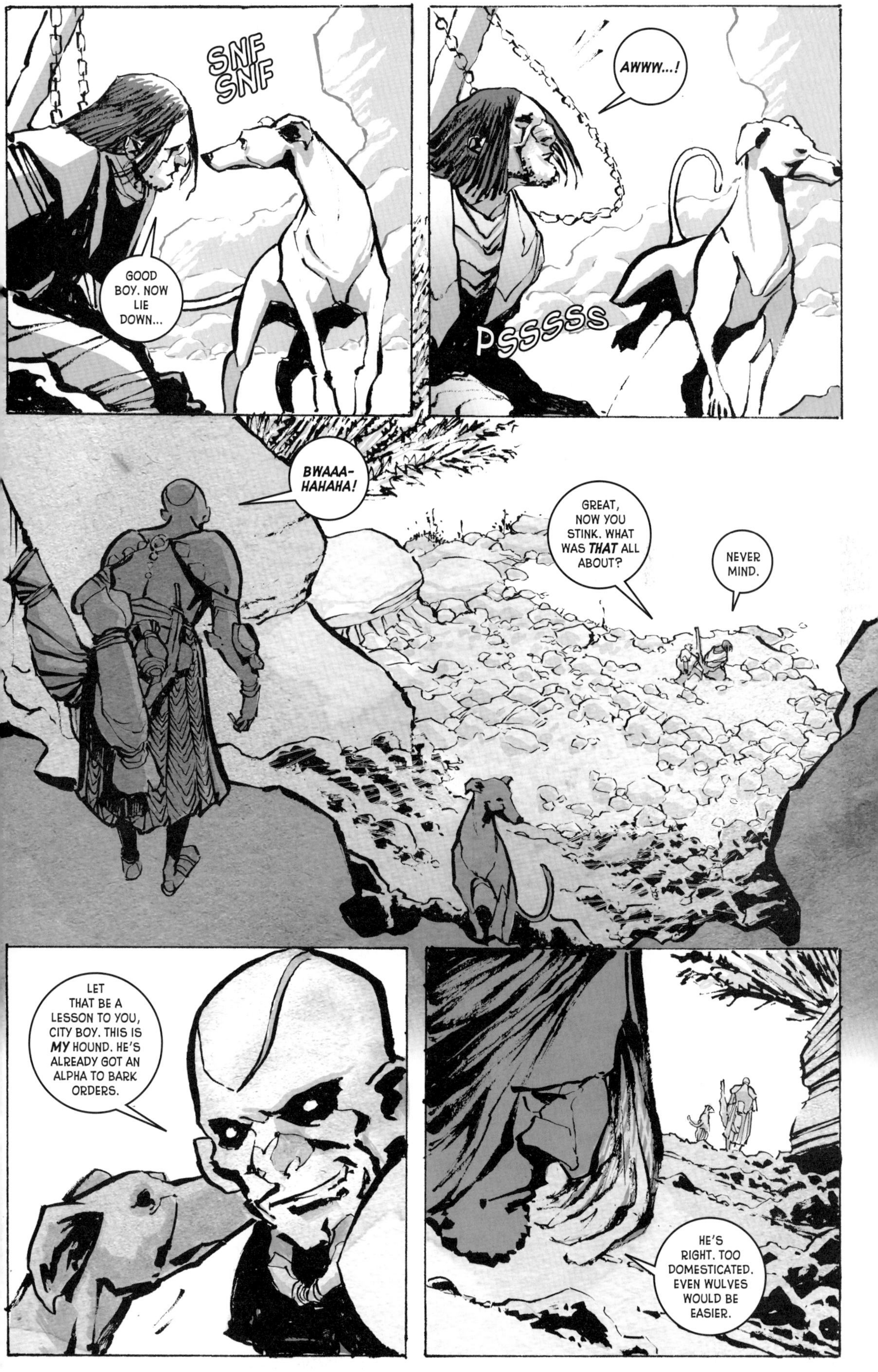
SNF SNF
GOOD BOY. NOW LIE DOWN...
AWWW...!
PSSSSS
BWAAA-HAHAHA!
GREAT, NOW YOU STINK. WHAT WAS THAT ALL ABOUT?
NEVER MIND.
LET THAT BE A LESSON TO YOU, CITY BOY. THIS IS MY HOUND. HE'S ALREADY GOT AN ALPHA TO BARK ORDERS.
HE'S RIGHT. TOO DOMESTICATED. EVEN WULVES WOULD BE EASIER.

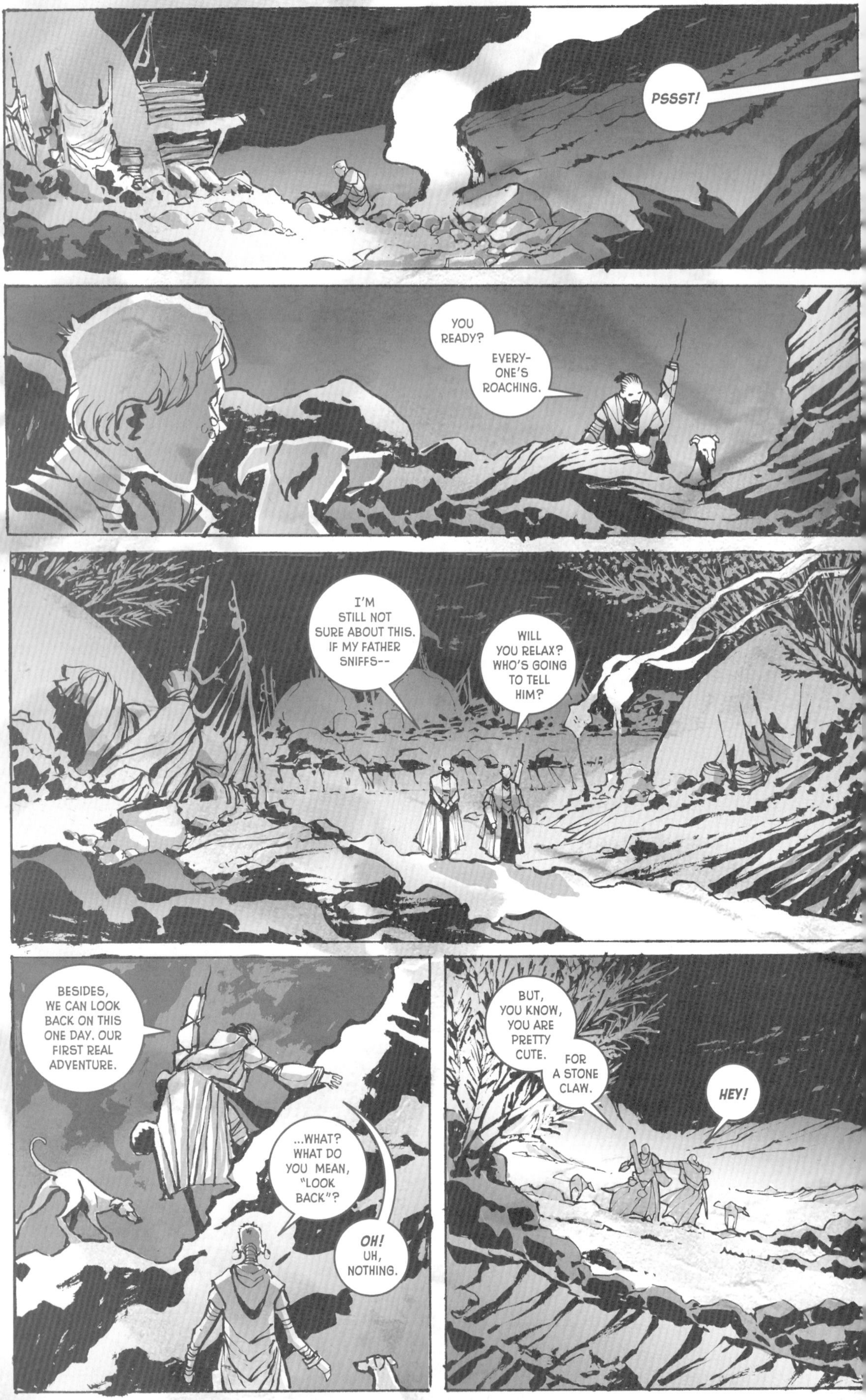
PSSST!
YOU READY?
EVERY-ONE'S ROACHING.
I'M STILL NOT SURE ABOUT THIS. IF MY FATHER SNIFFS--
WILL YOU RELAX? WHO'S GOING TO TELL HIM?
BESIDES, WE CAN LOOK BACK ON THIS ONE DAY. OUR FIRST REAL ADVENTURE.
...WHAT? WHAT DO YOU MEAN, "LOOK BACK"?
OH! UH, NOTHING.
BUT, YOU KNOW, YOU ARE PRETTY CUTE.
FOR A STONE CLAW.
HEY!

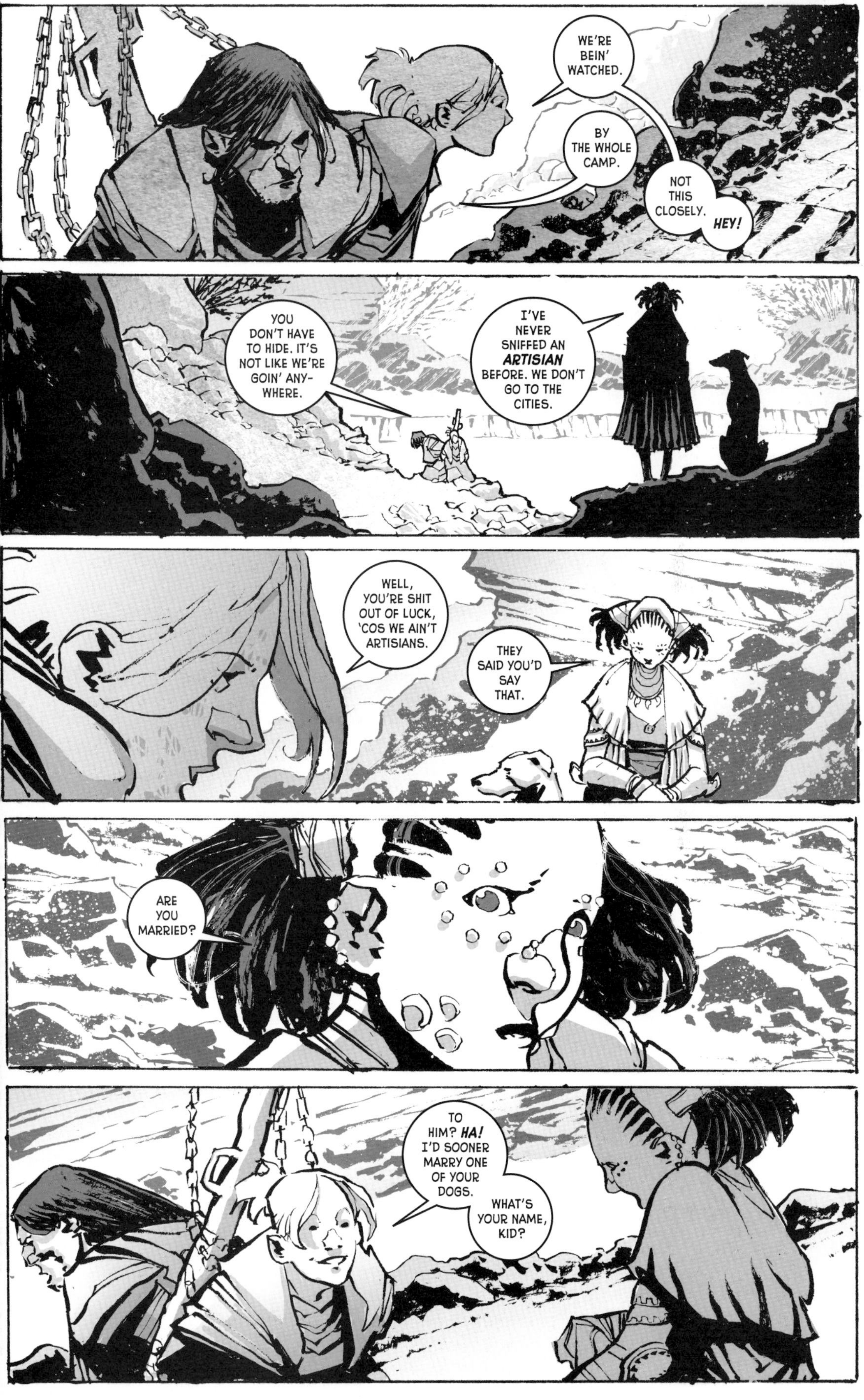
WE'RE BEIN' WATCHED.
BY THE WHOLE CAMP.
NOT THIS CLOSELY.
HEY!
YOU DON'T HAVE TO HIDE. IT'S NOT LIKE WE'RE GOIN' ANY-WHERE.
I'VE NEVER SNIFFED AN ARTISIAN BEFORE. WE DON'T GO TO THE CITIES.
WELL, YOU'RE SHIT OUT OF LUCK, 'COS WE AIN'T ARTISIANS.
THEY SAID YOU'D SAY THAT.
ARE YOU MARRIED?
TO HIM? HA! I'D SOONER MARRY ONE OF YOUR DOGS.
WHAT'S YOUR NAME, KID?

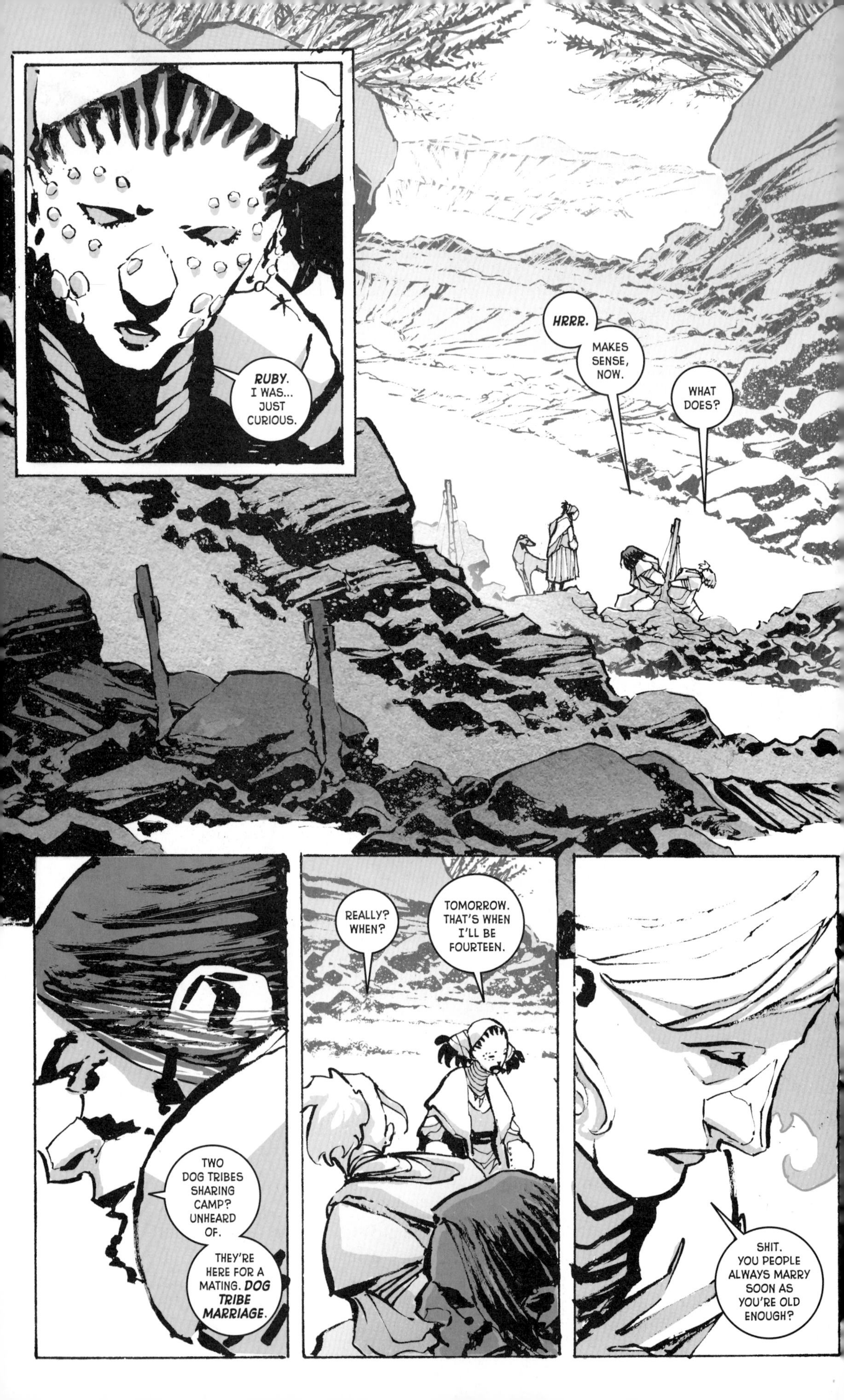
RUBY. I WAS... JUST CURIOUS.
HRRR.
MAKES SENSE, NOW.
WHAT DOES?
TWO DOG TRIBES SHARING CAMP? UNHEARD OF.
THEY'RE HERE FOR A MATING. DOG TRIBE MARRIAGE.
REALLY? WHEN?
TOMORROW. THAT'S WHEN I'LL BE FOURTEEN.
SHIT. YOU PEOPLE ALWAYS MARRY SOON AS YOU'RE OLD ENOUGH?

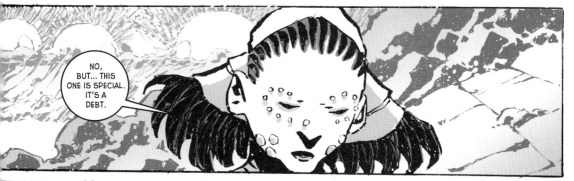

NO, BUT... THIS ONE IS SPECIAL. IT'S A DEBT.

THAT DON'T SOUND GOOD.

IT'S OKAY. I'VE JUST NEVER SNIFFED THE BOY I'M MATING. I'M A BIT NERVOUS.

HOLD ON A SECOND. YOU'RE MARRYIN' SOME GUY YOU'VE NEVER MET 'COS, LEMME GUESS, YOUR *PARENTS* OWE HIS FAMILY A DEBT?

THAT'S SUN-DAMNED *SLAVERY!*

HAPPENS ALL THE TIME. YOU WANT ADVICE, KID, ASK YOUR PARENTS.

MY FATHER'S THE TRIBE *ALPHA.* IT'S DIFFERENT FOR THEM.

SO GO TALK TO SOMEONE WHO ISN'T ALPHA. PLENTY TO CHOOSE FROM.

SHIT, MICHAEL, GO EASY ON THE GIRL. IT AIN'T HER FAULT WE'RE STUCK HERE.

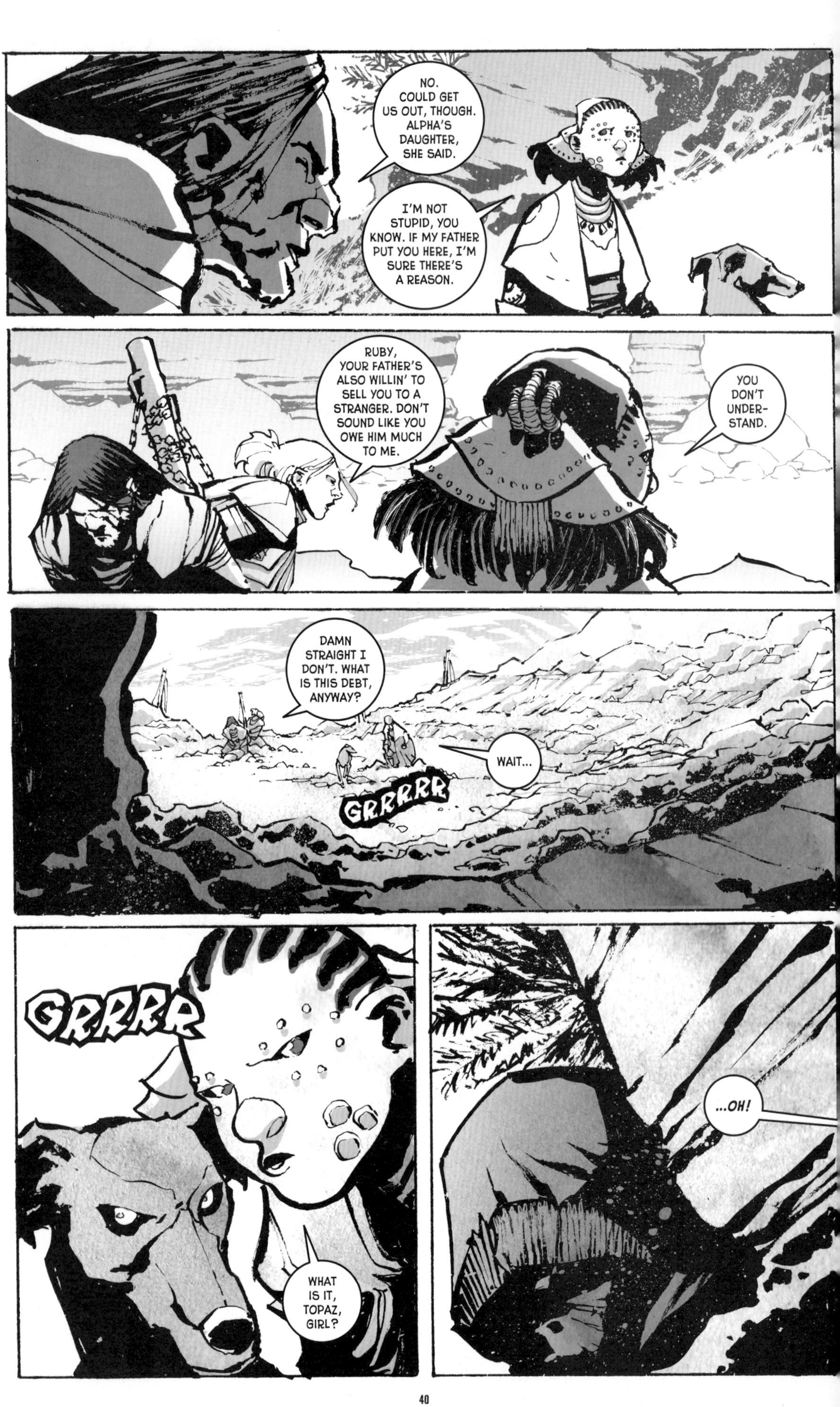
NO. COULD GET US OUT, THOUGH. ALPHA'S DAUGHTER, SHE SAID.
I'M NOT STUPID, YOU KNOW. IF MY FATHER PUT YOU HERE, I'M SURE THERE'S A REASON.
RUBY, YOUR FATHER'S ALSO WILLIN' TO SELL YOU TO A STRANGER. DON'T SOUND LIKE YOU OWE HIM MUCH TO ME.
YOU DON'T UNDER-STAND.
DAMN STRAIGHT I DON'T. WHAT IS THIS DEBT, ANYWAY?
WAIT...
GRRRRR
GRRRR
WHAT IS IT, TOPAZ, GIRL?
...OH!

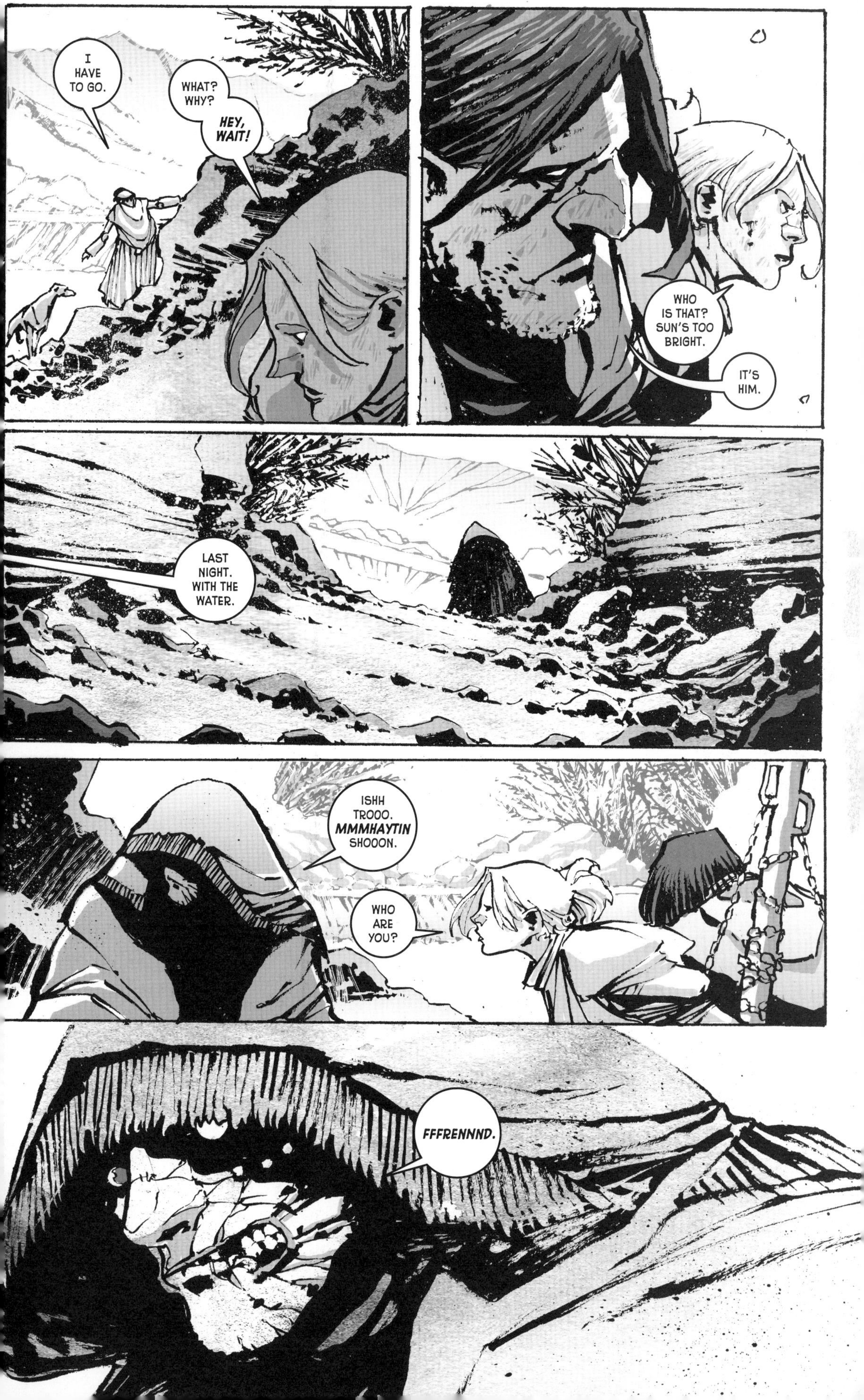

I HAVE TO GO.
WHAT? WHY?
HEY, WAIT!
WHO IS THAT? SUN'S TOO BRIGHT.
IT'S HIM.
LAST NIGHT. WITH THE WATER.
ISHH TROOO. MMMHAYTIN SHOOON.
WHO ARE YOU?
FFFRENNND.

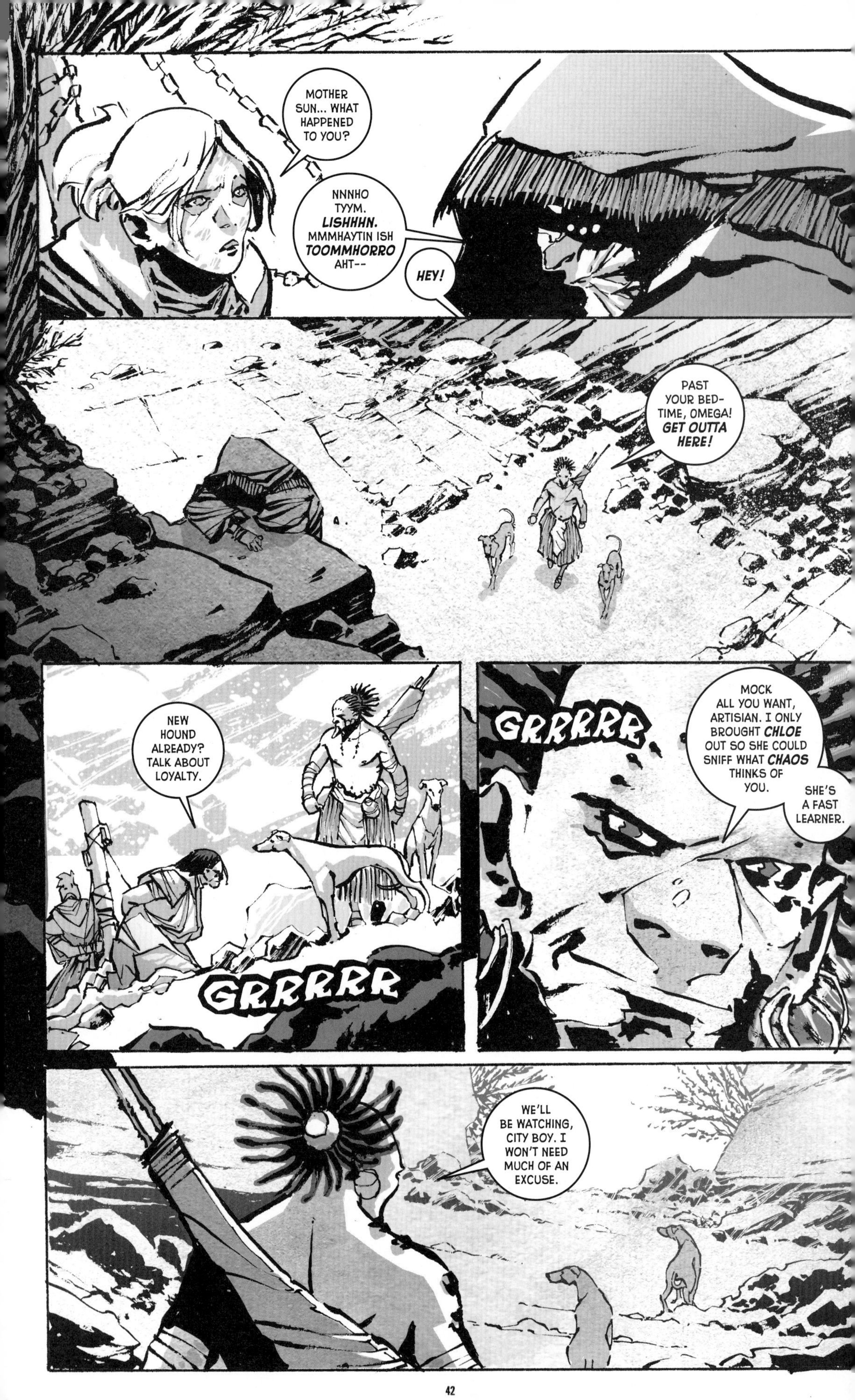
MOTHER SUN... WHAT HAPPENED TO YOU?
NNNHO TYYM. LISHHHN. MMMHAYTIN ISH TOOMMHORRO AHT--
HEY!
PAST YOUR BED-TIME, OMEGA! GET OUTTA HERE!
NEW HOUND ALREADY? TALK ABOUT LOYALTY.
GRRRRR
GRRRRR
MOCK ALL YOU WANT, ARTISIAN. I ONLY BROUGHT CHLOE OUT SO SHE COULD SNIFF WHAT CHAOS THINKS OF YOU.
SHE'S A FAST LEARNER.
WE'LL BE WATCHING, CITY BOY. I WON'T NEED MUCH OF AN EXCUSE.

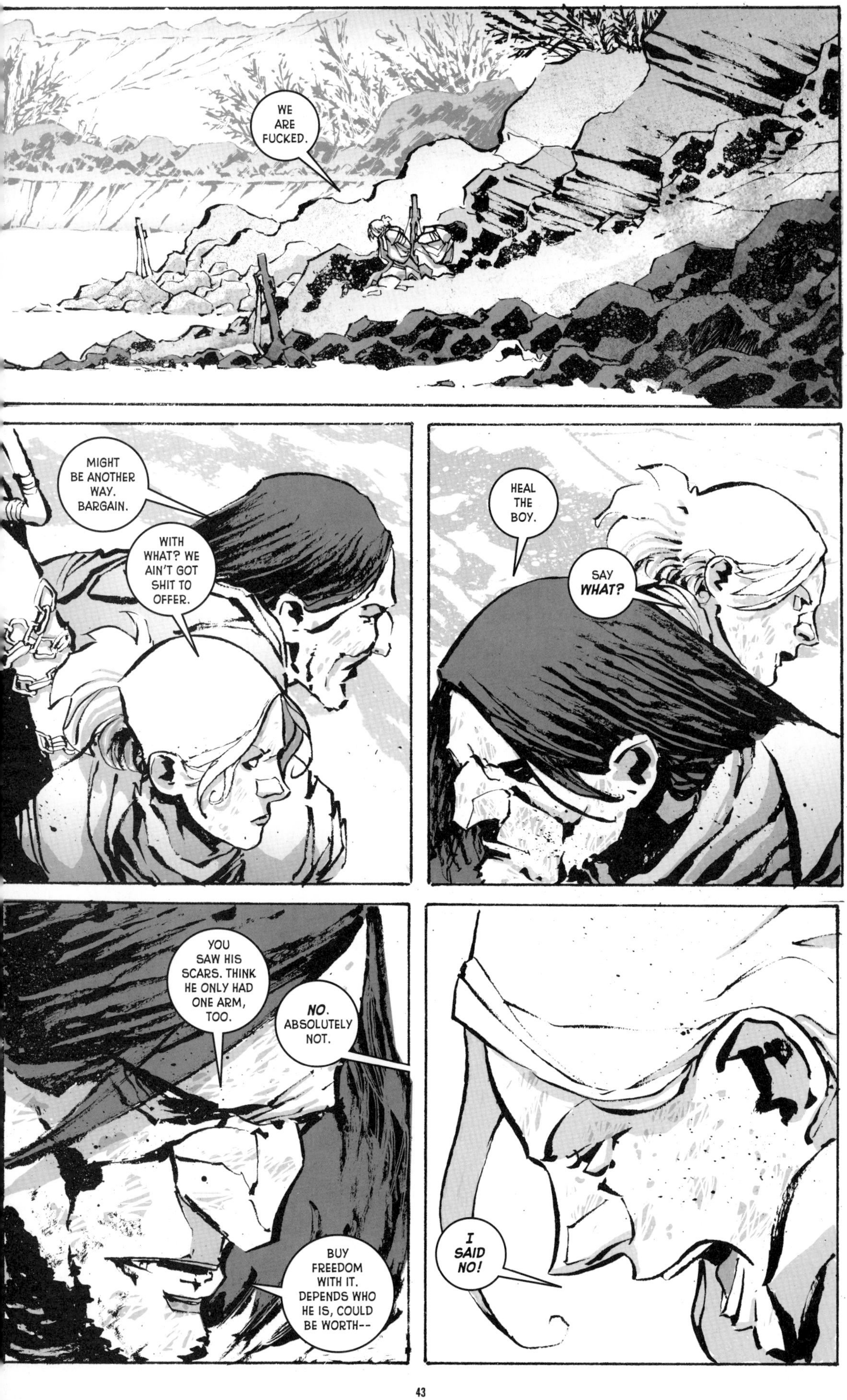

WE ARE FUCKED.
MIGHT BE ANOTHER WAY. BARGAIN.
WITH WHAT? WE AIN'T GOT SHIT TO OFFER.
HEAL THE BOY.
SAY *WHAT?*
YOU SAW HIS SCARS. THINK HE ONLY HAD ONE ARM, TOO.
NO. ABSOLUTELY NOT.
BUY FREEDOM WITH IT. DEPENDS WHO HE IS, COULD BE WORTH--
I SAID NO!

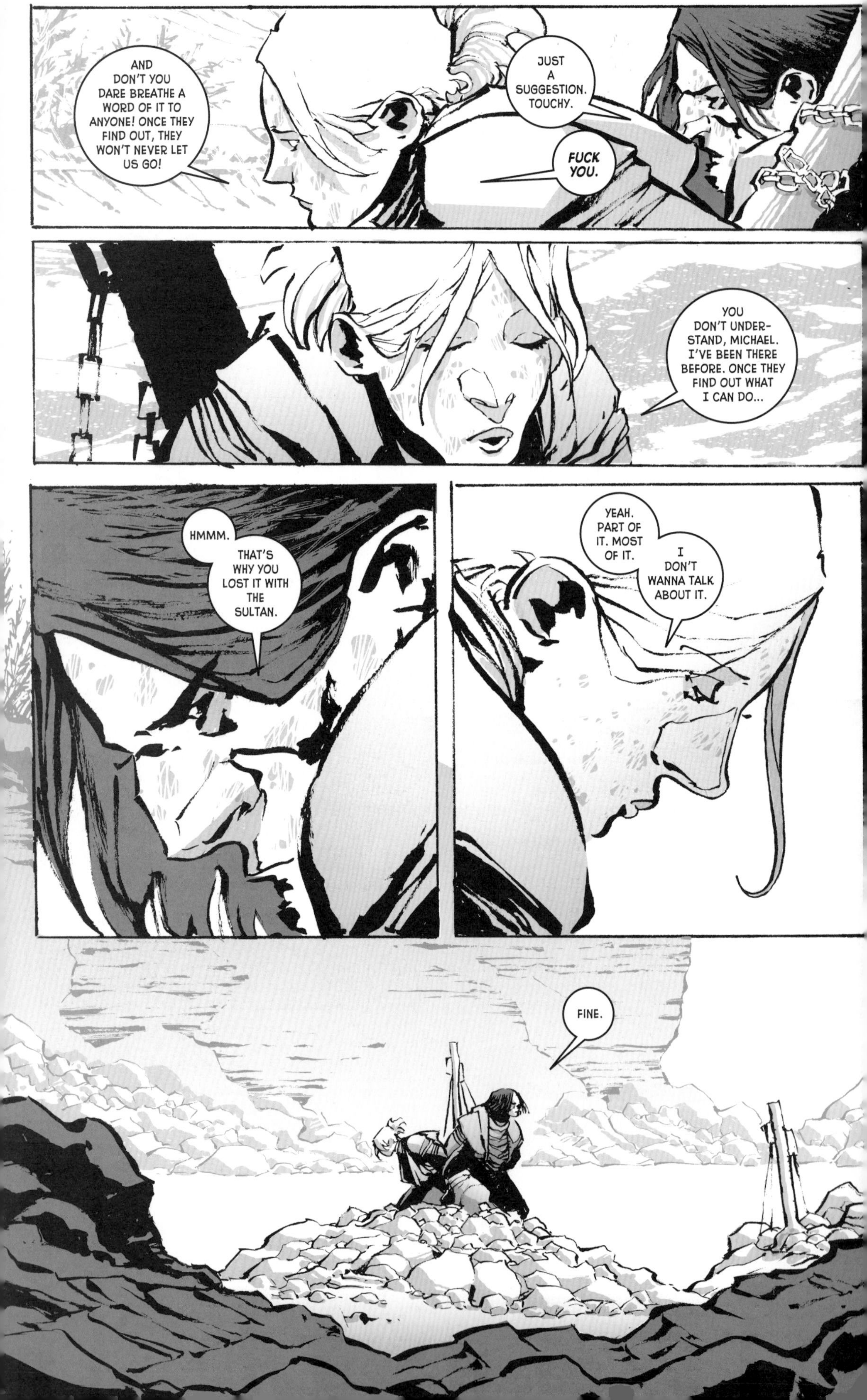
AND DON'T YOU DARE BREATHE A WORD OF IT TO ANYONE! ONCE THEY FIND OUT, THEY WON'T NEVER LET US GO!
JUST A SUGGESTION. TOUCHY.
FUCK YOU.
YOU DON'T UNDER-STAND, MICHAEL. I'VE BEEN THERE BEFORE. ONCE THEY FIND OUT WHAT I CAN DO...
HMMM.
THAT'S WHY YOU LOST IT WITH THE SULTAN.
YEAH. PART OF IT. MOST OF IT.
I DON'T WANNA TALK ABOUT IT.
FINE.

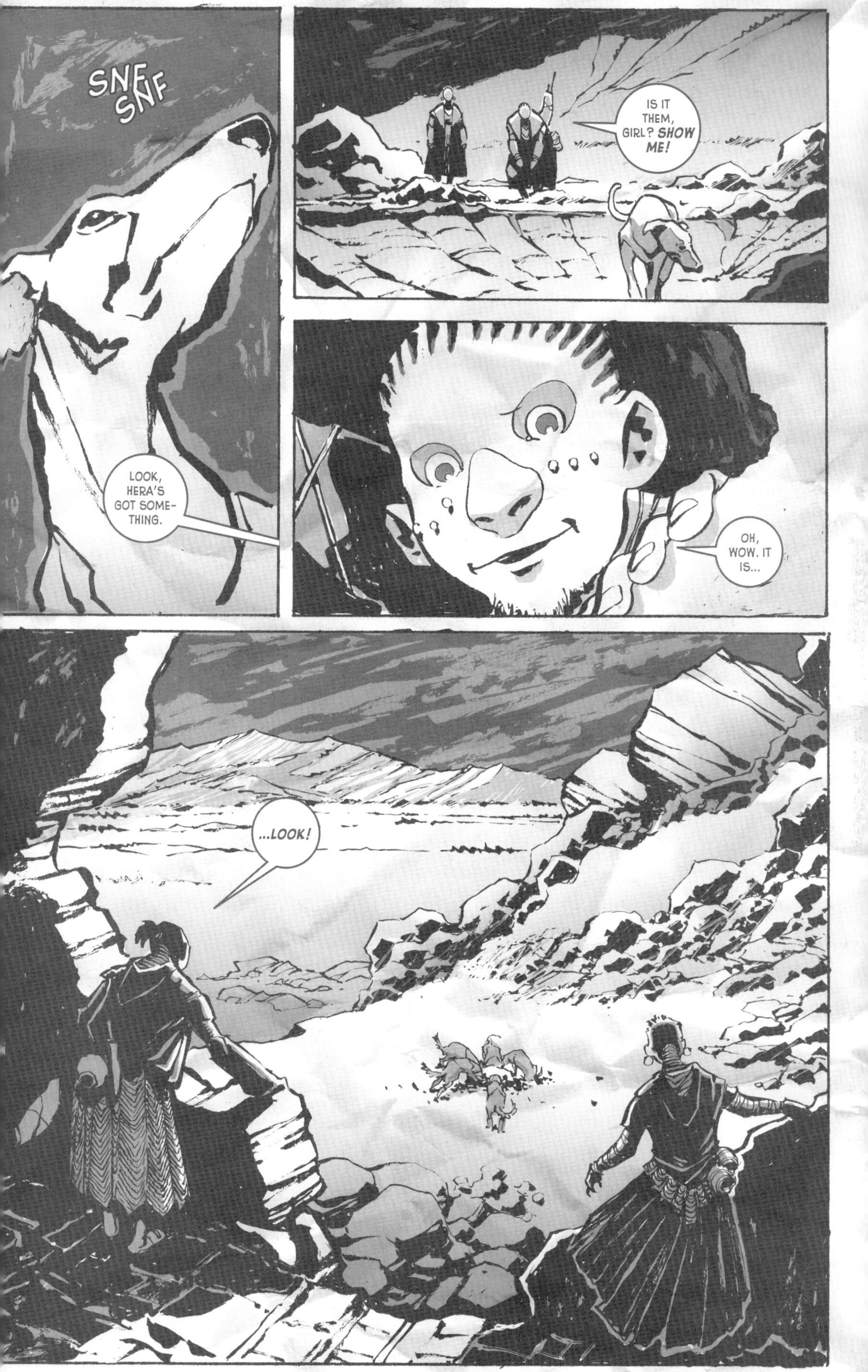
SNF SNF
IS IT THEM, GIRL? SHOW ME!
LOOK, HERA'S GOT SOME-THING.
OH, WOW. IT IS...
...LOOK!

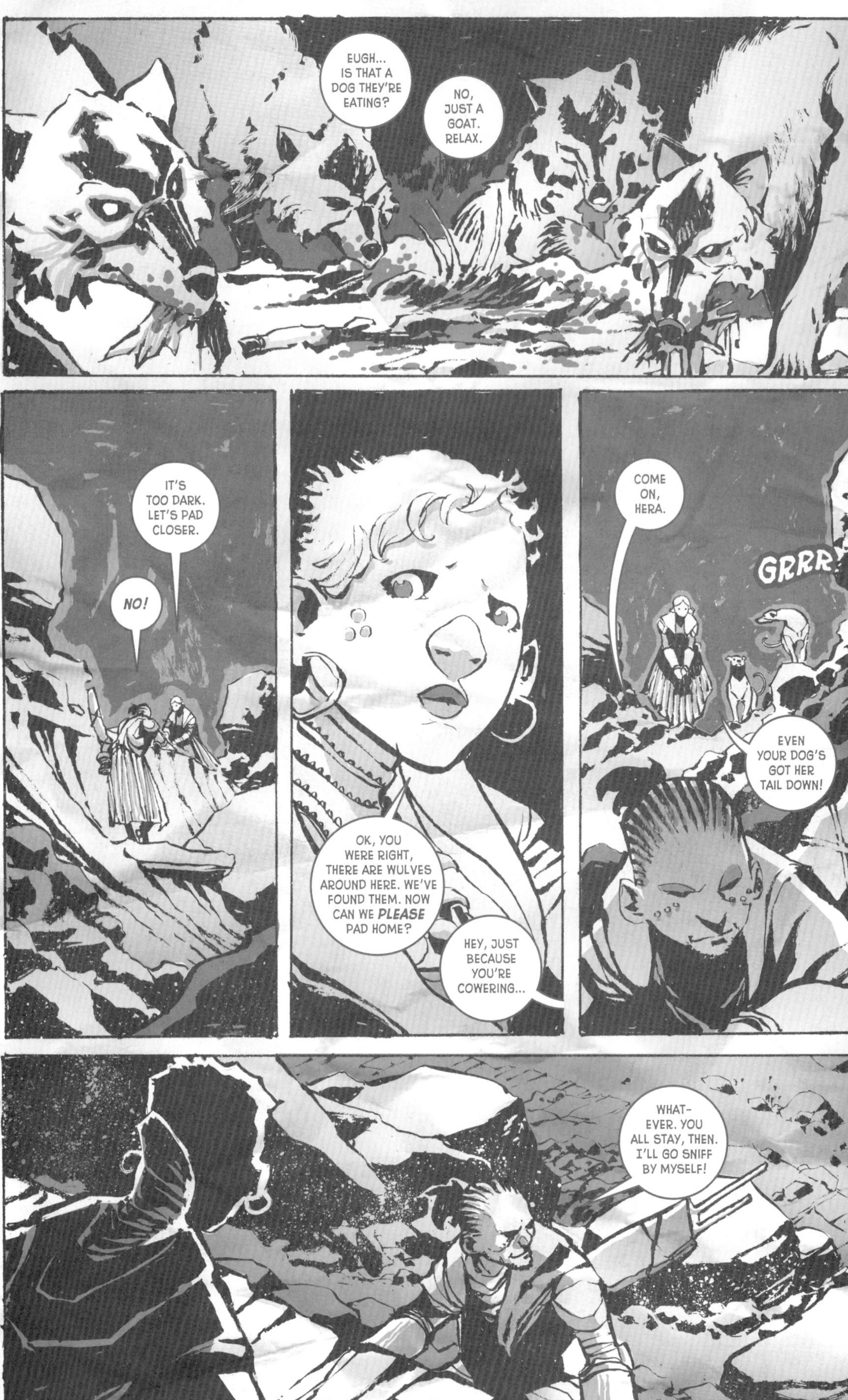
EUGH... IS THAT A DOG THEY'RE EATING?
NO, JUST A GOAT. RELAX.
IT'S TOO DARK. LET'S PAD CLOSER.
NO!
OK, YOU WERE RIGHT, THERE ARE WULVES AROUND HERE. WE'VE FOUND THEM. NOW CAN WE *PLEASE* PAD HOME?
HEY, JUST BECAUSE YOU'RE COWERING...
COME ON, HERA.
GRRR
EVEN YOUR DOG'S GOT HER TAIL DOWN!
WHAT-EVER. YOU ALL STAY, THEN. I'LL GO SNIFF BY MYSELF!

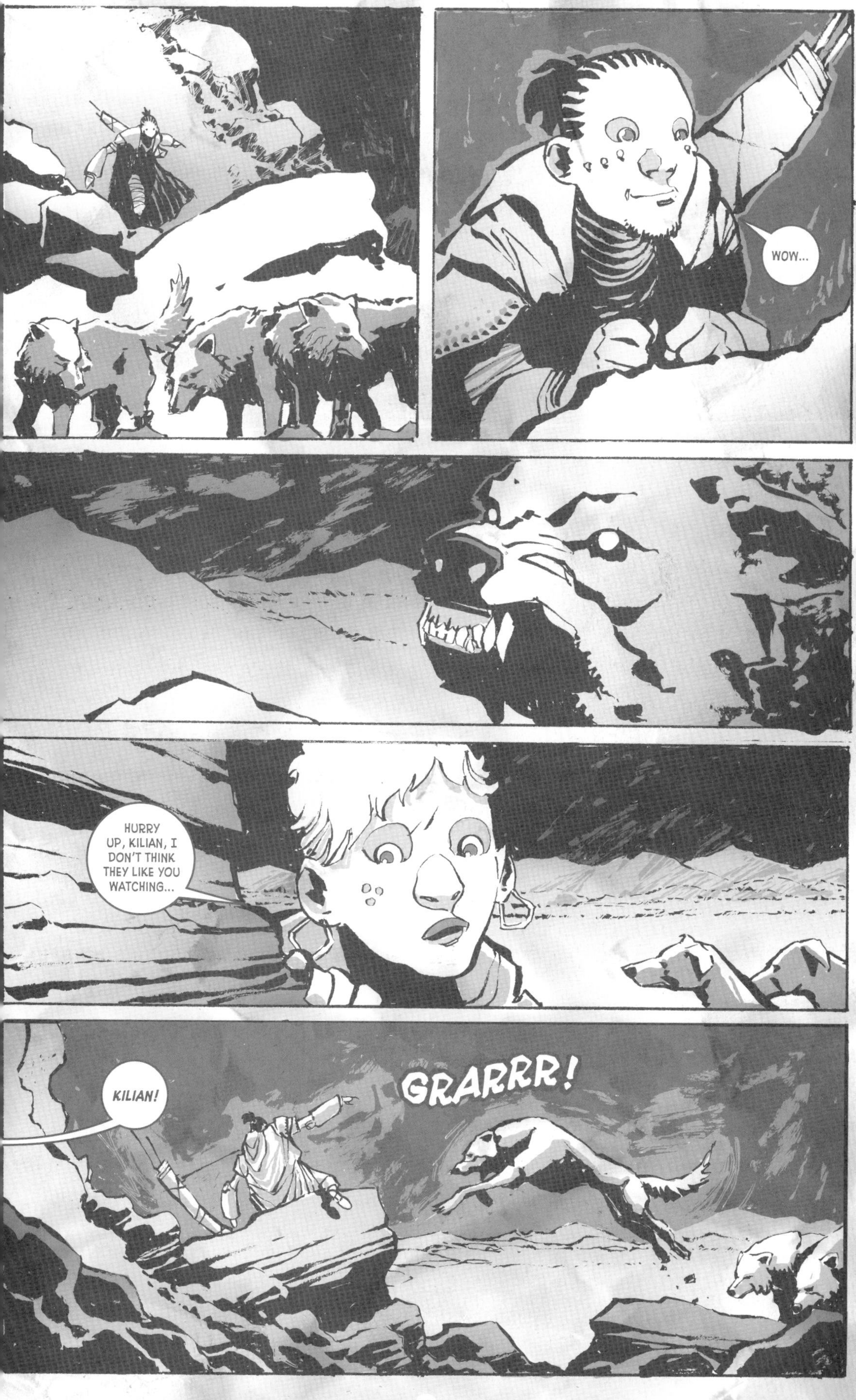
WOW...
HURRY UP, KILIAN, I DON'T THINK THEY LIKE YOU WATCHING...
KILIAN!
GRARRR!

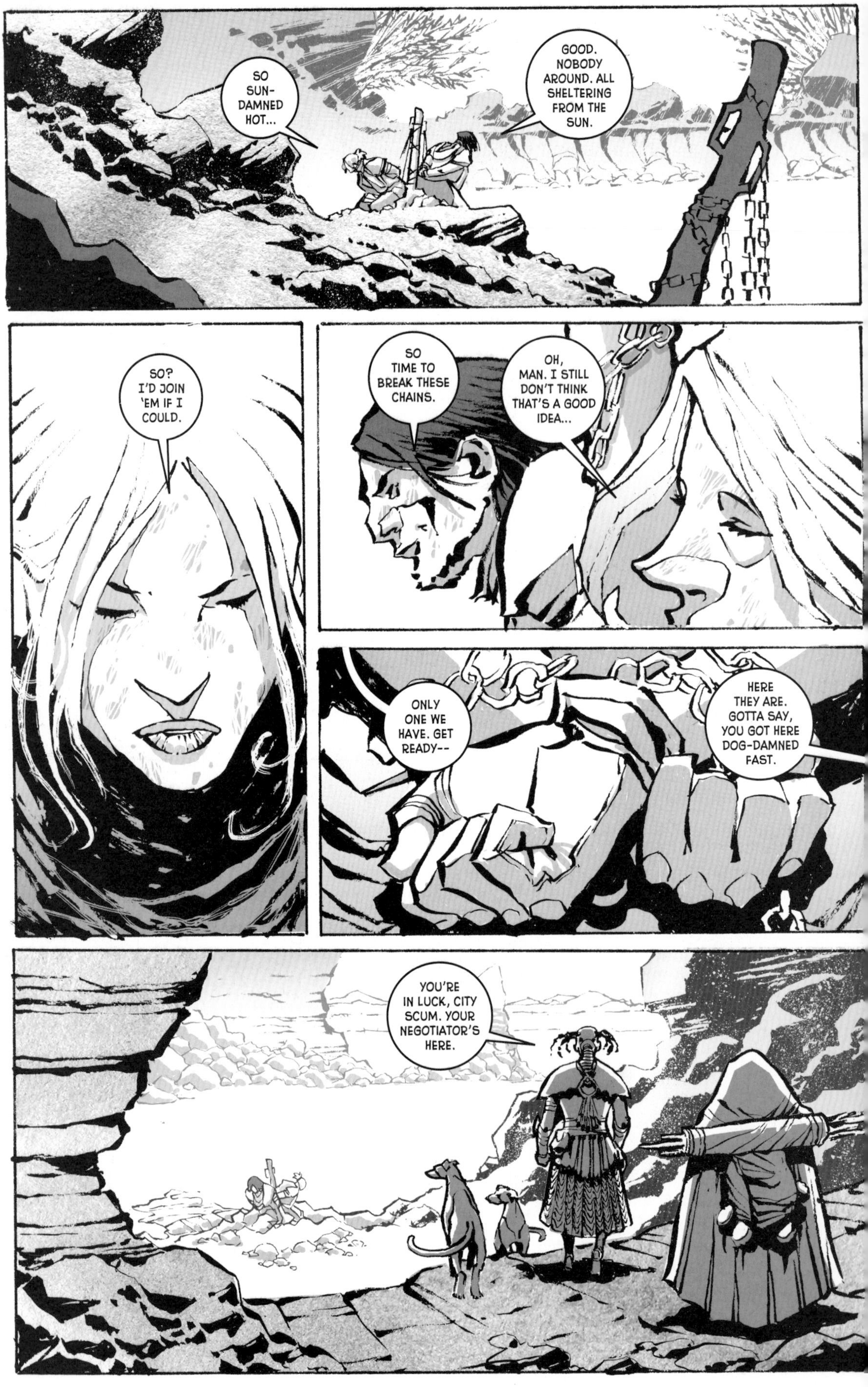
SO SUN-DAMNED HOT...
GOOD. NOBODY AROUND. ALL SHELTERING FROM THE SUN.
SO? I'D JOIN 'EM IF I COULD.
SO TIME TO BREAK THESE CHAINS.
OH, MAN. I STILL DON'T THINK THAT'S A GOOD IDEA...
ONLY ONE WE HAVE. GET READY--
HERE THEY ARE. GOTTA SAY, YOU GOT HERE DOG-DAMNED FAST.
YOU'RE IN LUCK, CITY SCUM. YOUR NEGOTIATOR'S HERE.

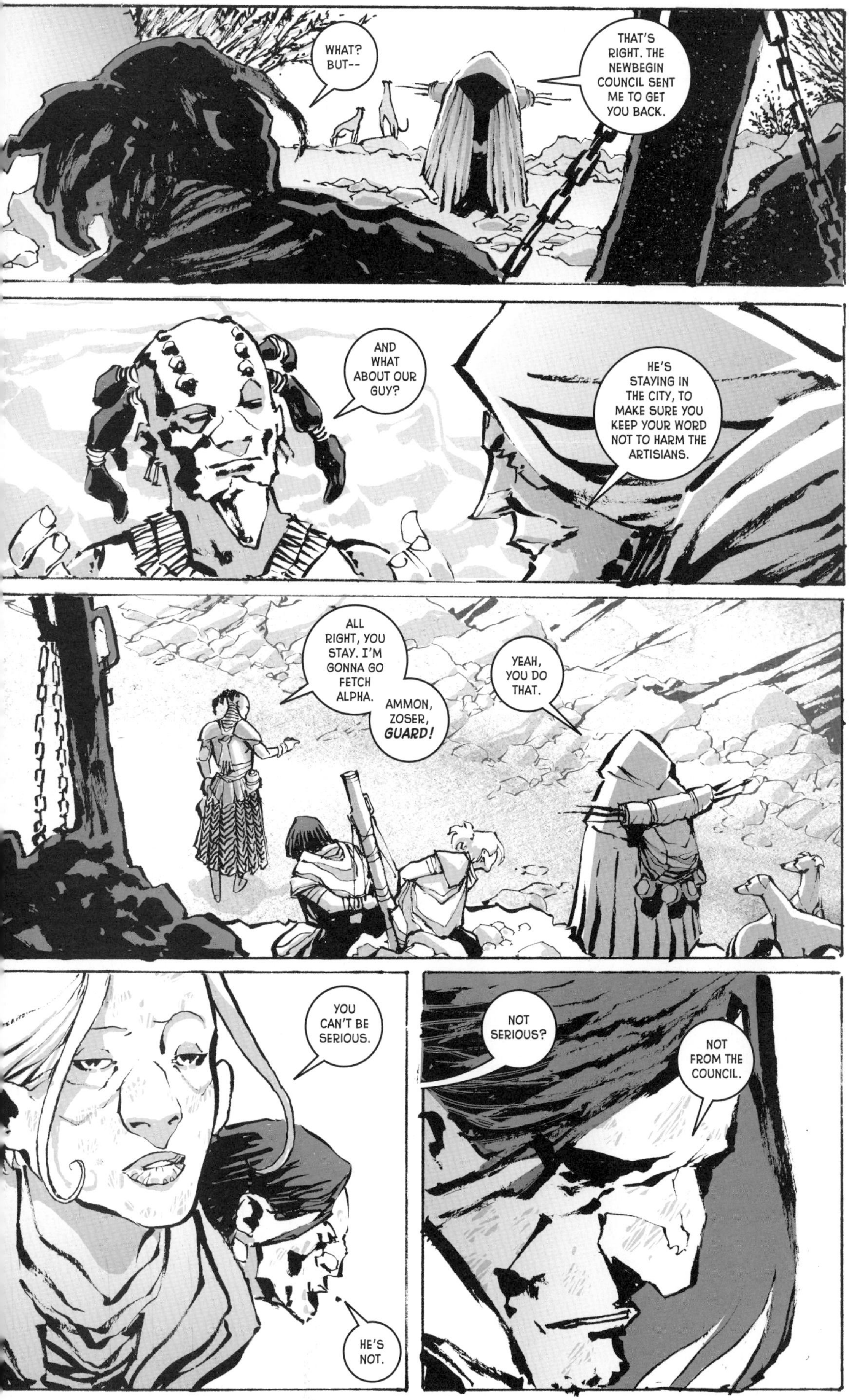
WHAT? BUT--
THAT'S RIGHT. THE NEWBEGIN COUNCIL SENT ME TO GET YOU BACK.
AND WHAT ABOUT OUR GUY?
HE'S STAYING IN THE CITY, TO MAKE SURE YOU KEEP YOUR WORD NOT TO HARM THE ARTISIANS.
ALL RIGHT, YOU STAY. I'M GONNA GO FETCH ALPHA.
AMMON, ZOSER, GUARD!
YEAH, YOU DO THAT.
YOU CAN'T BE SERIOUS.
HE'S NOT.
NOT SERIOUS?
NOT FROM THE COUNCIL.

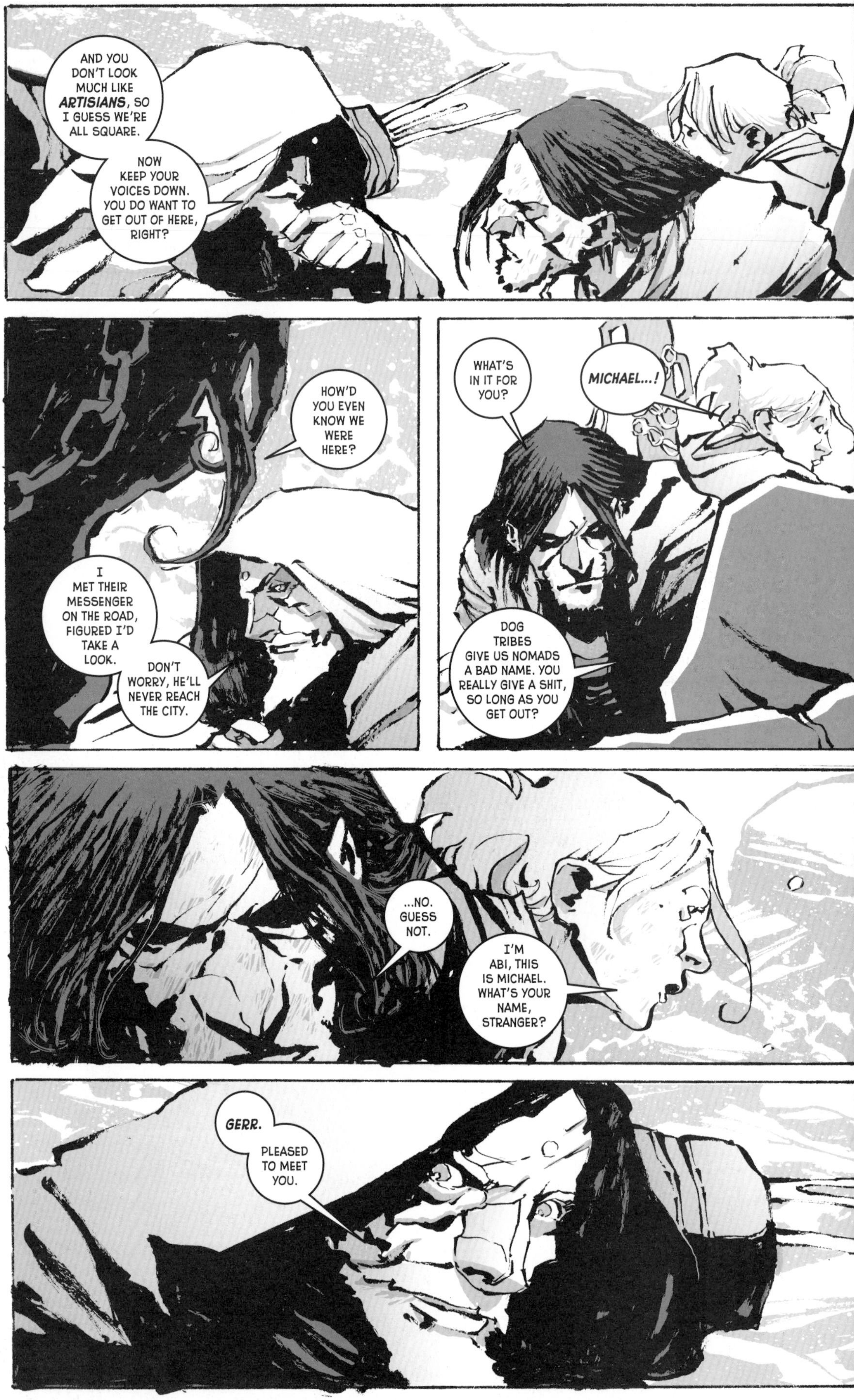
AND YOU DON'T LOOK MUCH LIKE ARTISIANS, SO I GUESS WE'RE ALL SQUARE.
NOW KEEP YOUR VOICES DOWN. YOU DO WANT TO GET OUT OF HERE, RIGHT?
HOW'D YOU EVEN KNOW WE WERE HERE?
I MET THEIR MESSENGER ON THE ROAD, FIGURED I'D TAKE A LOOK.
DON'T WORRY, HE'LL NEVER REACH THE CITY.
WHAT'S IN IT FOR YOU?
MICHAEL...!
DOG TRIBES GIVE US NOMADS A BAD NAME. YOU REALLY GIVE A SHIT, SO LONG AS YOU GET OUT?
...NO. GUESS NOT.
I'M ABI, THIS IS MICHAEL. WHAT'S YOUR NAME, STRANGER?
GERR.
PLEASED TO MEET YOU.

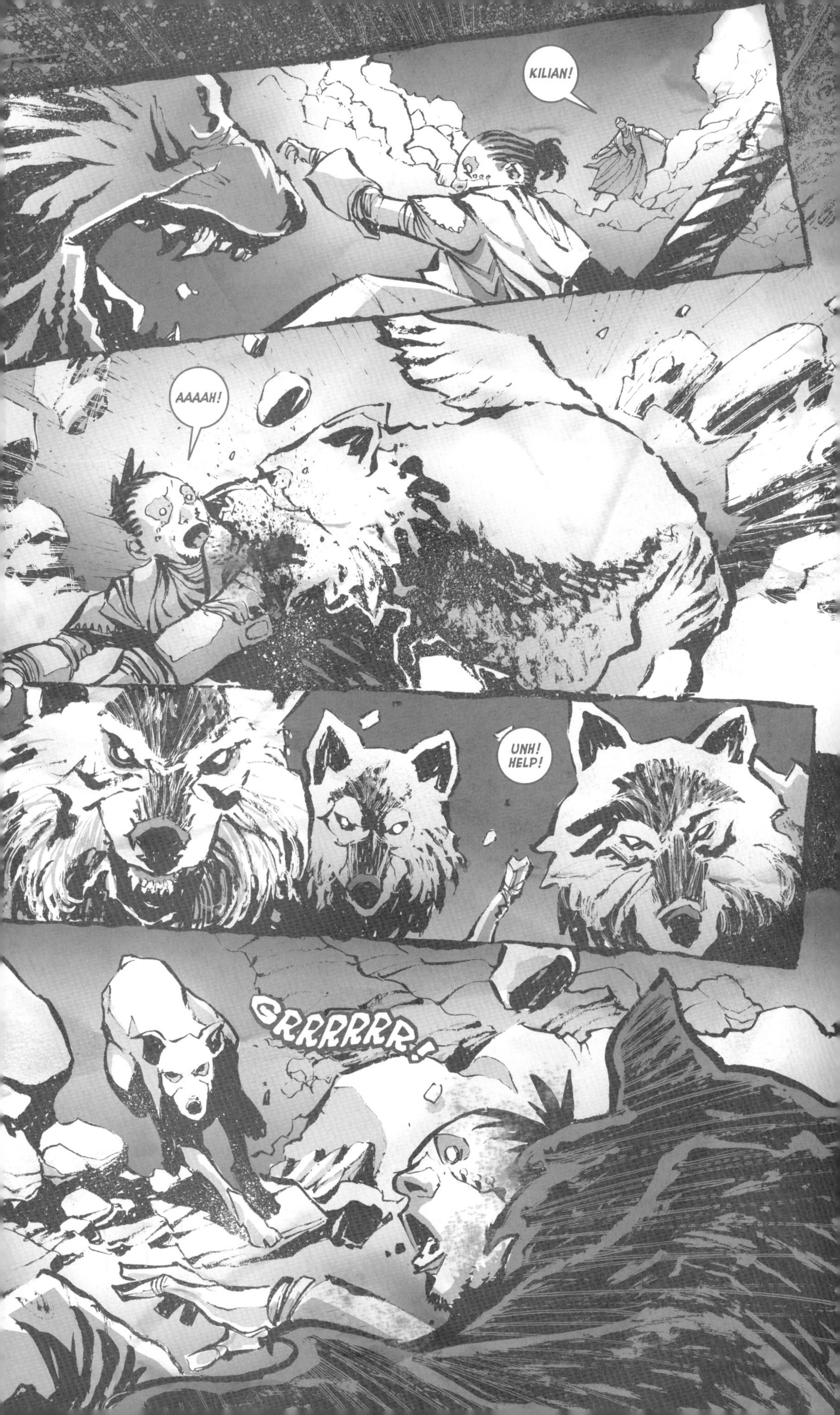
KILIAN!
AAAAH!
UNH! HELP!
GRRRRRR!

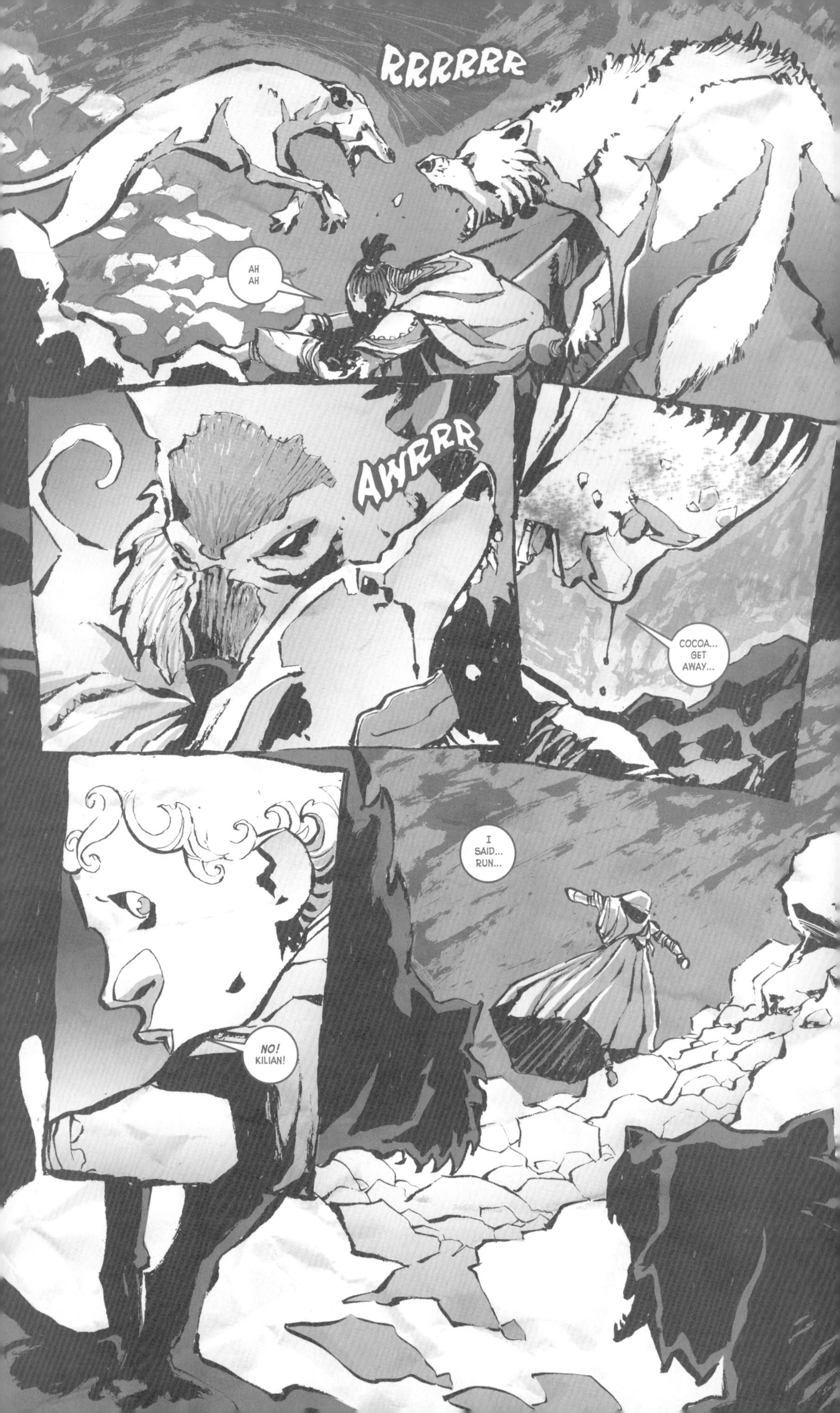
RRRRRR
AH AH
AWRRR
COCOA... GET AWAY...
NO! KILIAN!
I SAID... RUN...

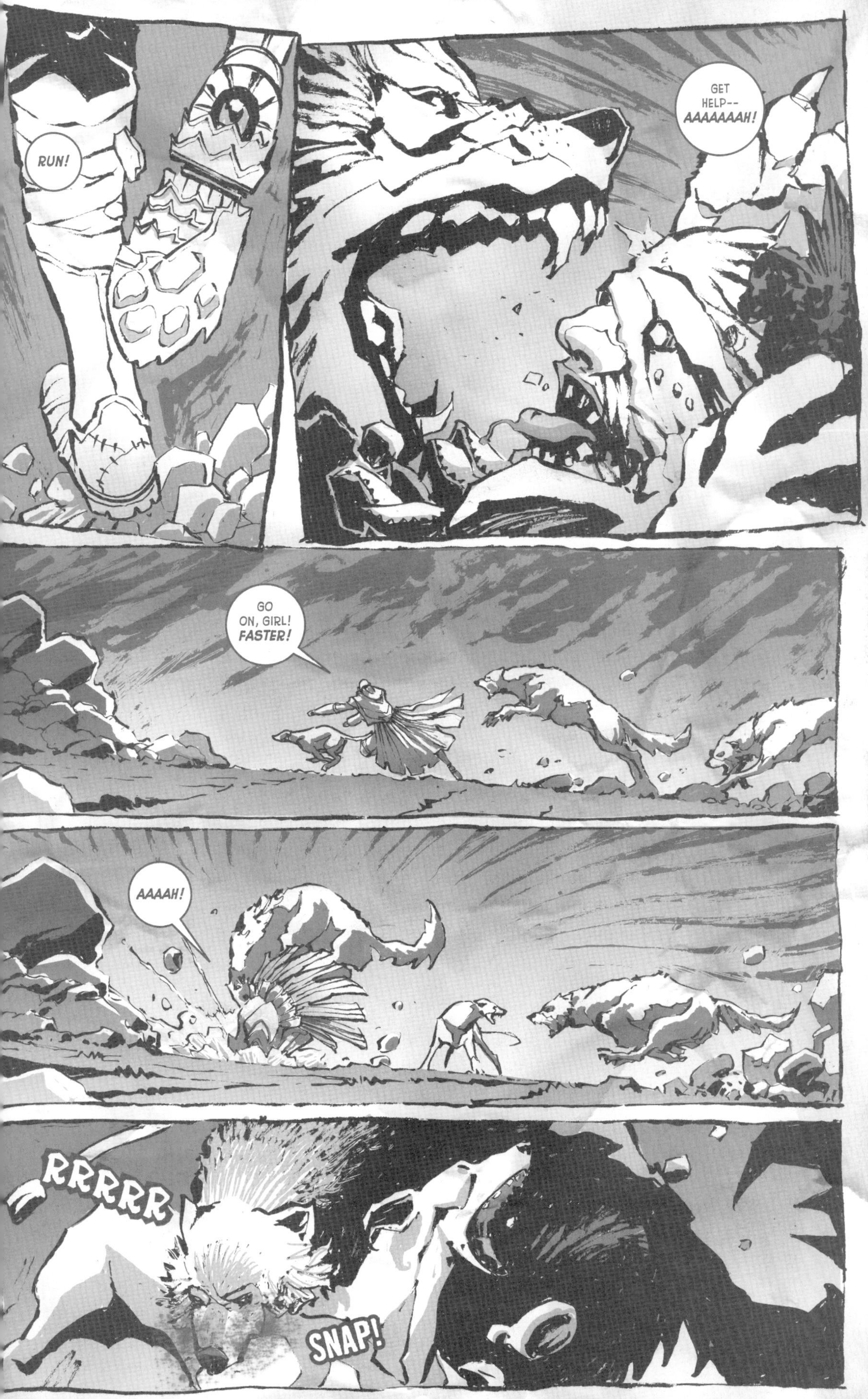
RUN!
GET HELP--
AAAAAAAH!
GO ON, GIRL!
FASTER!
AAAAH!
RRRRRR
SNAP!

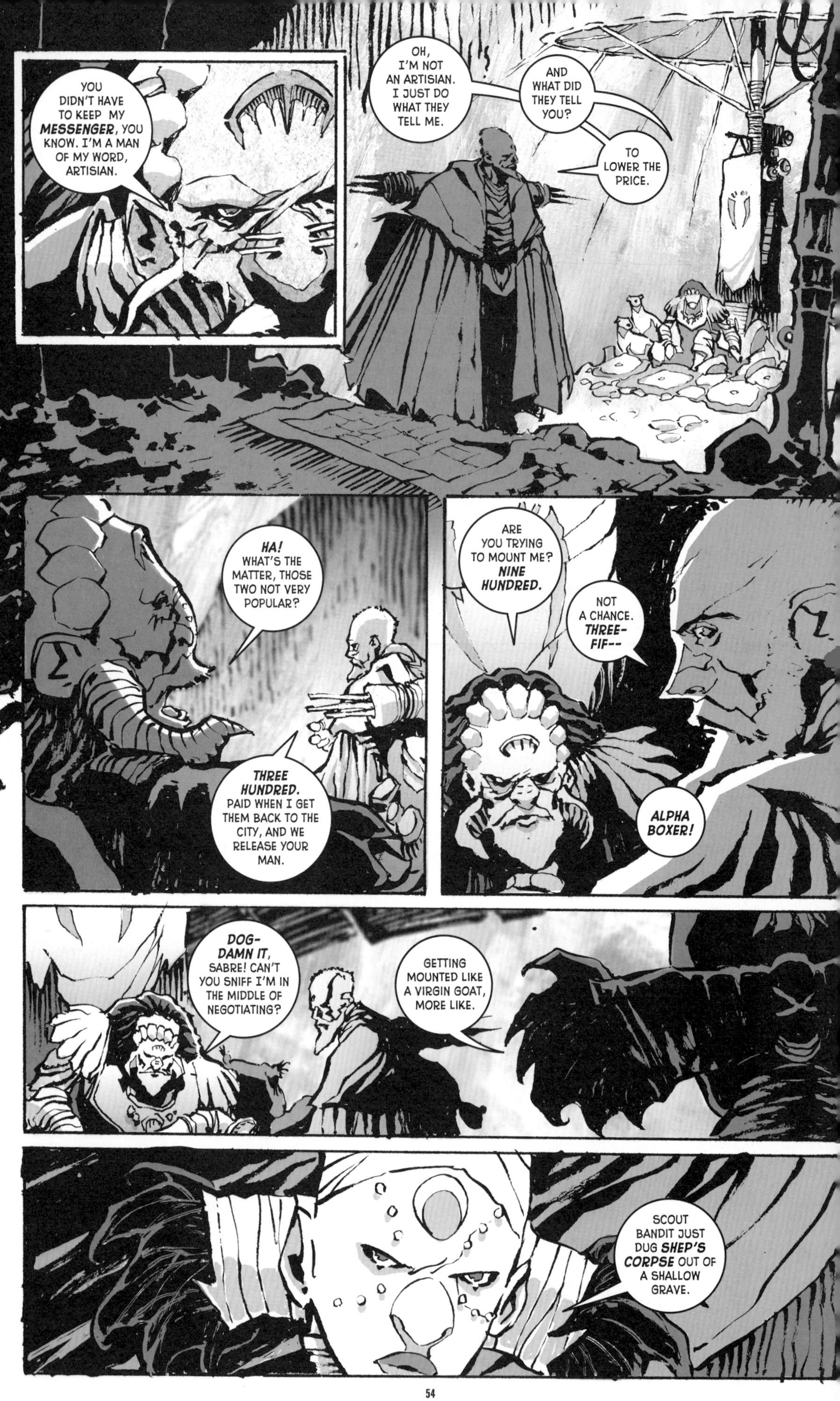
YOU DIDN'T HAVE TO KEEP MY **MESSENGER**, YOU KNOW. I'M A MAN OF MY WORD, ARTISIAN.
OH, I'M NOT AN ARTISIAN. I JUST DO WHAT THEY TELL ME.
AND WHAT DID THEY TELL YOU?
TO LOWER THE PRICE.
HA! WHAT'S THE MATTER, THOSE TWO NOT VERY POPULAR?
THREE HUNDRED. PAID WHEN I GET THEM BACK TO THE CITY, AND WE RELEASE YOUR MAN.
ARE YOU TRYING TO MOUNT ME? **NINE HUNDRED.**
NOT A CHANCE. **THREE-FIF--**
ALPHA BOXER!
DOG-DAMN IT, SABRE! CAN'T YOU SNIFF I'M IN THE MIDDLE OF NEGOTIATING?
GETTING MOUNTED LIKE A VIRGIN GOAT, MORE LIKE.
SCOUT BANDIT JUST DUG **SHEP'S CORPSE** OUT OF A SHALLOW GRAVE.

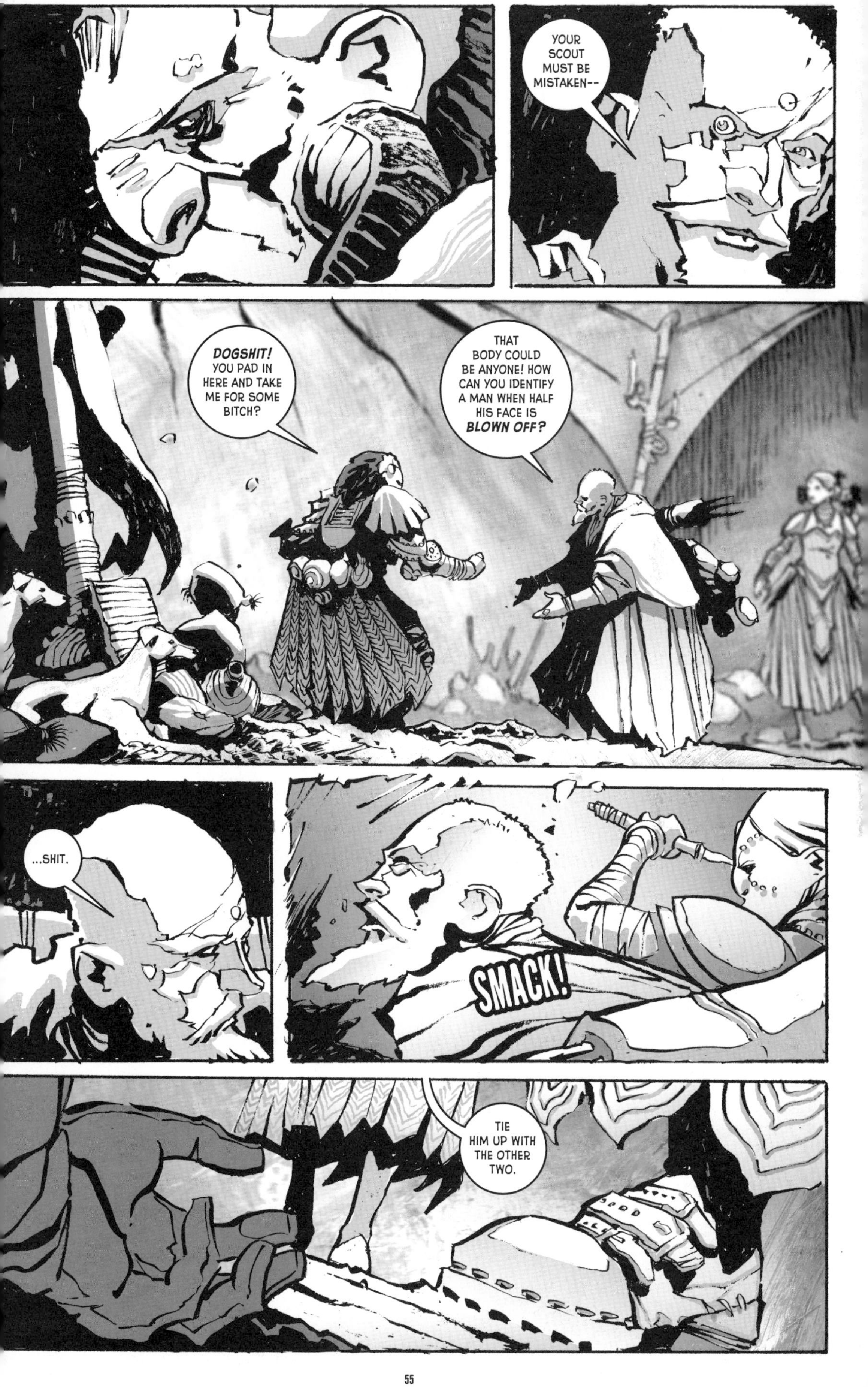
YOUR SCOUT MUST BE MISTAKEN--
DOGSHIT! YOU PAD IN HERE AND TAKE ME FOR SOME BITCH?
THAT BODY COULD BE ANYONE! HOW CAN YOU IDENTIFY A MAN WHEN HALF HIS FACE IS BLOWN OFF?
...SHIT.
SMACK!
TIE HIM UP WITH THE OTHER TWO.

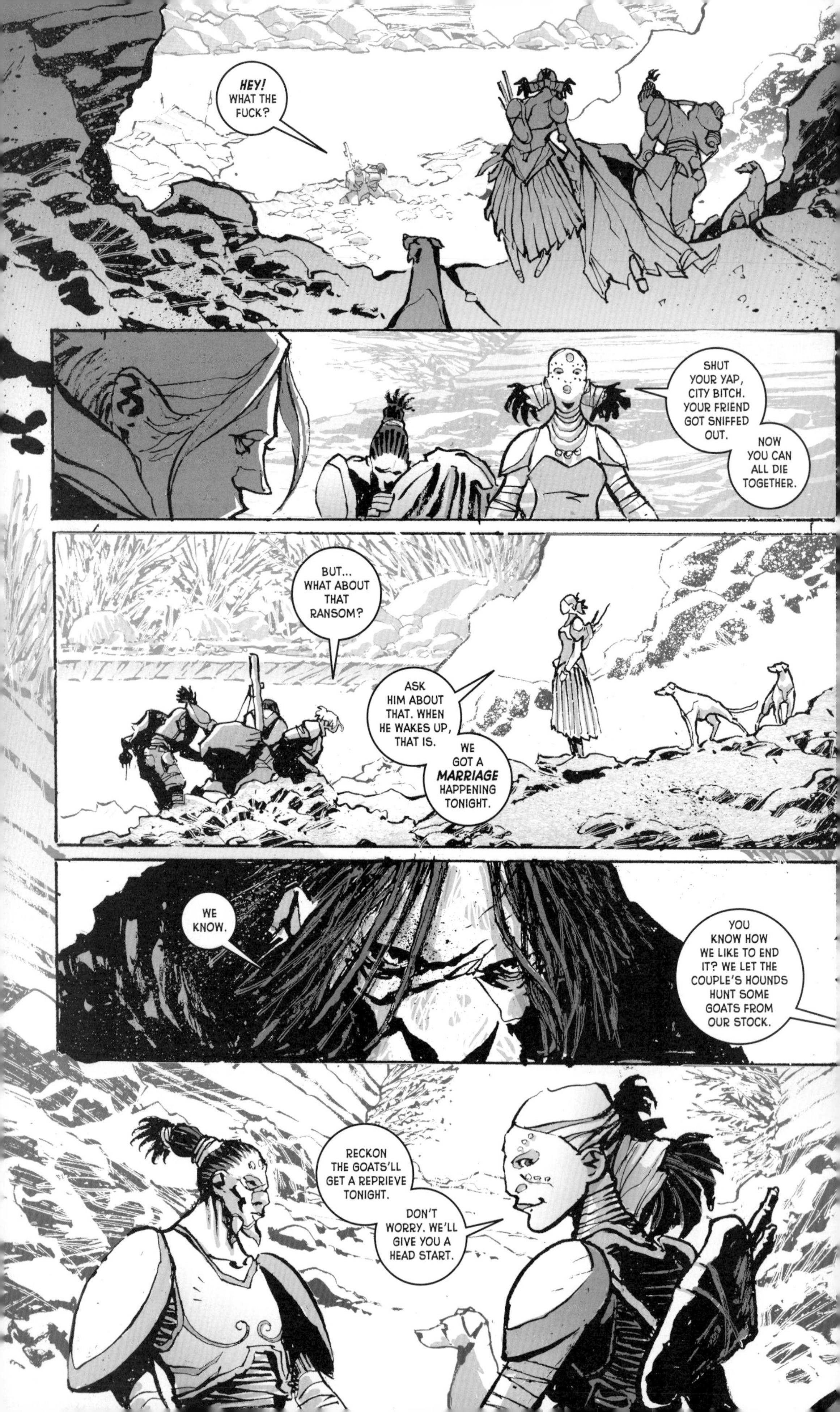

HEY! WHAT THE FUCK?
SHUT YOUR YAP, CITY BITCH. YOUR FRIEND GOT SNIFFED OUT.
NOW YOU CAN ALL DIE TOGETHER.
BUT... WHAT ABOUT THAT RANSOM?
ASK HIM ABOUT THAT. WHEN HE WAKES UP, THAT IS.
WE GOT A *MARRIAGE* HAPPENING TONIGHT.
WE KNOW.
YOU KNOW HOW WE LIKE TO END IT? WE LET THE COUPLE'S HOUNDS HUNT SOME GOATS FROM OUR STOCK.
RECKON THE GOATS'LL GET A REPRIEVE TONIGHT.
DON'T WORRY. WE'LL GIVE YOU A HEAD START.

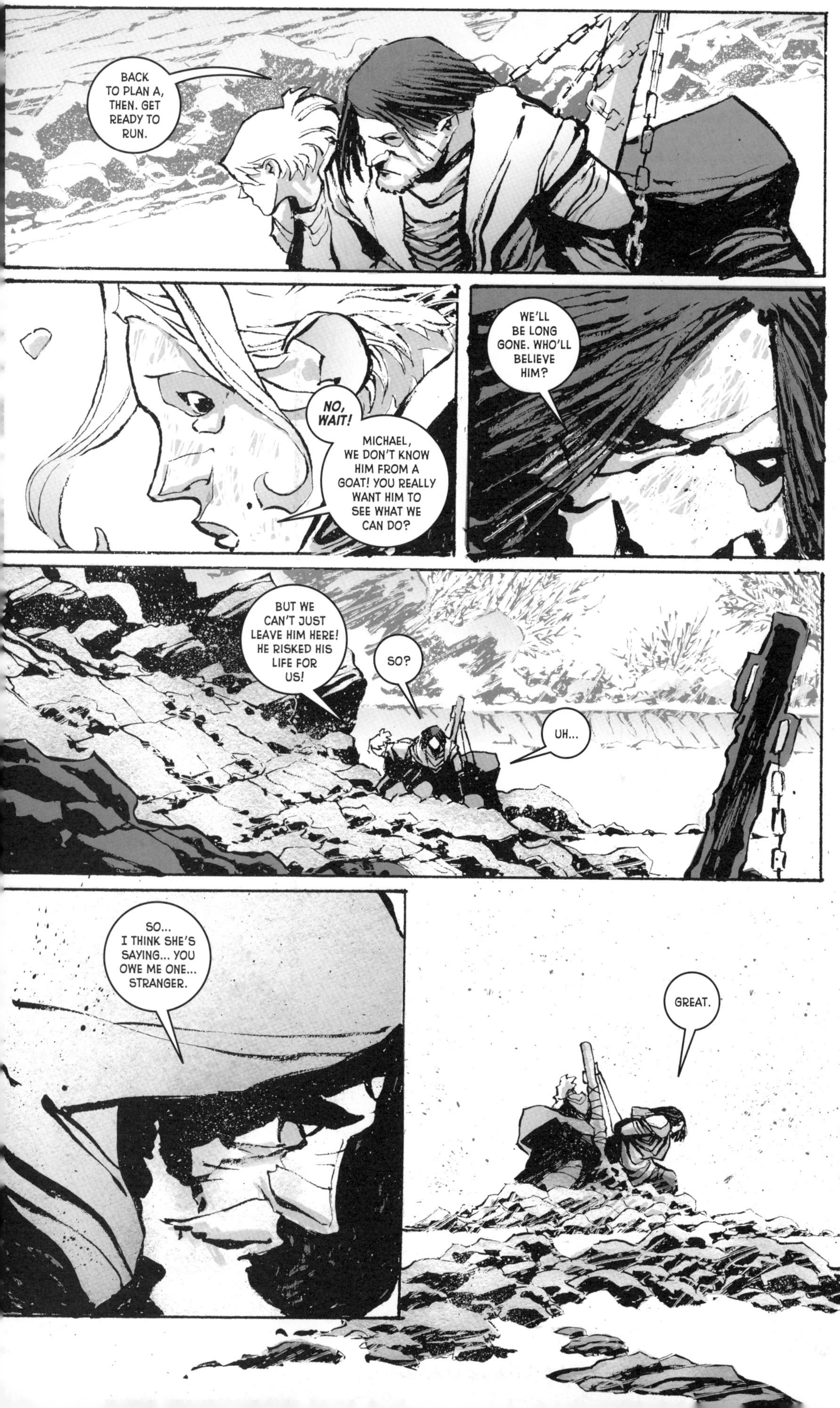
BACK TO PLAN A, THEN. GET READY TO RUN.
NO, WAIT!
MICHAEL, WE DON'T KNOW HIM FROM A GOAT! YOU REALLY WANT HIM TO SEE WHAT WE CAN DO?
WE'LL BE LONG GONE. WHO'LL BELIEVE HIM?
BUT WE CAN'T JUST LEAVE HIM HERE! HE RISKED HIS LIFE FOR US!
SO?
UH...
SO... I THINK SHE'S SAYING... YOU OWE ME ONE... STRANGER.
GREAT.

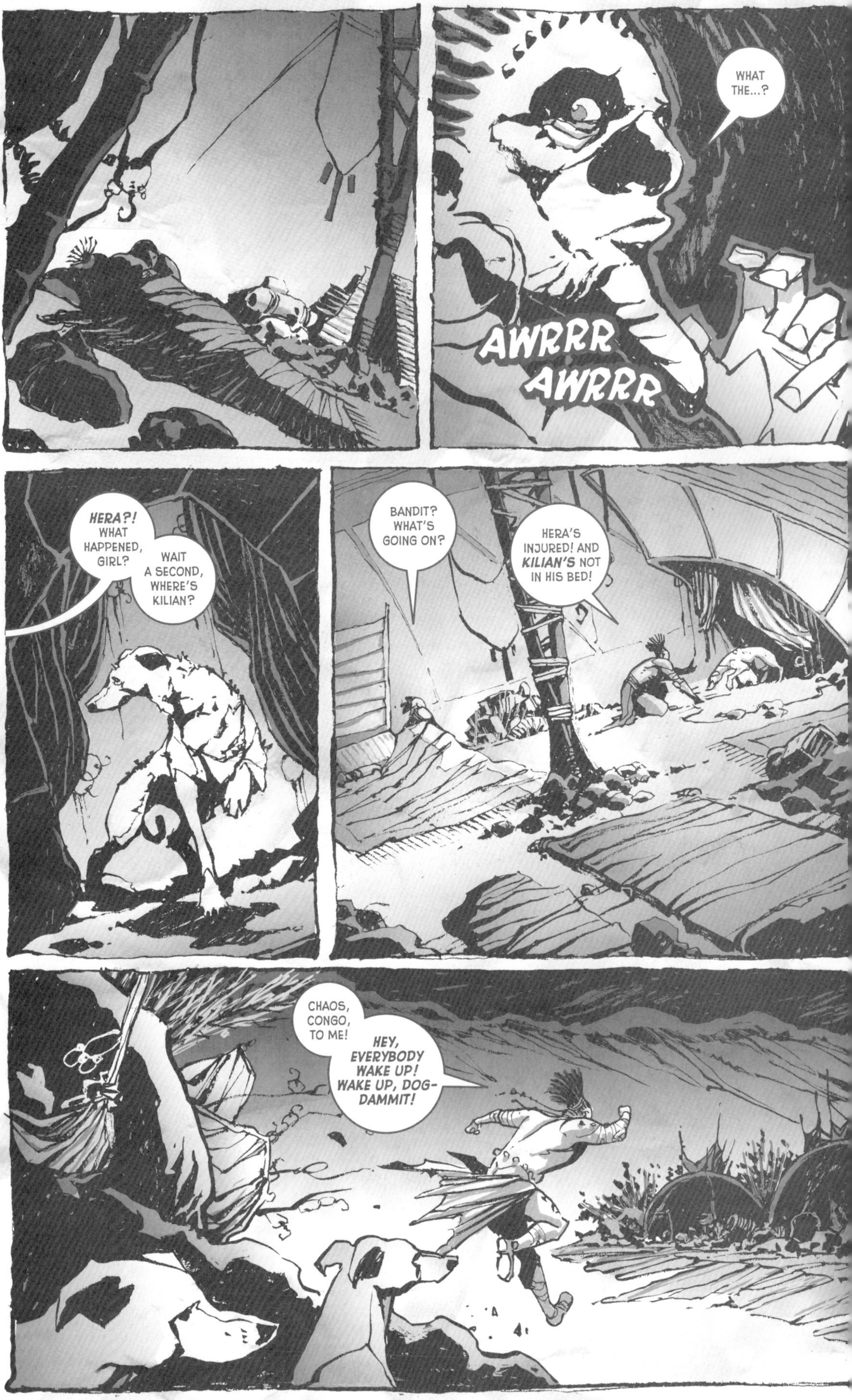
WHAT THE...?
AWRRR AWRRR
HERA?! WHAT HAPPENED, GIRL?
WAIT A SECOND, WHERE'S KILIAN?
BANDIT? WHAT'S GOING ON?
HERA'S INJURED! AND KILIAN'S NOT IN HIS BED!
CHAOS, CONGO, TO ME!
HEY, EVERYBODY WAKE UP! WAKE UP, DOG-DAMMIT!

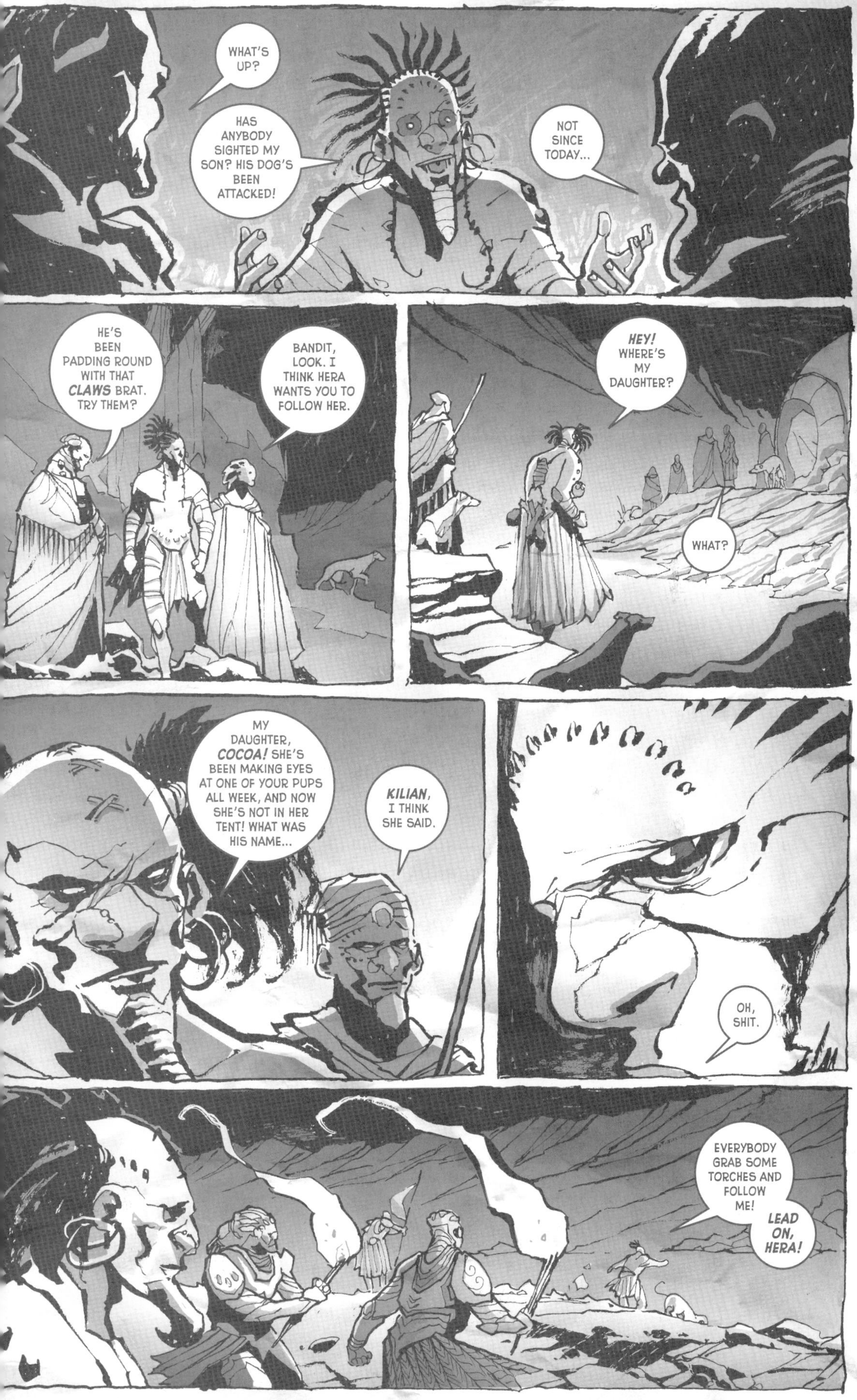
WHAT'S UP?
HAS ANYBODY SIGHTED MY SON? HIS DOG'S BEEN ATTACKED!
NOT SINCE TODAY...
HE'S BEEN PADDING ROUND WITH THAT CLAWS BRAT. TRY THEM?
BANDIT, LOOK. I THINK HERA WANTS YOU TO FOLLOW HER.
HEY! WHERE'S MY DAUGHTER?
WHAT?
MY DAUGHTER, COCOA! SHE'S BEEN MAKING EYES AT ONE OF YOUR PUPS ALL WEEK, AND NOW SHE'S NOT IN HER TENT! WHAT WAS HIS NAME...
KILIAN, I THINK SHE SAID.
OH, SHIT.
EVERYBODY GRAB SOME TORCHES AND FOLLOW ME!
LEAD ON, HERA!

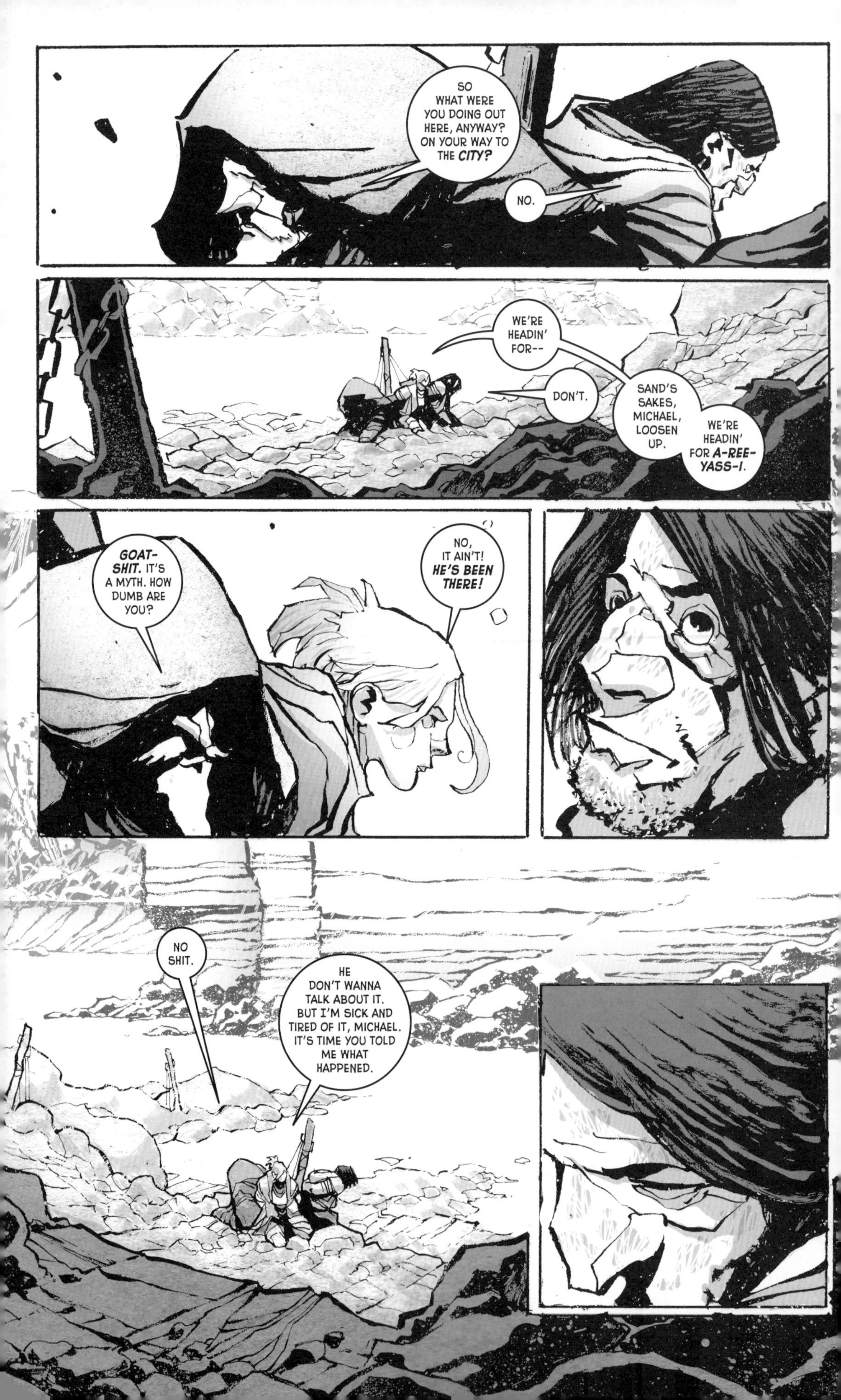
SO WHAT WERE YOU DOING OUT HERE, ANYWAY? ON YOUR WAY TO THE *CITY?*
NO.
WE'RE HEADIN' FOR--
DON'T.
SAND'S SAKES, MICHAEL, LOOSEN UP.
WE'RE HEADIN' FOR ***A-REE-YASS-I***.
GOAT-SHIT. IT'S A MYTH. HOW DUMB ARE YOU?
NO, IT AIN'T! ***HE'S BEEN THERE!***
NO SHIT.
HE DON'T WANNA TALK ABOUT IT. BUT I'M SICK AND TIRED OF IT, MICHAEL. IT'S TIME YOU TOLD ME WHAT HAPPENED.

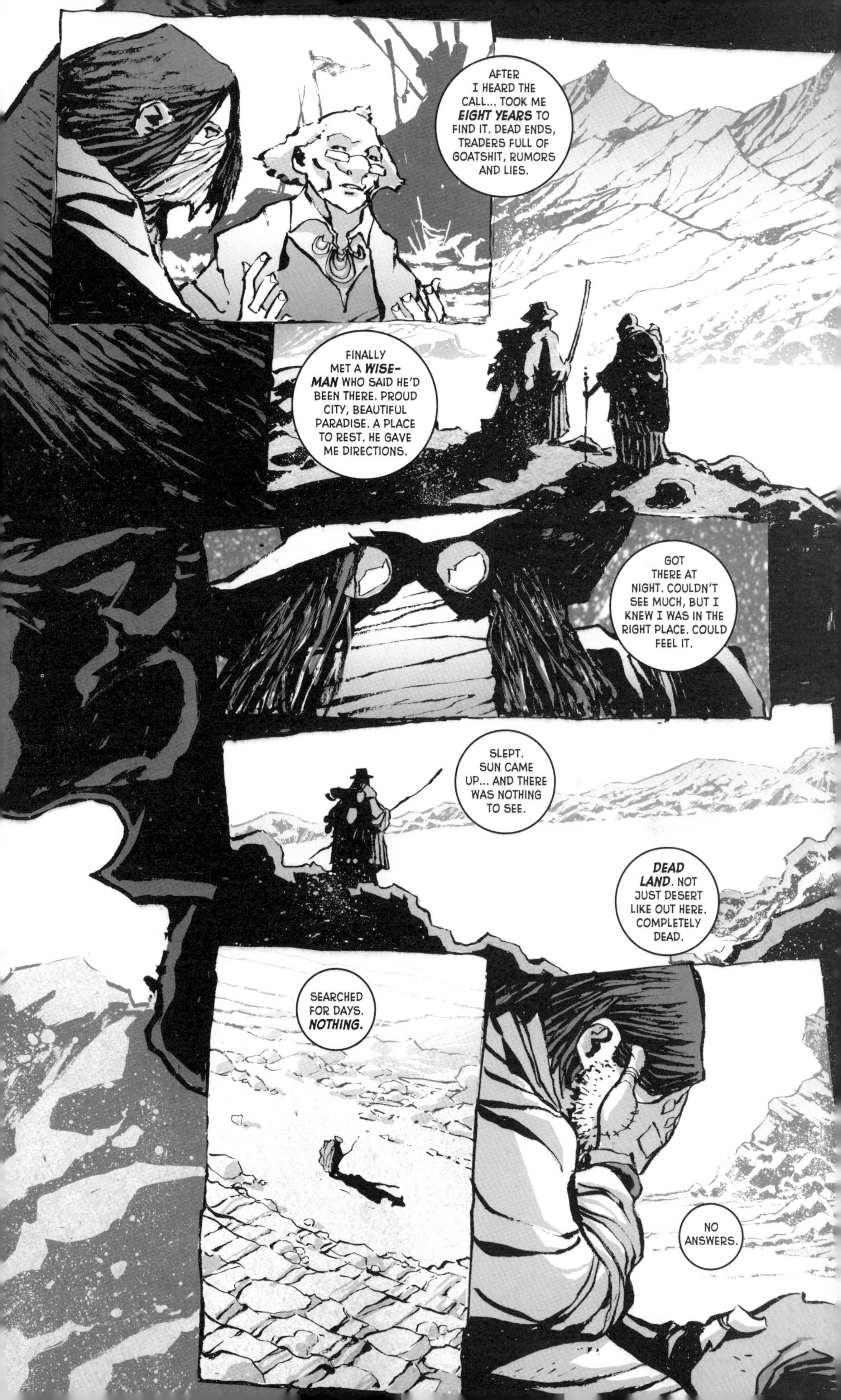
AFTER I HEARD THE CALL... TOOK ME EIGHT YEARS TO FIND IT. DEAD ENDS, TRADERS FULL OF GOATSHIT, RUMORS AND LIES.
FINALLY MET A WISE-MAN WHO SAID HE'D BEEN THERE. PROUD CITY, BEAUTIFUL PARADISE. A PLACE TO REST. HE GAVE ME DIRECTIONS.
GOT THERE AT NIGHT. COULDN'T SEE MUCH, BUT I KNEW I WAS IN THE RIGHT PLACE. COULD FEEL IT.
SLEPT. SUN CAME UP... AND THERE WAS NOTHING TO SEE.
DEAD LAND. NOT JUST DESERT LIKE OUT HERE. COMPLETELY DEAD.
SEARCHED FOR DAYS. NOTHING.
NO ANSWERS.

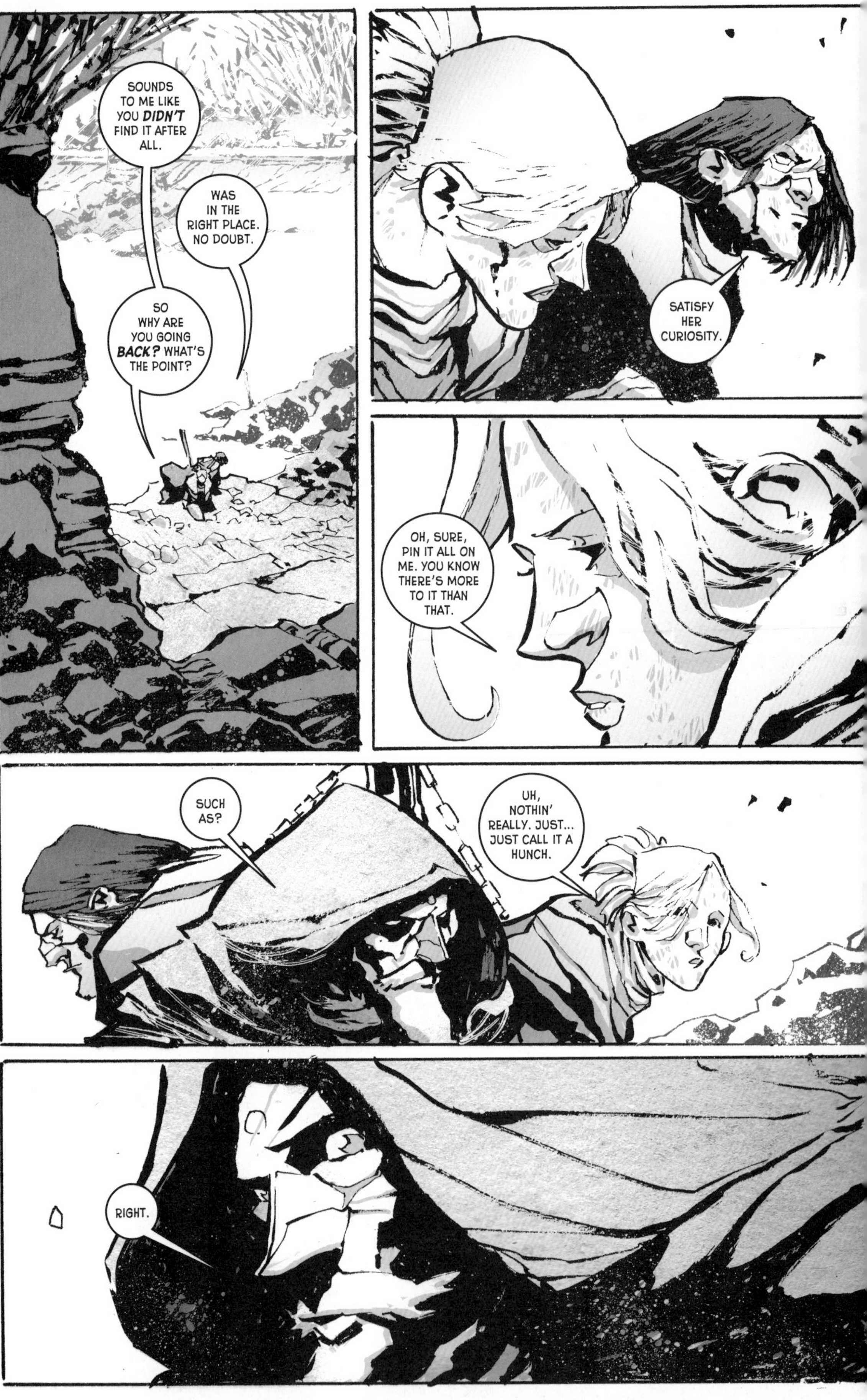
SOUNDS TO ME LIKE YOU *DIDN'T* FIND IT AFTER ALL.
WAS IN THE RIGHT PLACE. NO DOUBT.
SO WHY ARE YOU GOING *BACK?* WHAT'S THE POINT?
SATISFY HER CURIOSITY.
OH, SURE, PIN IT ALL ON ME. YOU KNOW THERE'S MORE TO IT THAN THAT.
SUCH AS?
UH, NOTHIN' REALLY. JUST... JUST CALL IT A HUNCH.
RIGHT.

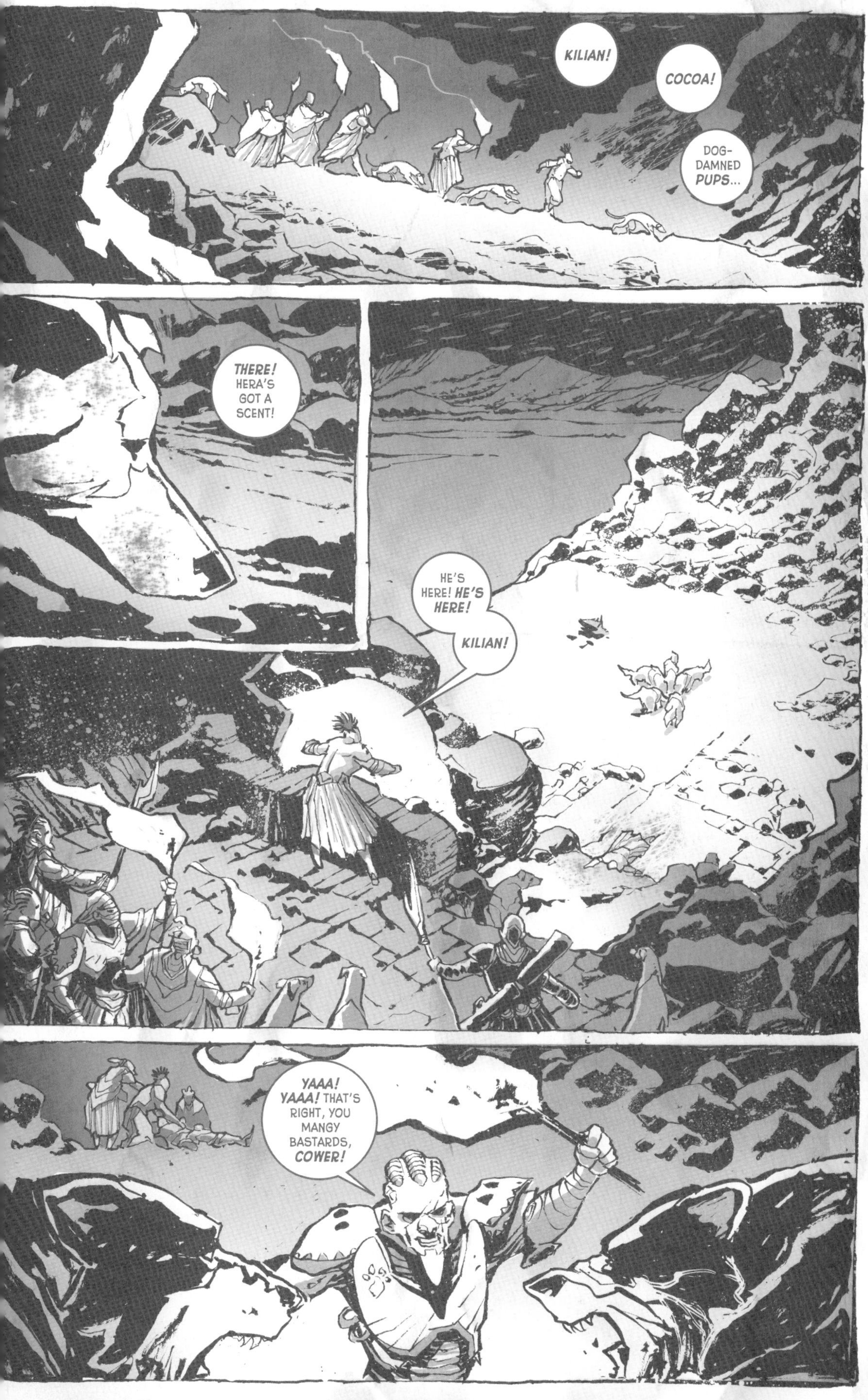
KILIAN!
COCOA!
DOG-DAMNED PUPS...
THERE! HERA'S GOT A SCENT!
HE'S HERE! HE'S HERE!
KILIAN!
YAAA! YAAA! THAT'S RIGHT, YOU MANGY BASTARDS, COWER!

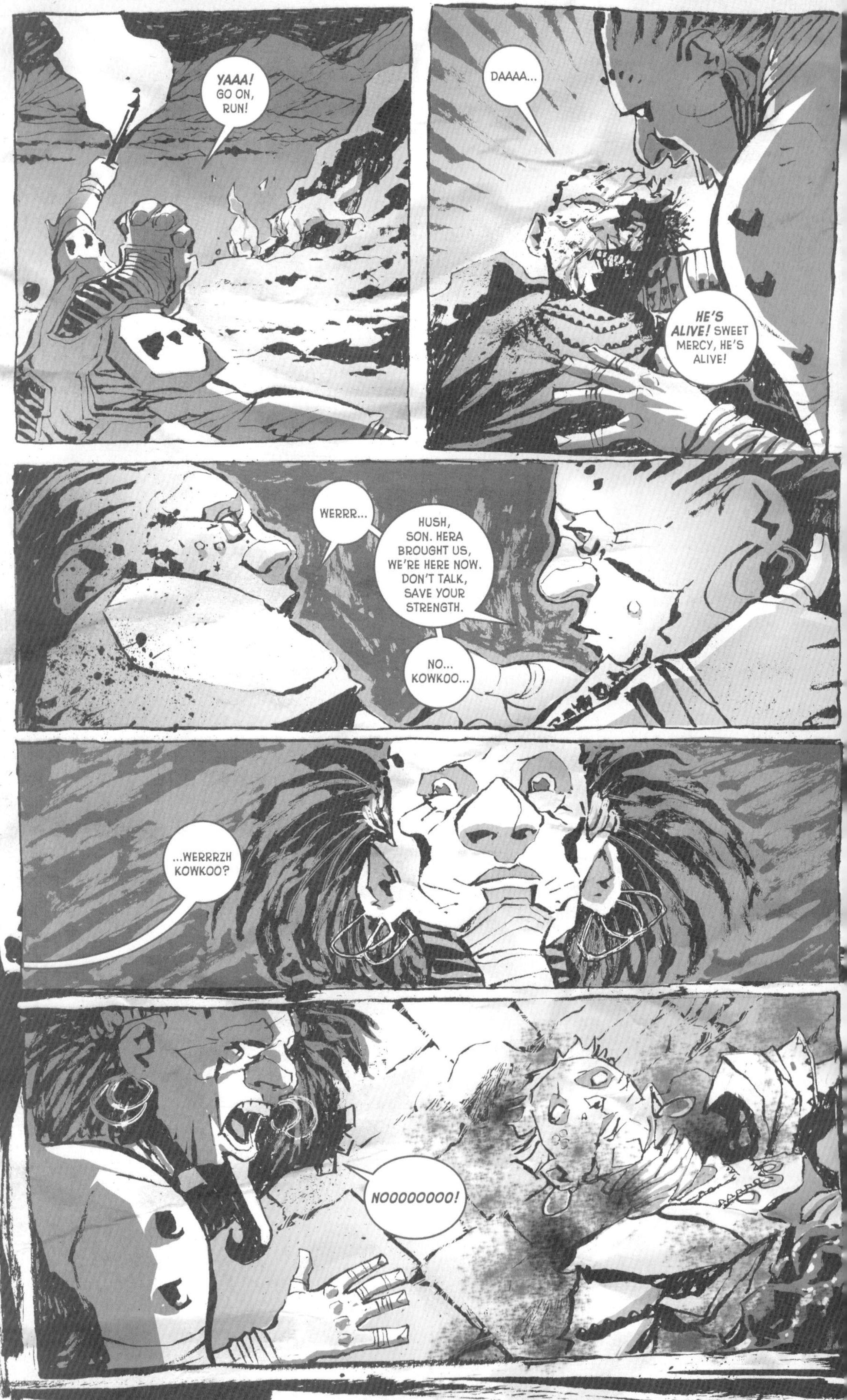
YAAA! GO ON, RUN!
DAAAA...
HE'S ALIVE! SWEET MERCY, HE'S ALIVE!
WERRR...
HUSH, SON. HERA BROUGHT US, WE'RE HERE NOW. DON'T TALK, SAVE YOUR STRENGTH.
NO... KOWKOO...
...WERRRZH KOWKOO?
NOOOOOOOO!

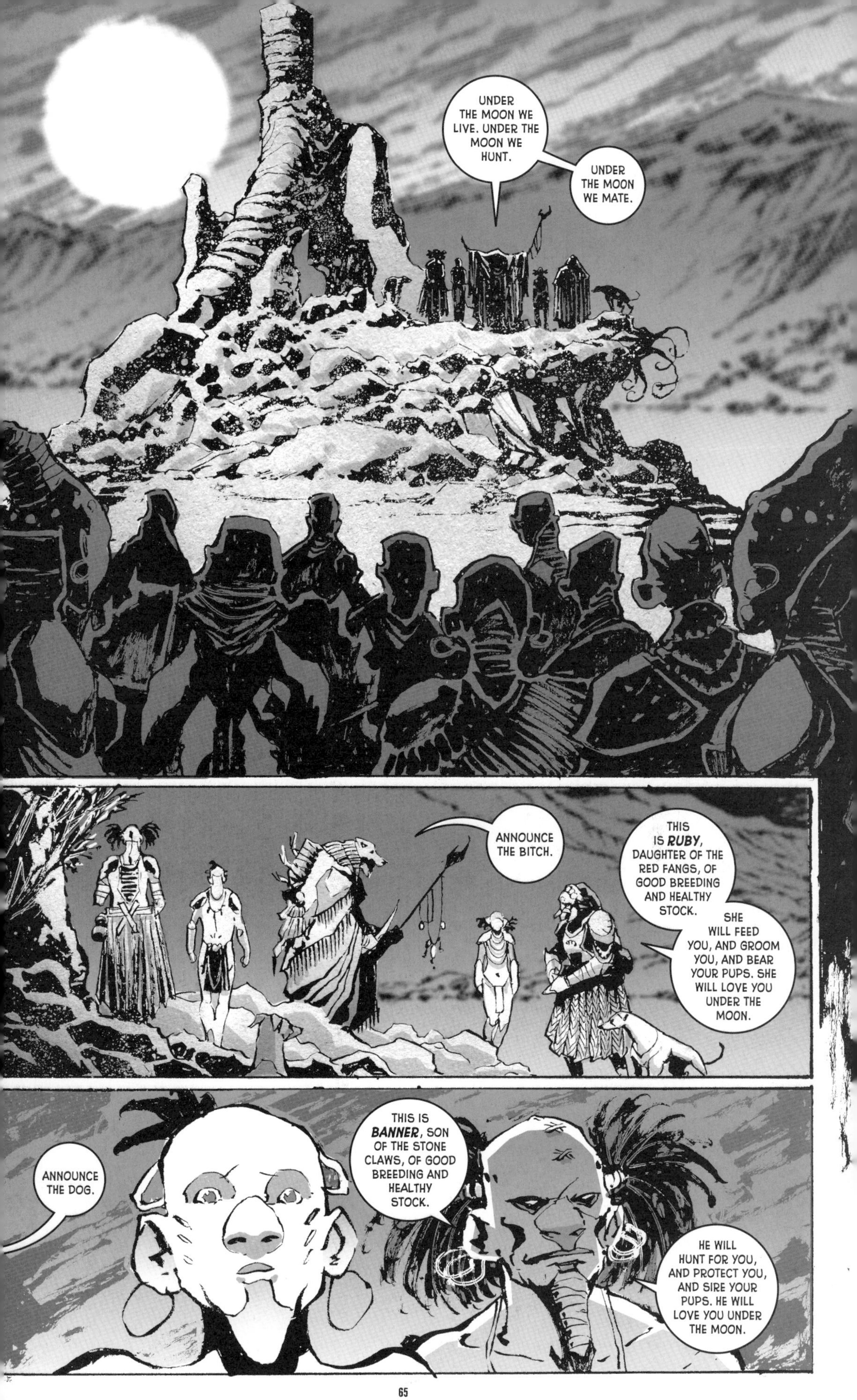
UNDER THE MOON WE LIVE. UNDER THE MOON WE HUNT.
UNDER THE MOON WE MATE.
ANNOUNCE THE BITCH.
THIS IS RUBY, DAUGHTER OF THE RED FANGS, OF GOOD BREEDING AND HEALTHY STOCK.
SHE WILL FEED YOU, AND GROOM YOU, AND BEAR YOUR PUPS. SHE WILL LOVE YOU UNDER THE MOON.
ANNOUNCE THE DOG.
THIS IS BANNER, SON OF THE STONE CLAWS, OF GOOD BREEDING AND HEALTHY STOCK.
HE WILL HUNT FOR YOU, AND PROTECT YOU, AND SIRE YOUR PUPS. HE WILL LOVE YOU UNDER THE MOON.

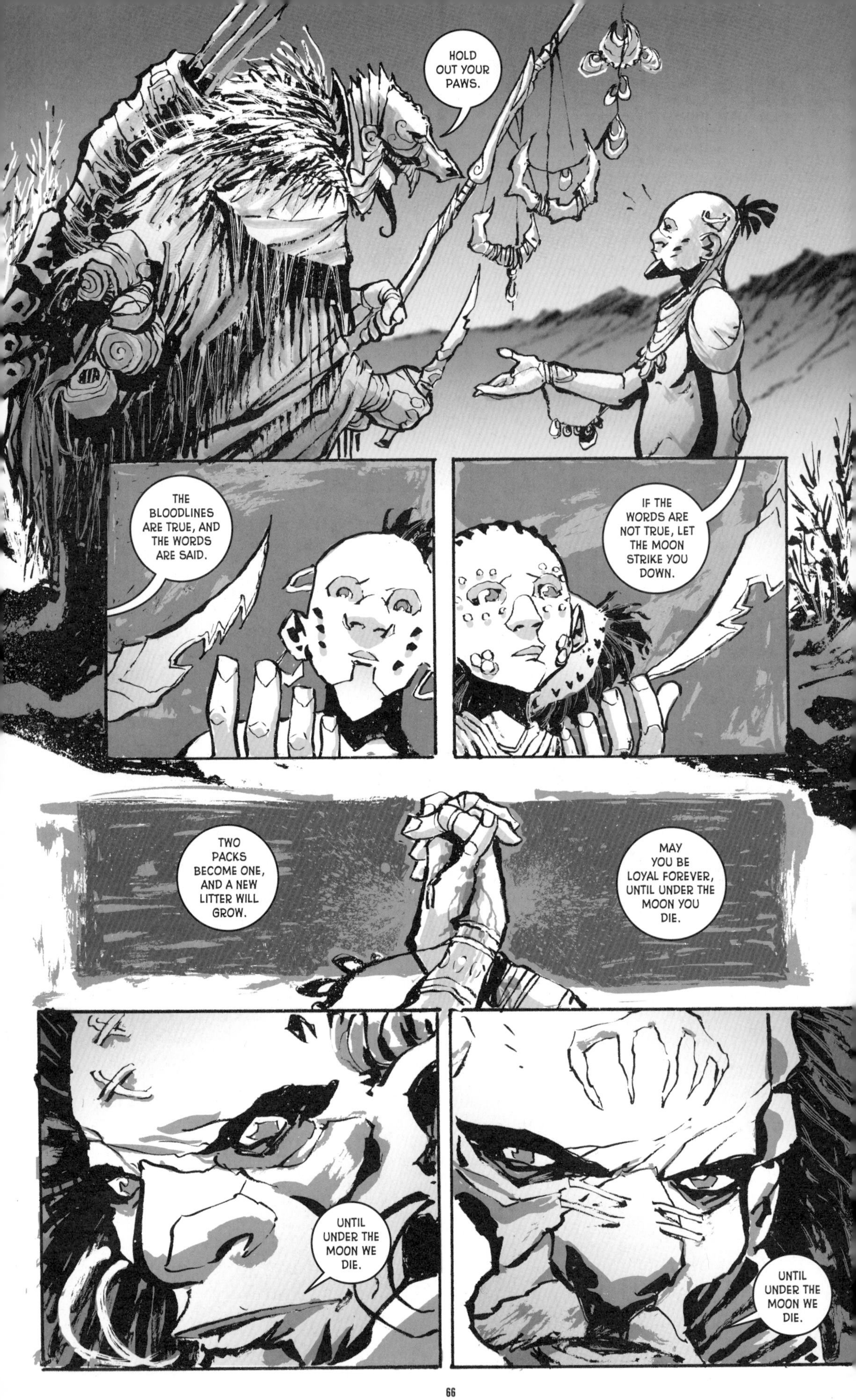
HOLD OUT YOUR PAWS.
THE BLOODLINES ARE TRUE, AND THE WORDS ARE SAID.
IF THE WORDS ARE NOT TRUE, LET THE MOON STRIKE YOU DOWN.
TWO PACKS BECOME ONE, AND A NEW LITTER WILL GROW.
MAY YOU BE LOYAL FOREVER, UNTIL UNDER THE MOON YOU DIE.
UNTIL UNDER THE MOON WE DIE.
UNTIL UNDER THE MOON WE DIE.

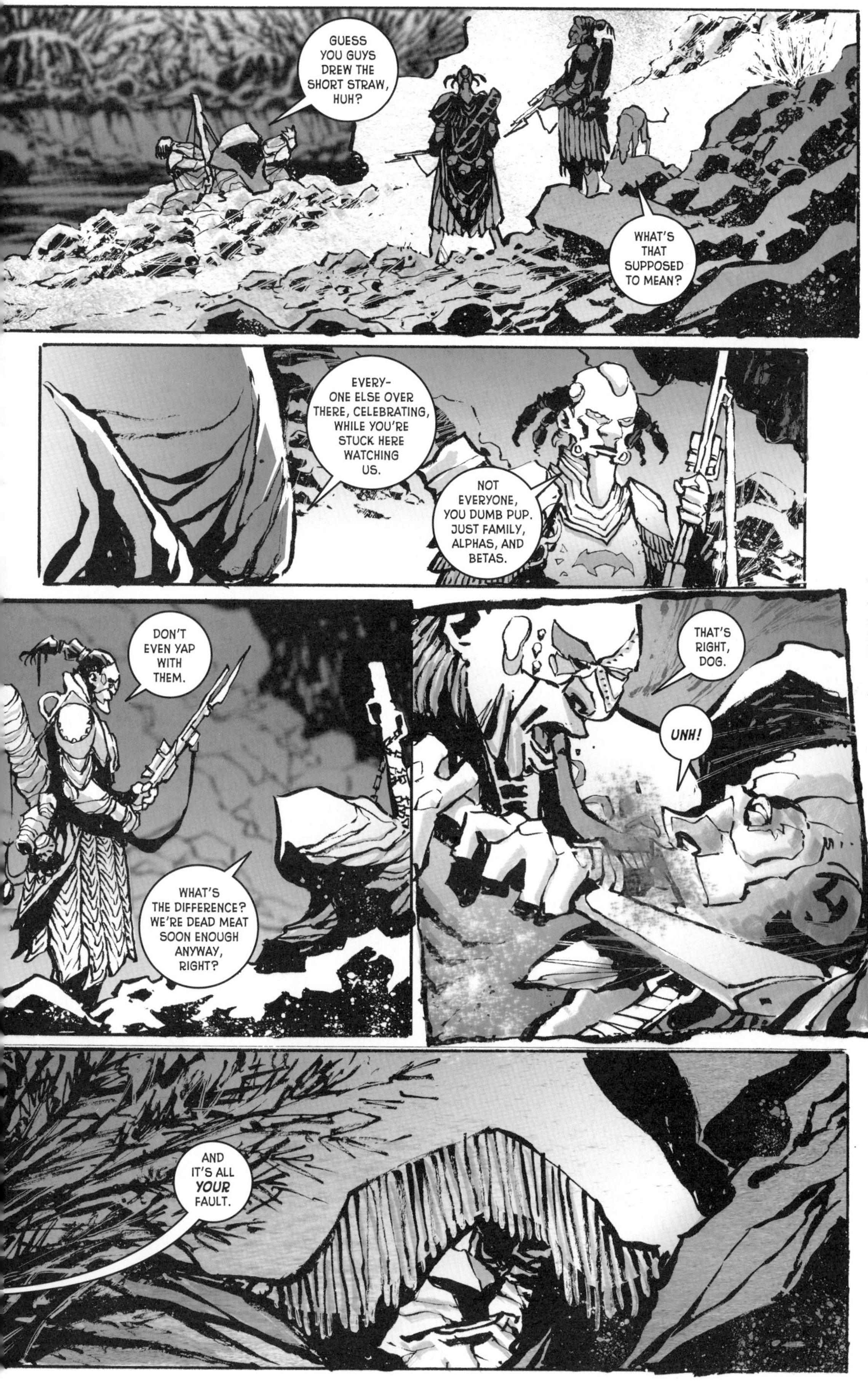
GUESS YOU GUYS DREW THE SHORT STRAW, HUH?
WHAT'S THAT SUPPOSED TO MEAN?
EVERY-ONE ELSE OVER THERE, CELEBRATING, WHILE YOU'RE STUCK HERE WATCHING US.
NOT EVERYONE, YOU DUMB PUP. JUST FAMILY, ALPHAS, AND BETAS.
DON'T EVEN YAP WITH THEM.
WHAT'S THE DIFFERENCE? WE'RE DEAD MEAT SOON ENOUGH ANYWAY, RIGHT?
THAT'S RIGHT, DOG.
UNH!
AND IT'S ALL *YOUR* FAULT.

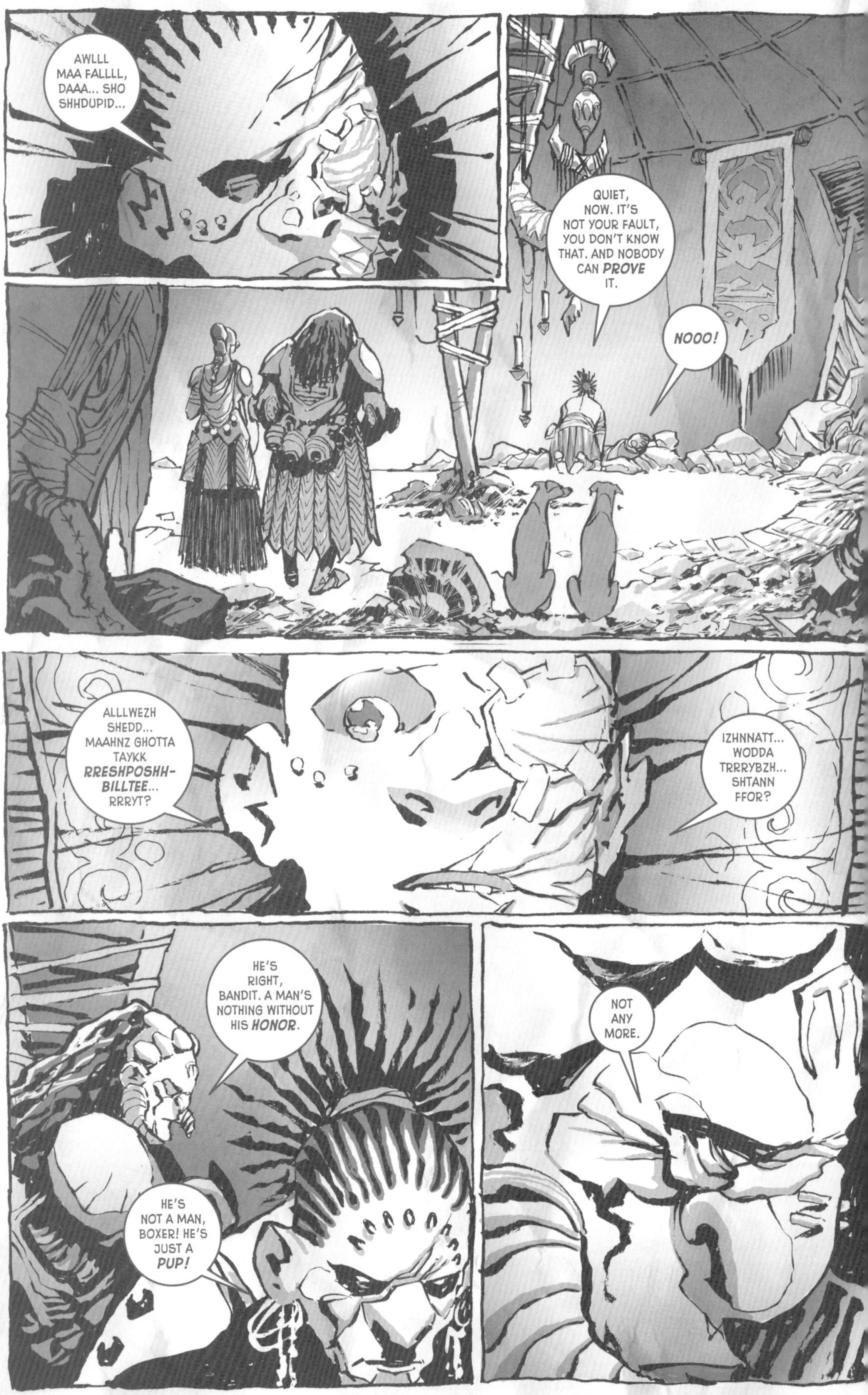
AWLLL MAA FALLLL, DAAA... SHO SHHDUPID...
QUIET, NOW. IT'S NOT YOUR FAULT, YOU DON'T KNOW THAT. AND NOBODY CAN PROVE IT.
NOOO!
ALLLWEZH SHEDD... MAAHNZ GHOTTA TAYKK RRESHPOSHH-BILLTEE... RRRYT?
IZHNNATT... WODDA TRRRYBZH... SHTANN FFOR?
HE'S RIGHT, BANDIT. A MAN'S NOTHING WITHOUT HIS HONOR.
HE'S NOT A MAN, BOXER! HE'S JUST A PUP!
NOT ANY MORE.

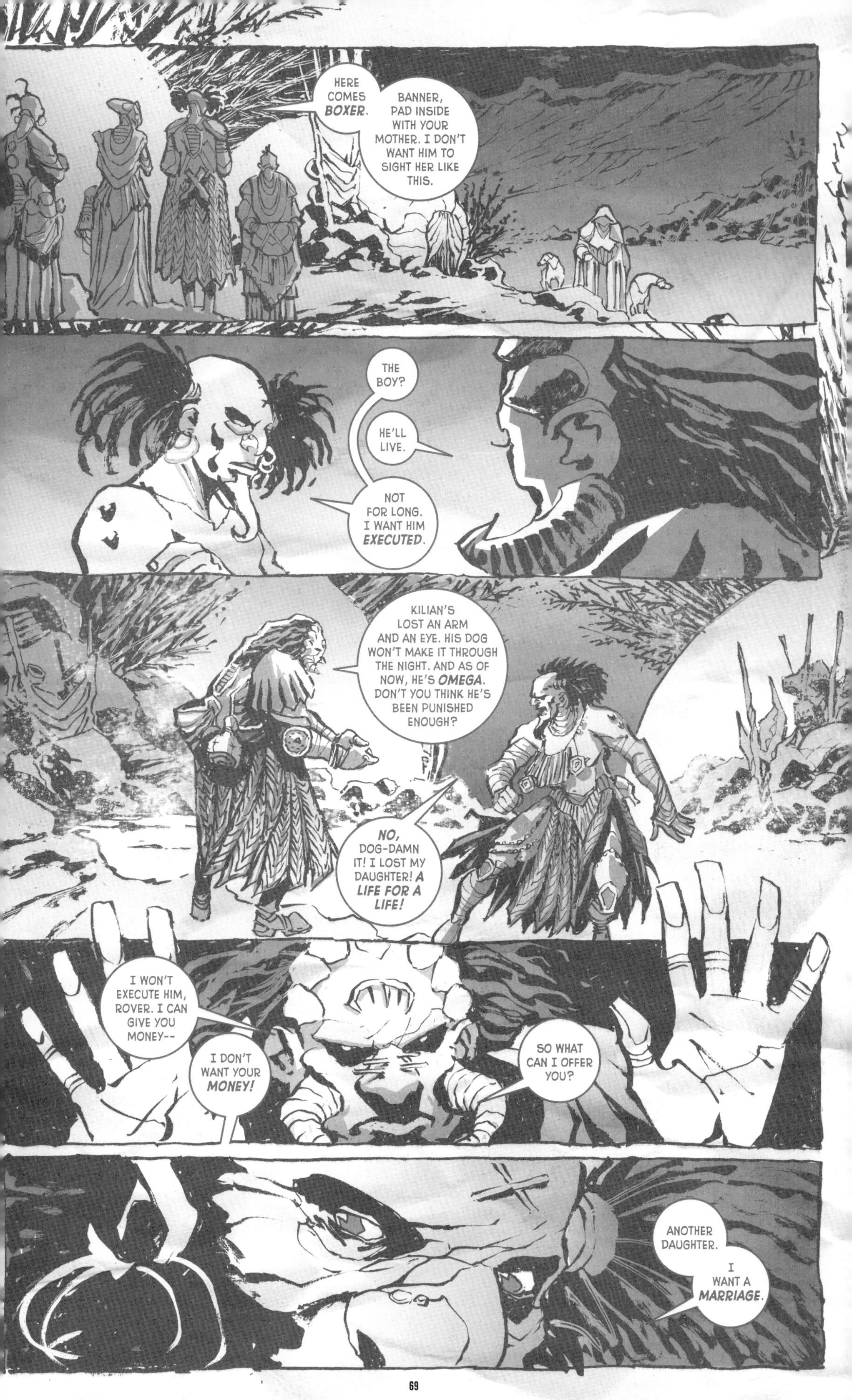
HERE COMES BOXER.
BANNER, PAD INSIDE WITH YOUR MOTHER. I DON'T WANT HIM TO SIGHT HER LIKE THIS.
THE BOY?
HE'LL LIVE.
NOT FOR LONG. I WANT HIM EXECUTED.
KILIAN'S LOST AN ARM AND AN EYE. HIS DOG WON'T MAKE IT THROUGH THE NIGHT. AND AS OF NOW, HE'S OMEGA. DON'T YOU THINK HE'S BEEN PUNISHED ENOUGH?
NO, DOG-DAMN IT! I LOST MY DAUGHTER! A LIFE FOR A LIFE!
I WON'T EXECUTE HIM, ROVER. I CAN GIVE YOU MONEY--
I DON'T WANT YOUR MONEY!
SO WHAT CAN I OFFER YOU?
ANOTHER DAUGHTER.
I WANT A MARRIAGE.

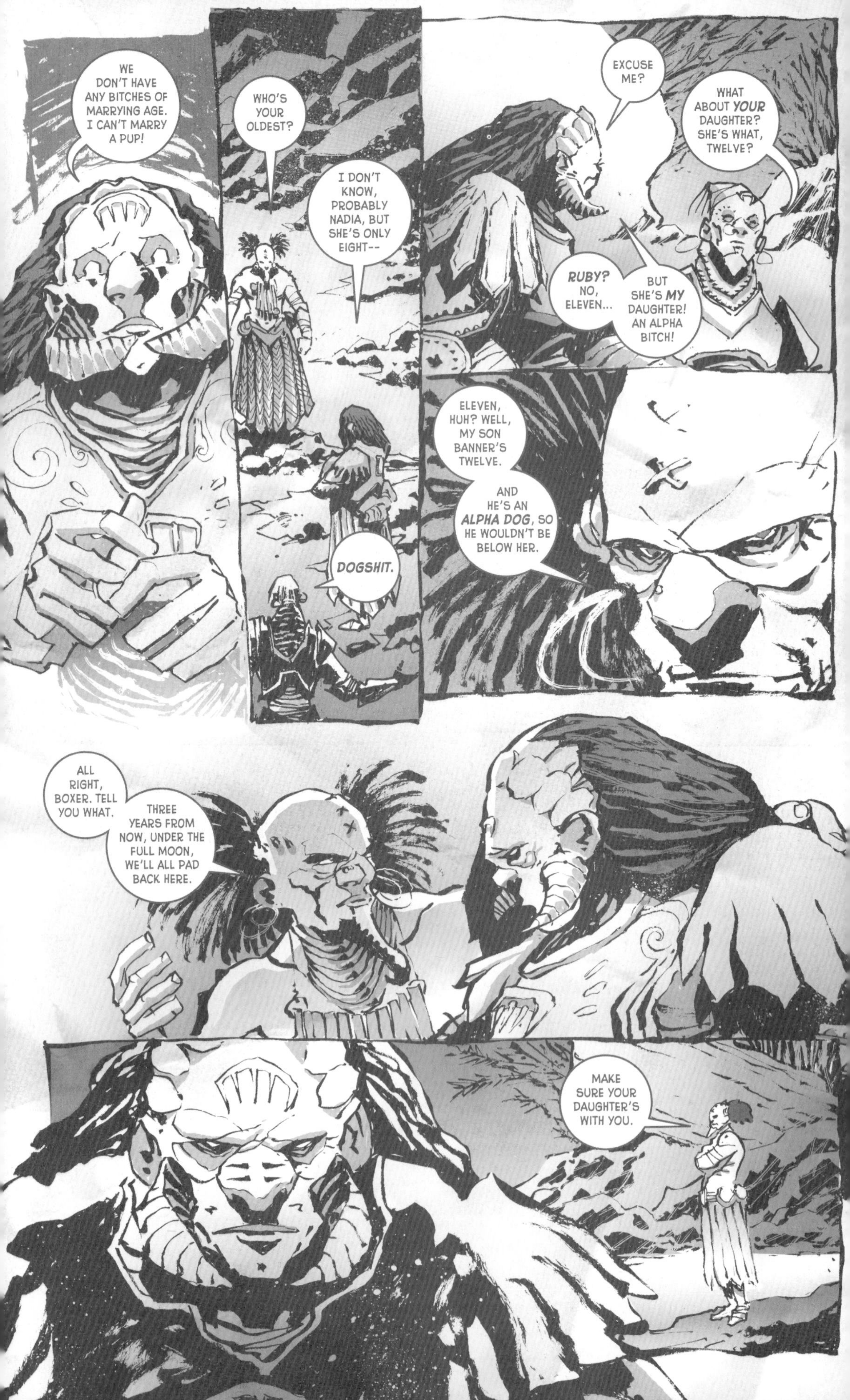
WE DON'T HAVE ANY BITCHES OF MARRYING AGE. I CAN'T MARRY A PUP!
WHO'S YOUR OLDEST?
I DON'T KNOW, PROBABLY NADIA, BUT SHE'S ONLY EIGHT--
DOGSHIT.
EXCUSE ME?
WHAT ABOUT YOUR DAUGHTER? SHE'S WHAT, TWELVE?
RUBY? NO, ELEVEN...
BUT SHE'S MY DAUGHTER! AN ALPHA BITCH!
ELEVEN, HUH? WELL, MY SON BANNER'S TWELVE.
AND HE'S AN ALPHA DOG, SO HE WOULDN'T BE BELOW HER.
ALL RIGHT, BOXER. TELL YOU WHAT.
THREE YEARS FROM NOW, UNDER THE FULL MOON, WE'LL ALL PAD BACK HERE.
MAKE SURE YOUR DAUGHTER'S WITH YOU.

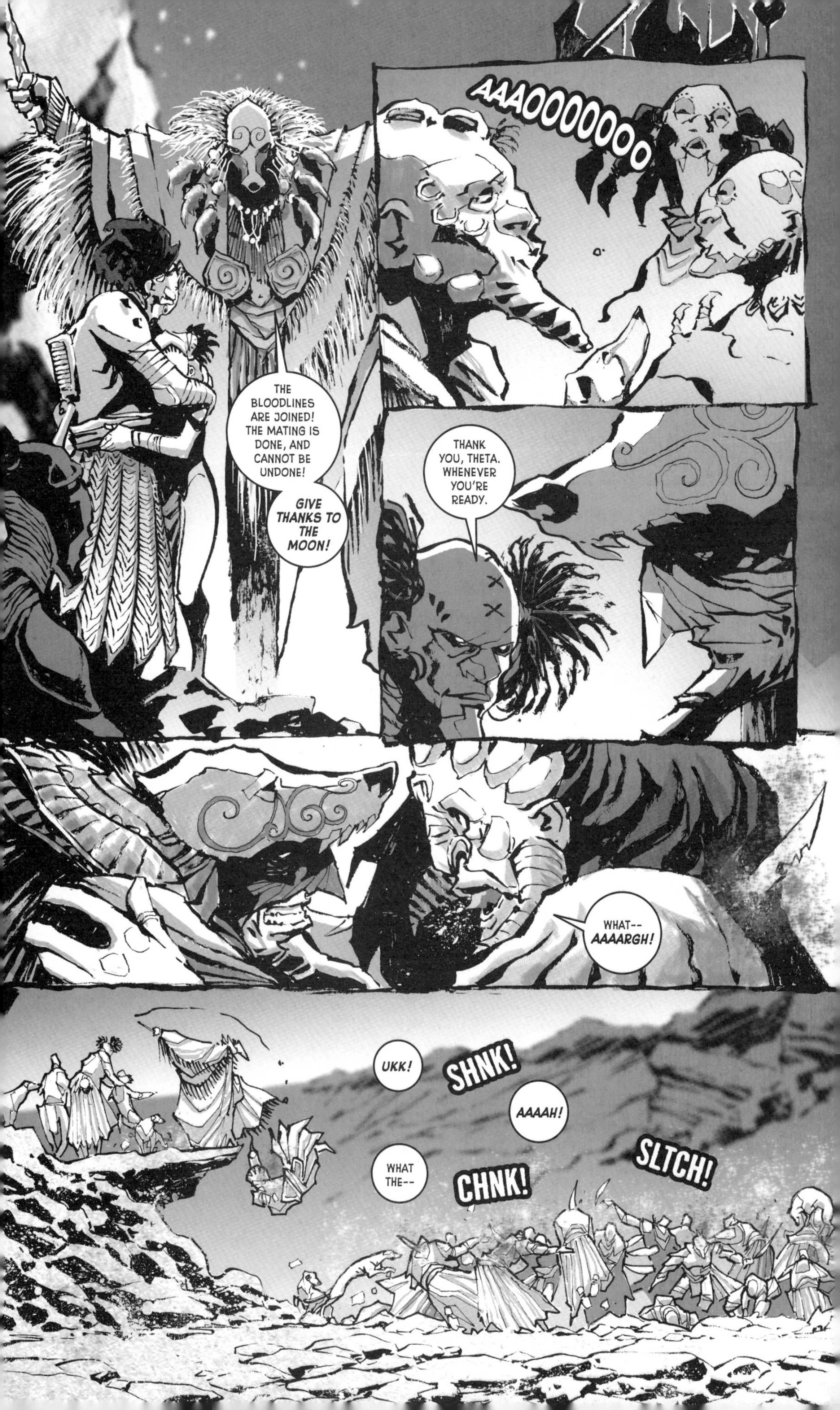
AAAOOOOOOOO
THE BLOODLINES ARE JOINED! THE MATING IS DONE, AND CANNOT BE UNDONE!
GIVE THANKS TO THE MOON!
THANK YOU, THETA. WHENEVER YOU'RE READY.
WHAT-- AAAARGH!
UKK!
SHNK!
AAAAH!
WHAT THE--
CHNK!
SLTCH!

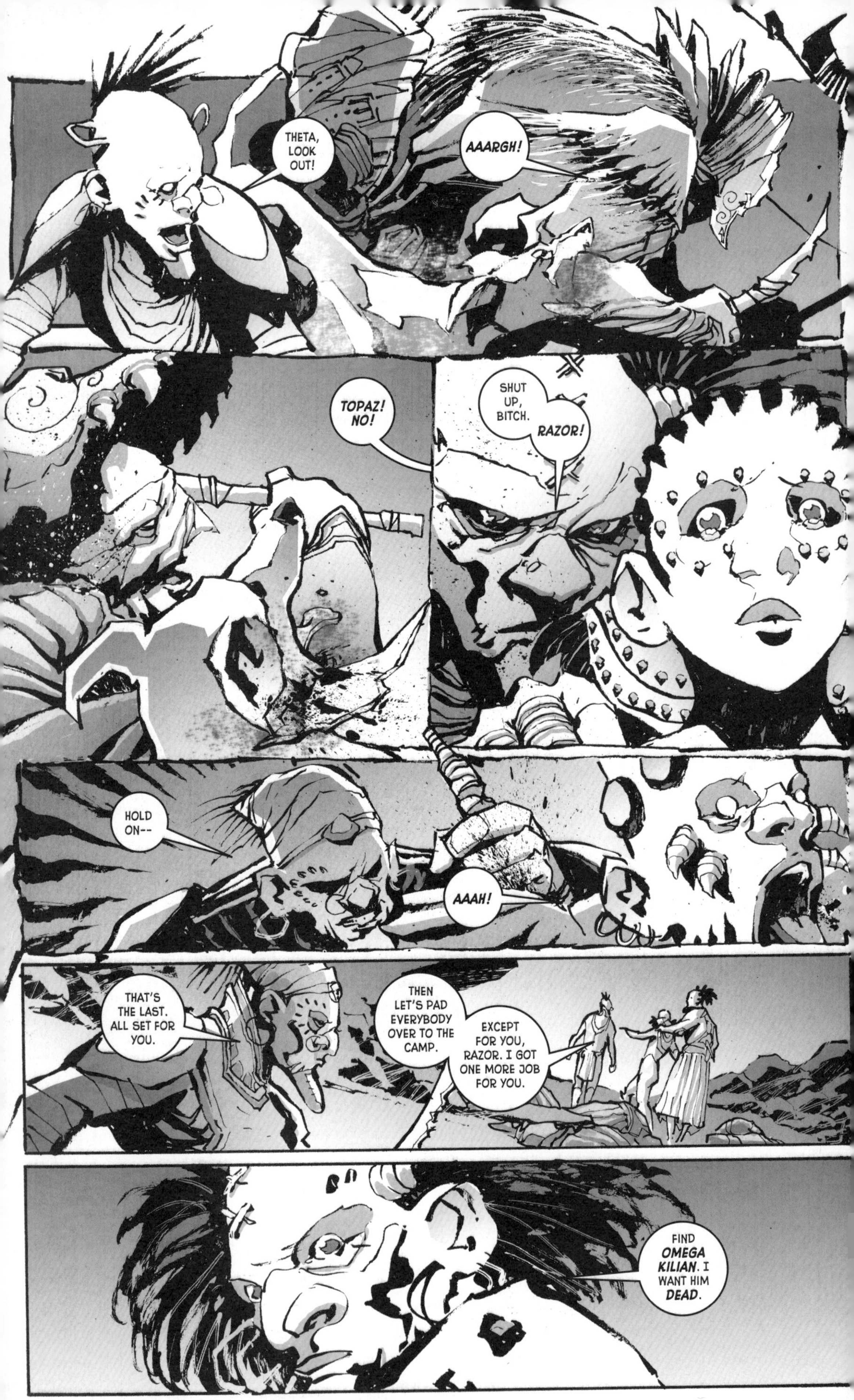
THETA, LOOK OUT!
AAARGH!
TOPAZ! NO!
SHUT UP, BITCH.
RAZOR!
HOLD ON--
AAAH!
THAT'S THE LAST. ALL SET FOR YOU.
THEN LET'S PAD EVERYBODY OVER TO THE CAMP.
EXCEPT FOR YOU, RAZOR. I GOT ONE MORE JOB FOR YOU.
FIND OMEGA KILIAN. I WANT HIM DEAD.

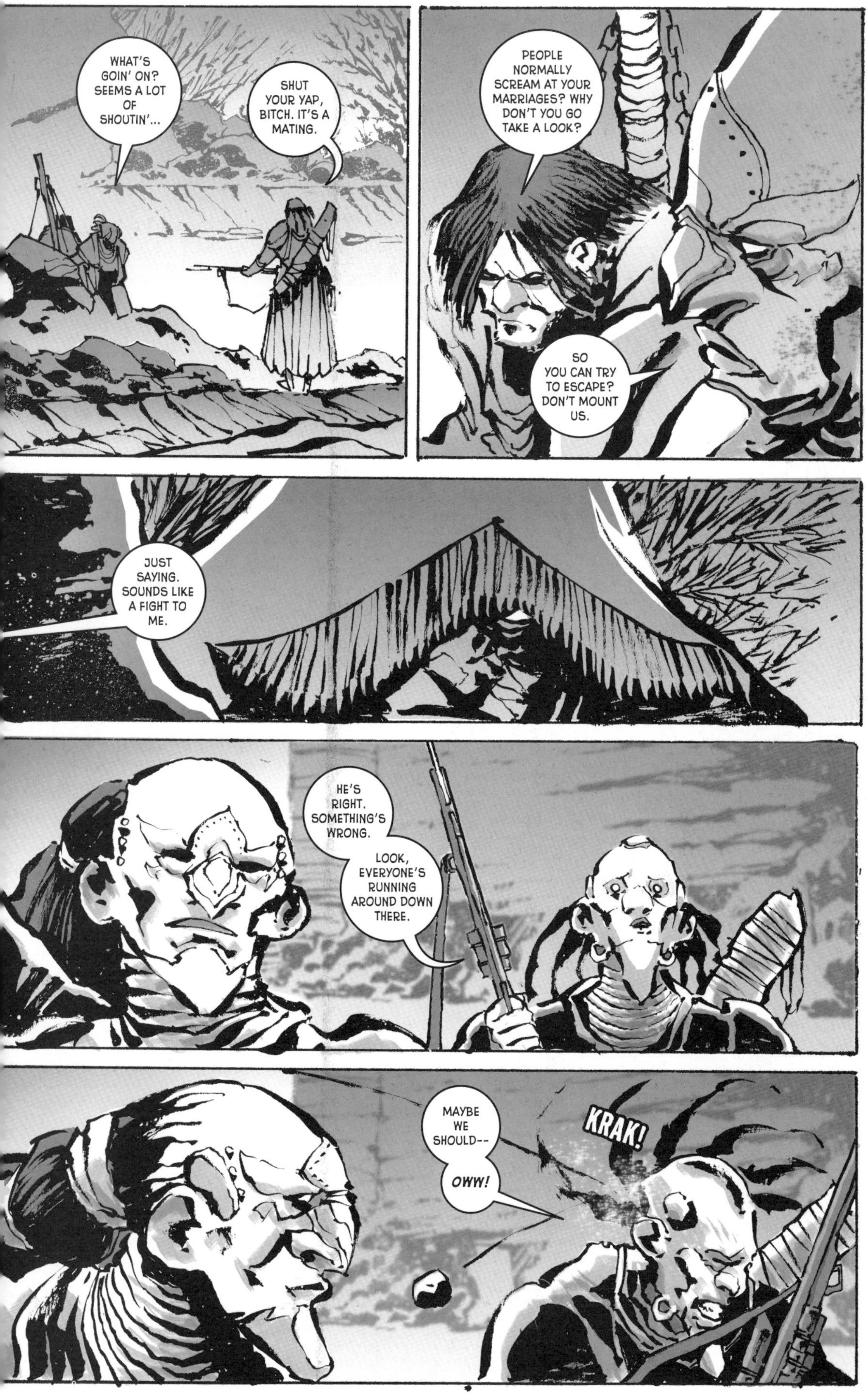
WHAT'S GOIN' ON? SEEMS A LOT OF SHOUTIN'...
SHUT YOUR YAP, BITCH. IT'S A MATING.
PEOPLE NORMALLY SCREAM AT YOUR MARRIAGES? WHY DON'T YOU GO TAKE A LOOK?
SO YOU CAN TRY TO ESCAPE? DON'T MOUNT US.
JUST SAYING. SOUNDS LIKE A FIGHT TO ME.
HE'S RIGHT. SOMETHING'S WRONG.
LOOK, EVERYONE'S RUNNING AROUND DOWN THERE.
MAYBE WE SHOULD--
KRAK!
OWW!

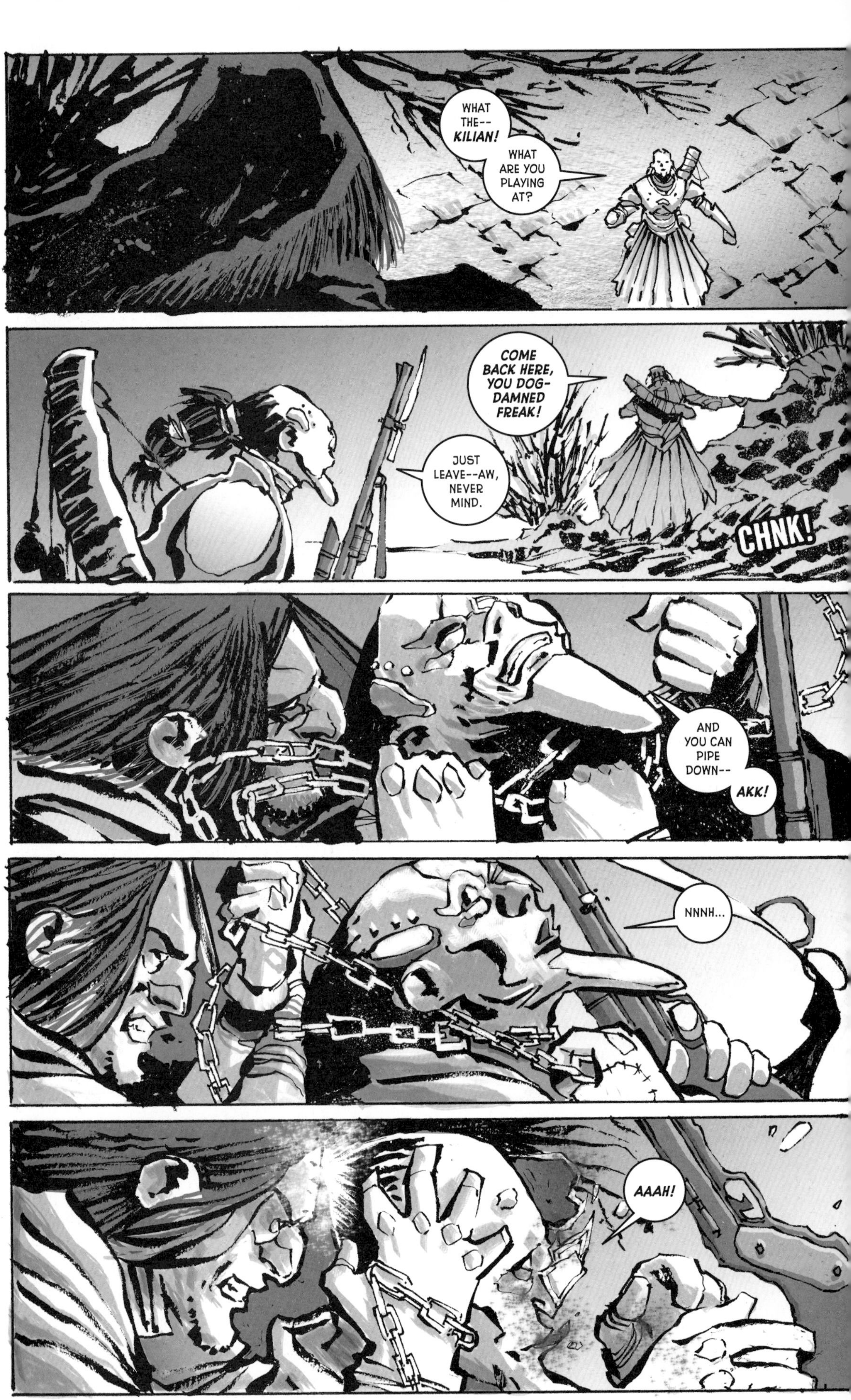
WHAT THE-- KILIAN!
WHAT ARE YOU PLAYING AT?
COME BACK HERE, YOU DOG-DAMNED FREAK!
JUST LEAVE--AW, NEVER MIND.
CHNK!
AND YOU CAN PIPE DOWN--
AKK!
NNNH...
AAAH!

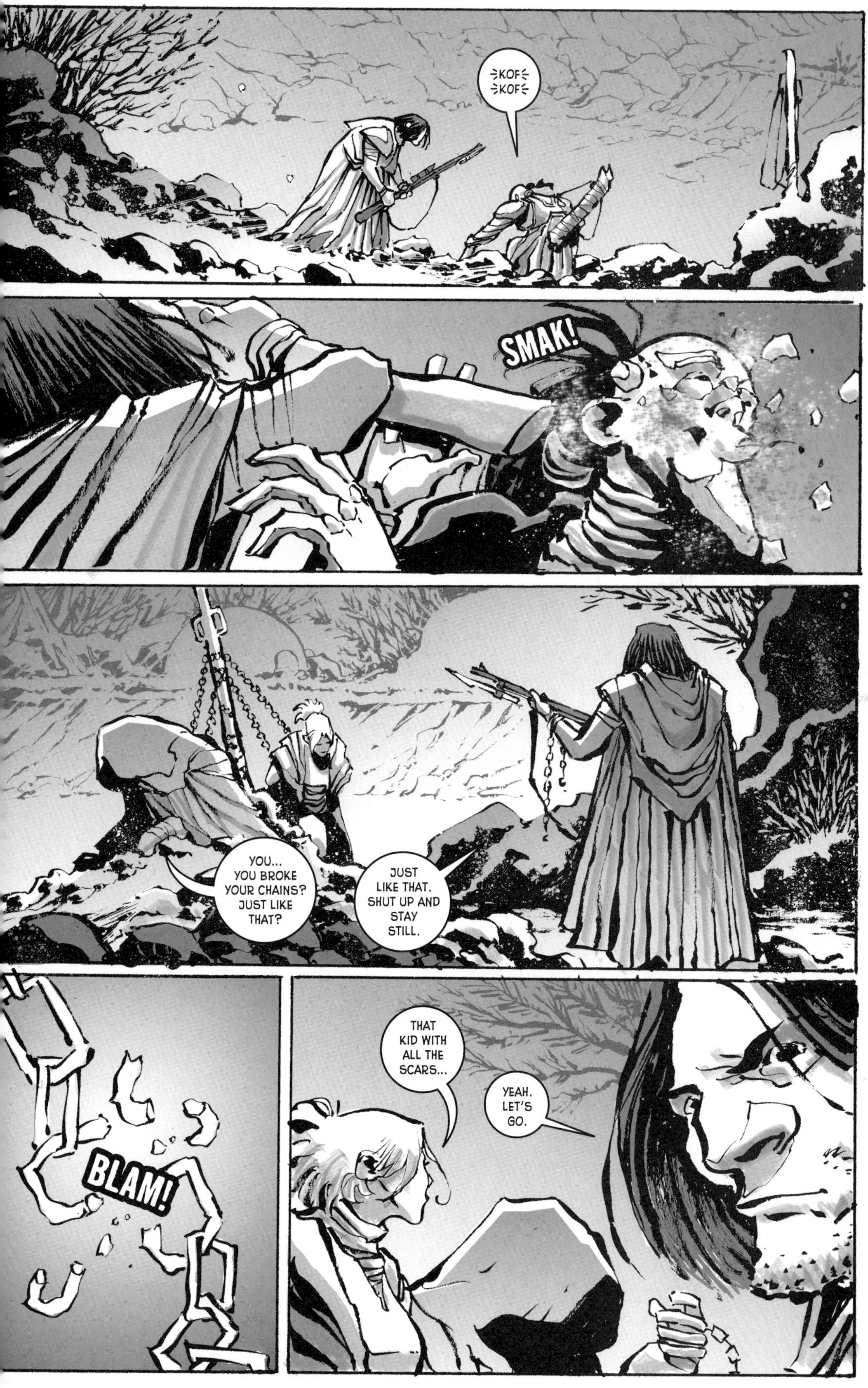

KOF
KOF
SMAK!
YOU... YOU BROKE YOUR CHAINS? JUST LIKE THAT?
JUST LIKE THAT. SHUT UP AND STAY STILL.
BLAM!
THAT KID WITH ALL THE SCARS...
YEAH. LET'S GO.

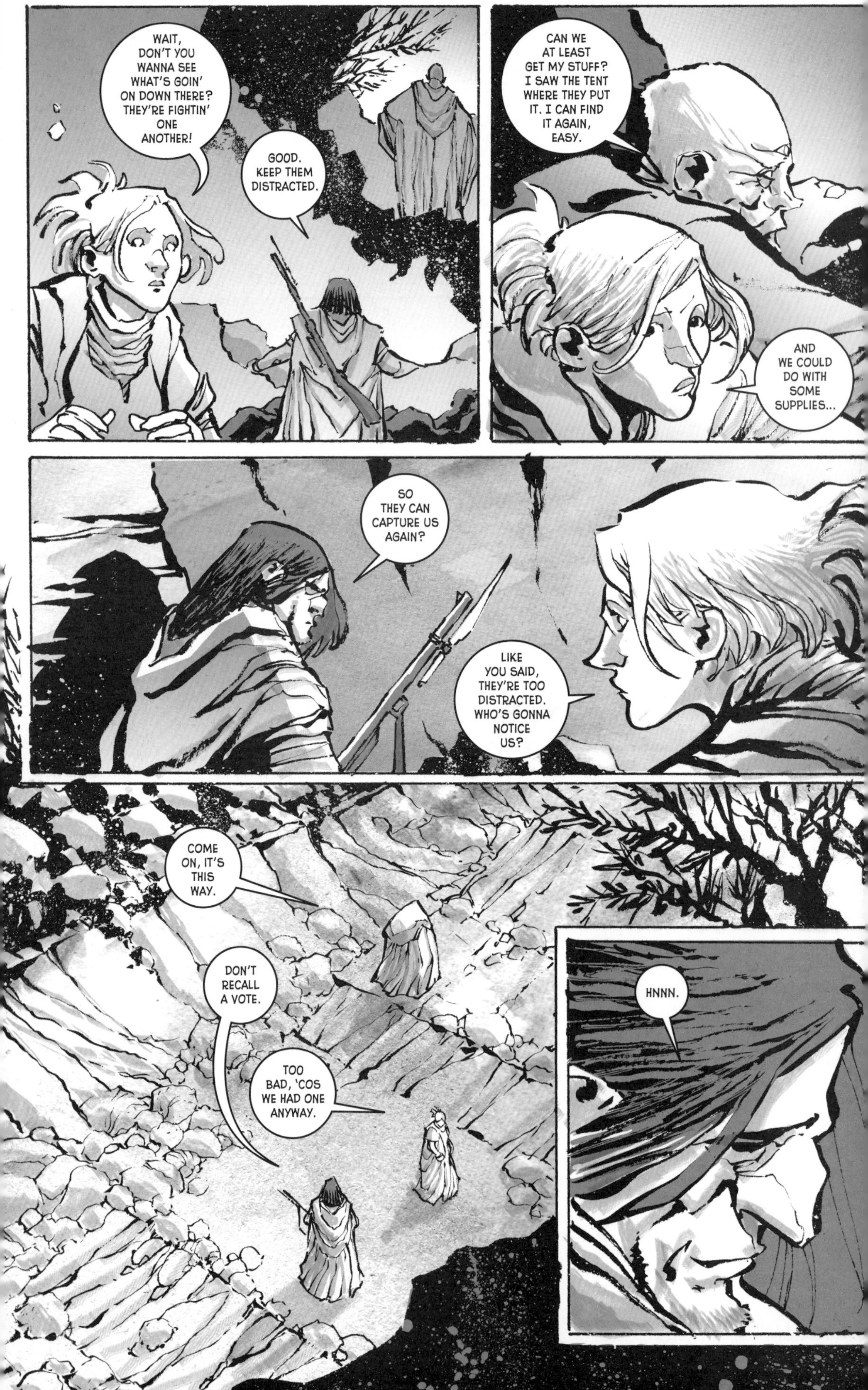
WAIT, DON'T YOU WANNA SEE WHAT'S GOIN' ON DOWN THERE? THEY'RE FIGHTIN' ONE ANOTHER!
GOOD. KEEP THEM DISTRACTED.
CAN WE AT LEAST GET MY STUFF? I SAW THE TENT WHERE THEY PUT IT. I CAN FIND IT AGAIN, EASY.
AND WE COULD DO WITH SOME SUPPLIES...
SO THEY CAN CAPTURE US AGAIN?
LIKE YOU SAID, THEY'RE TOO DISTRACTED. WHO'S GONNA NOTICE US?
COME ON, IT'S THIS WAY.
DON'T RECALL A VOTE.
TOO BAD, 'COS WE HAD ONE ANYWAY.
HNNN.

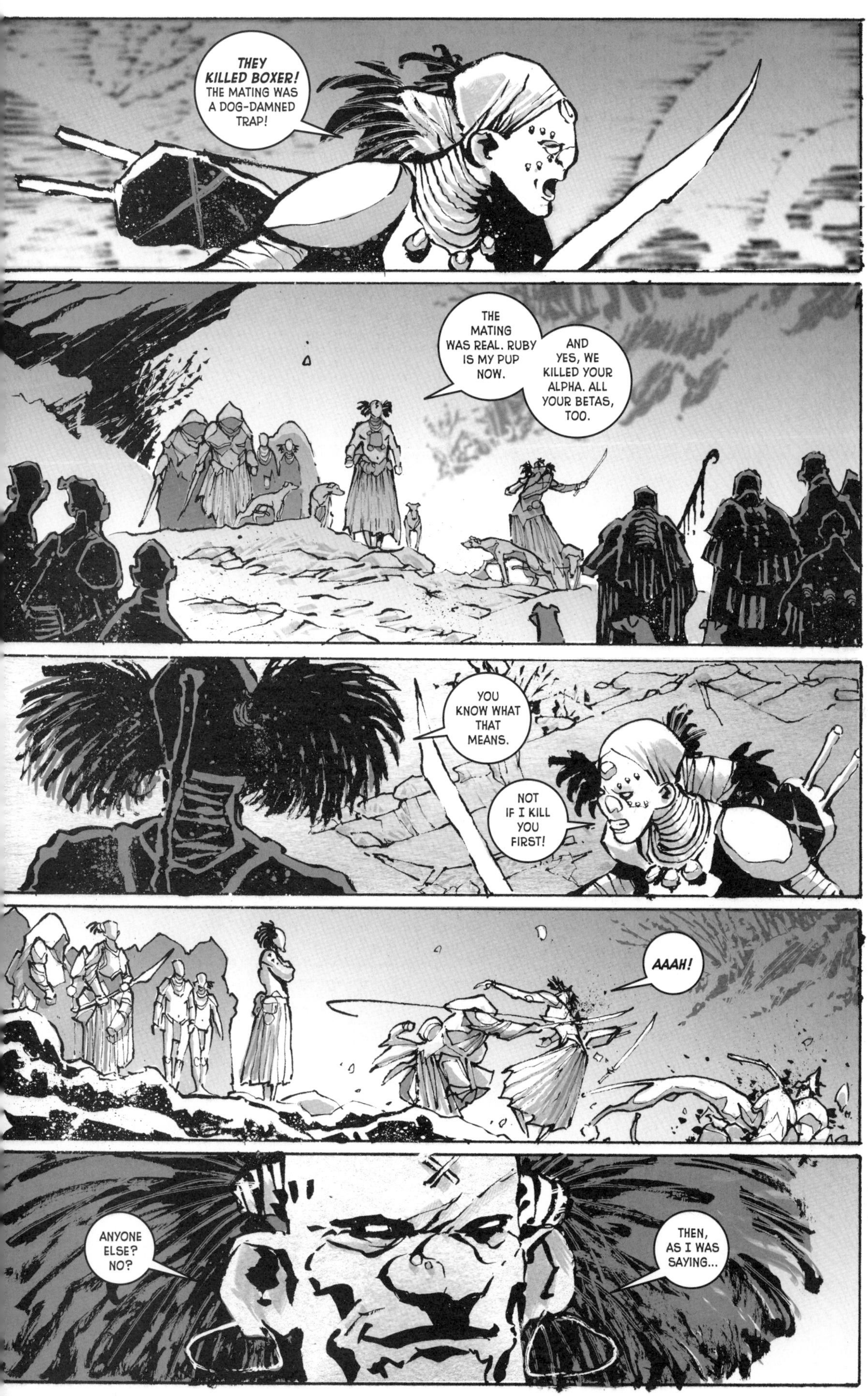
THEY KILLED BOXER! THE MATING WAS A DOG-DAMNED TRAP!
THE MATING WAS REAL. RUBY IS MY PUP NOW.
AND YES, WE KILLED YOUR ALPHA. ALL YOUR BETAS, TOO.
YOU KNOW WHAT THAT MEANS.
NOT IF I KILL YOU FIRST!
AAAH!
ANYONE ELSE? NO?
THEN, AS I WAS SAYING...

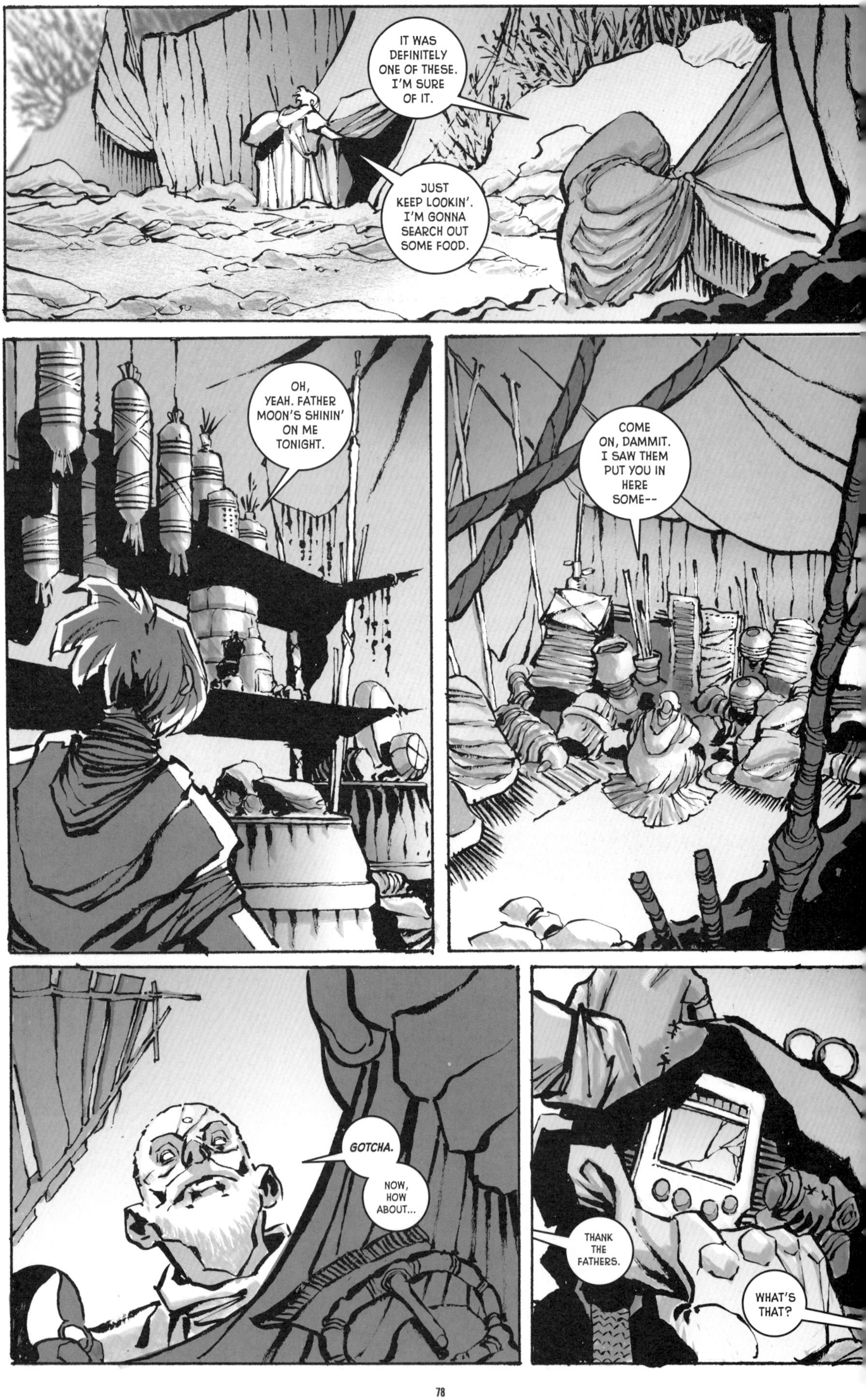
IT WAS DEFINITELY ONE OF THESE. I'M SURE OF IT.
JUST KEEP LOOKIN'. I'M GONNA SEARCH OUT SOME FOOD.
OH, YEAH. FATHER MOON'S SHININ' ON ME TONIGHT.
COME ON, DAMMIT. I SAW THEM PUT YOU IN HERE SOME--
GOTCHA.
NOW, HOW ABOUT...
THANK THE FATHERS.
WHAT'S THAT?

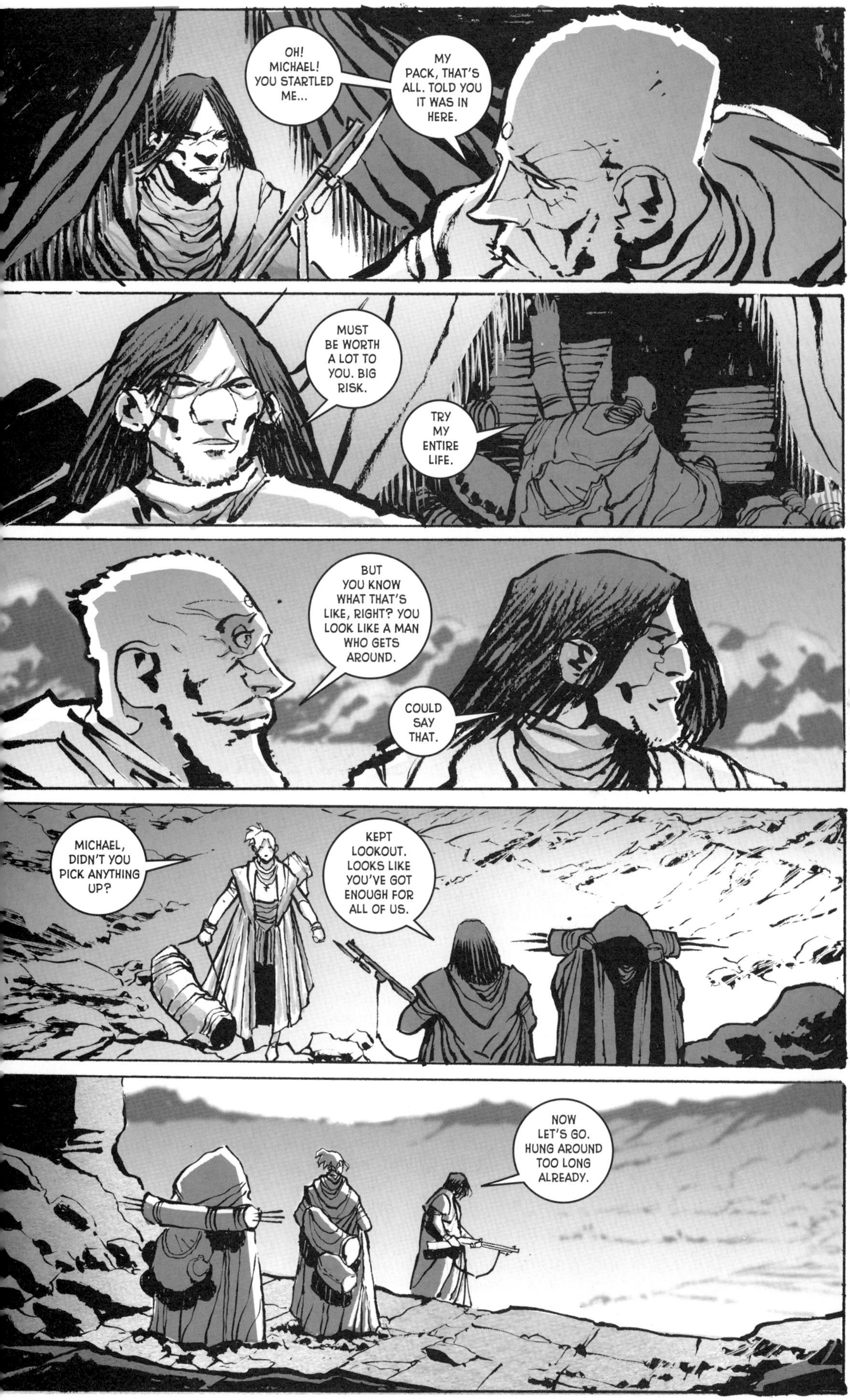
OH! MICHAEL! YOU STARTLED ME...
MY PACK, THAT'S ALL. TOLD YOU IT WAS IN HERE.
MUST BE WORTH A LOT TO YOU. BIG RISK.
TRY MY ENTIRE LIFE.
BUT YOU KNOW WHAT THAT'S LIKE, RIGHT? YOU LOOK LIKE A MAN WHO GETS AROUND.
COULD SAY THAT.
MICHAEL, DIDN'T YOU PICK ANYTHING UP?
KEPT LOOKOUT. LOOKS LIKE YOU'VE GOT ENOUGH FOR ALL OF US.
NOW LET'S GO. HUNG AROUND TOO LONG ALREADY.

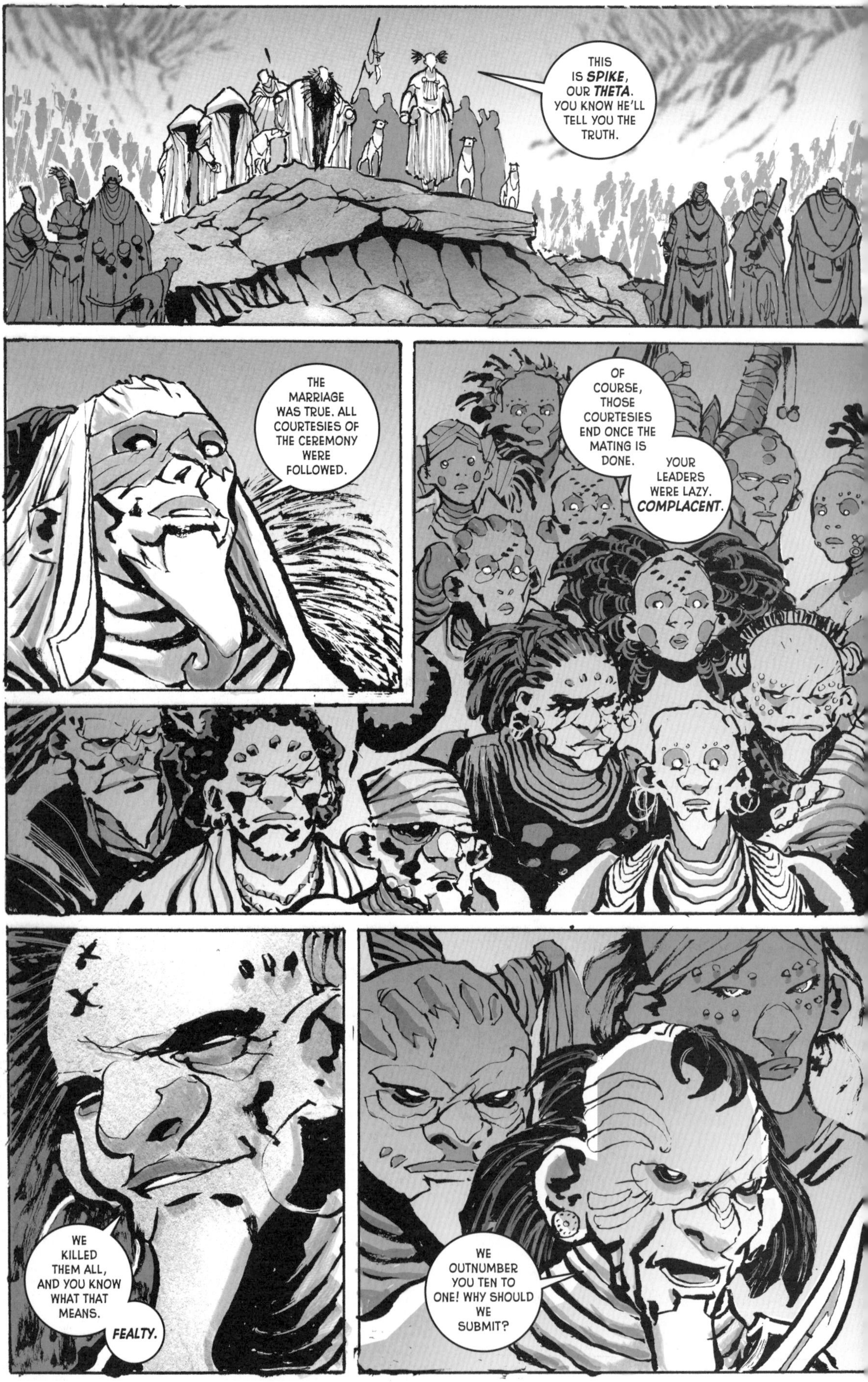

THIS IS SPIKE, OUR THETA. YOU KNOW HE'LL TELL YOU THE TRUTH.
THE MARRIAGE WAS TRUE. ALL COURTESIES OF THE CEREMONY WERE FOLLOWED.
OF COURSE, THOSE COURTESIES END ONCE THE MATING IS DONE.
YOUR LEADERS WERE LAZY. COMPLACENT.
WE KILLED THEM ALL, AND YOU KNOW WHAT THAT MEANS.
FEALTY.
WE OUTNUMBER YOU TEN TO ONE! WHY SHOULD WE SUBMIT?

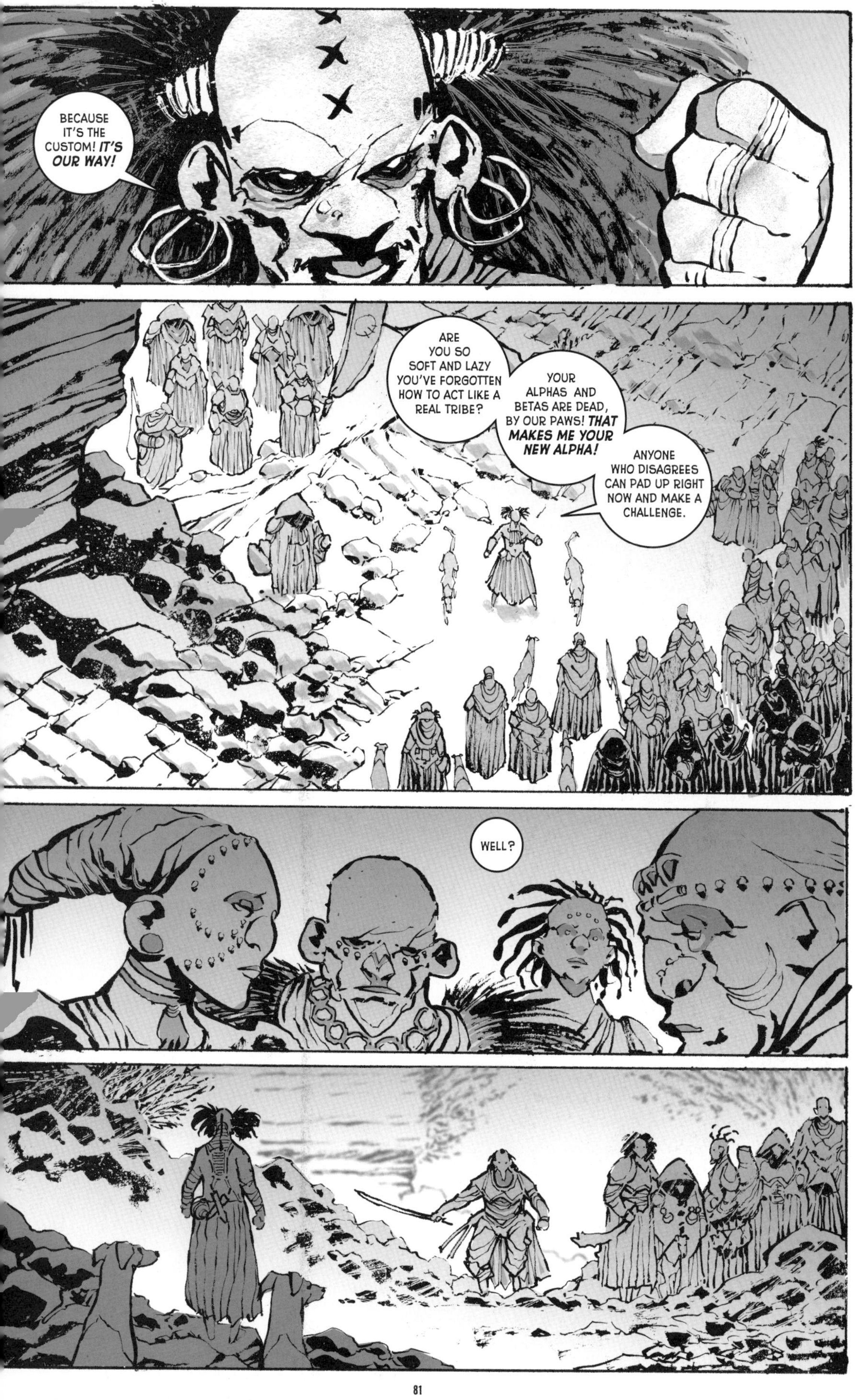
BECAUSE IT'S THE CUSTOM! IT'S OUR WAY!
ARE YOU SO SOFT AND LAZY YOU'VE FORGOTTEN HOW TO ACT LIKE A REAL TRIBE?
YOUR ALPHAS AND BETAS ARE DEAD, BY OUR PAWS! THAT MAKES ME YOUR NEW ALPHA!
ANYONE WHO DISAGREES CAN PAD UP RIGHT NOW AND MAKE A CHALLENGE.
WELL?

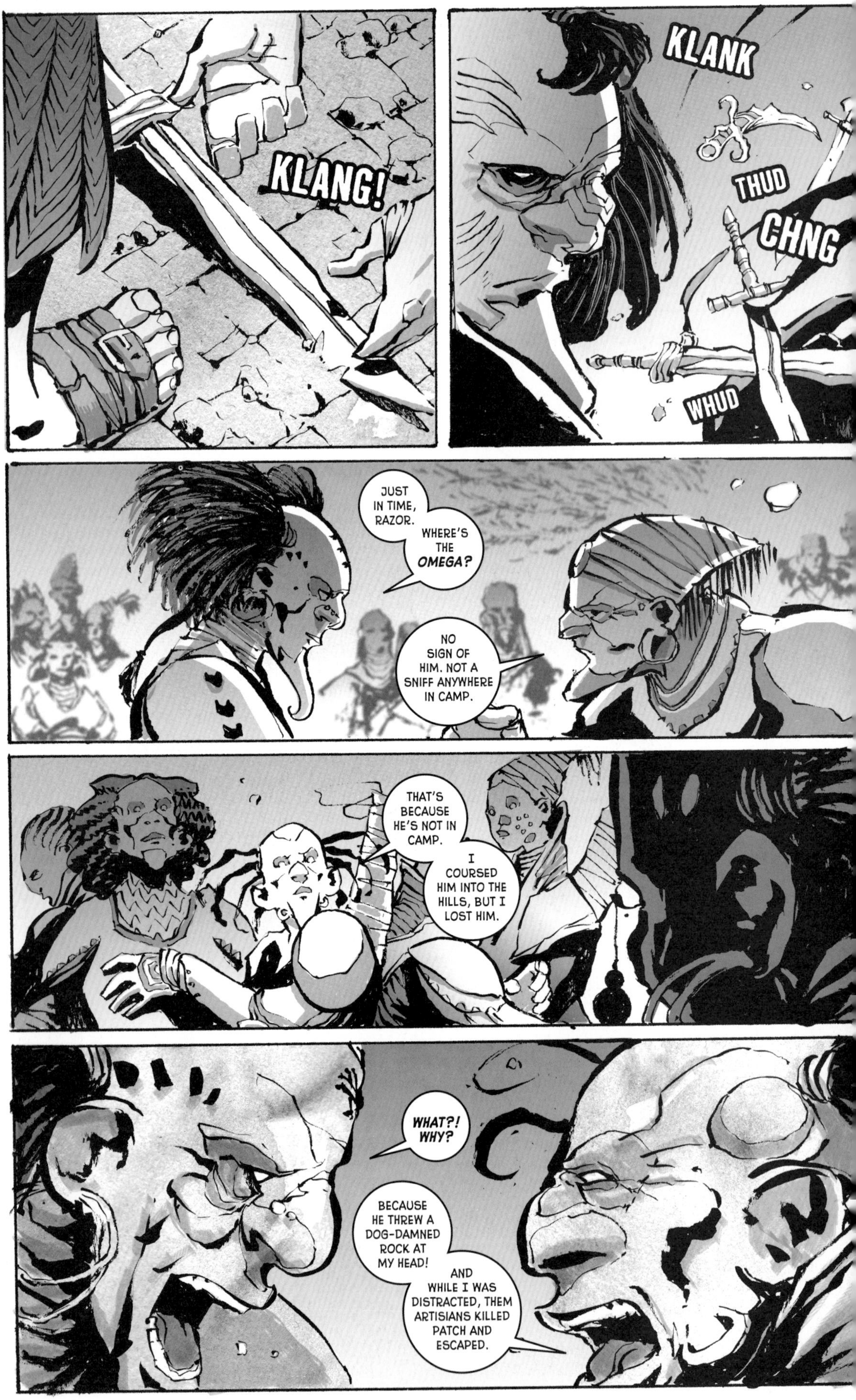
KLANG!
KLANK
THUD
CHNG
WHUD
JUST IN TIME, RAZOR.
WHERE'S THE *OMEGA?*
NO SIGN OF HIM. NOT A SNIFF ANYWHERE IN CAMP.
THAT'S BECAUSE HE'S NOT IN CAMP.
I COURSED HIM INTO THE HILLS, BUT I LOST HIM.
WHAT?! WHY?
BECAUSE HE THREW A DOG-DAMNED ROCK AT MY HEAD!
AND WHILE I WAS DISTRACTED, THEM ARTISIANS KILLED PATCH AND ESCAPED.

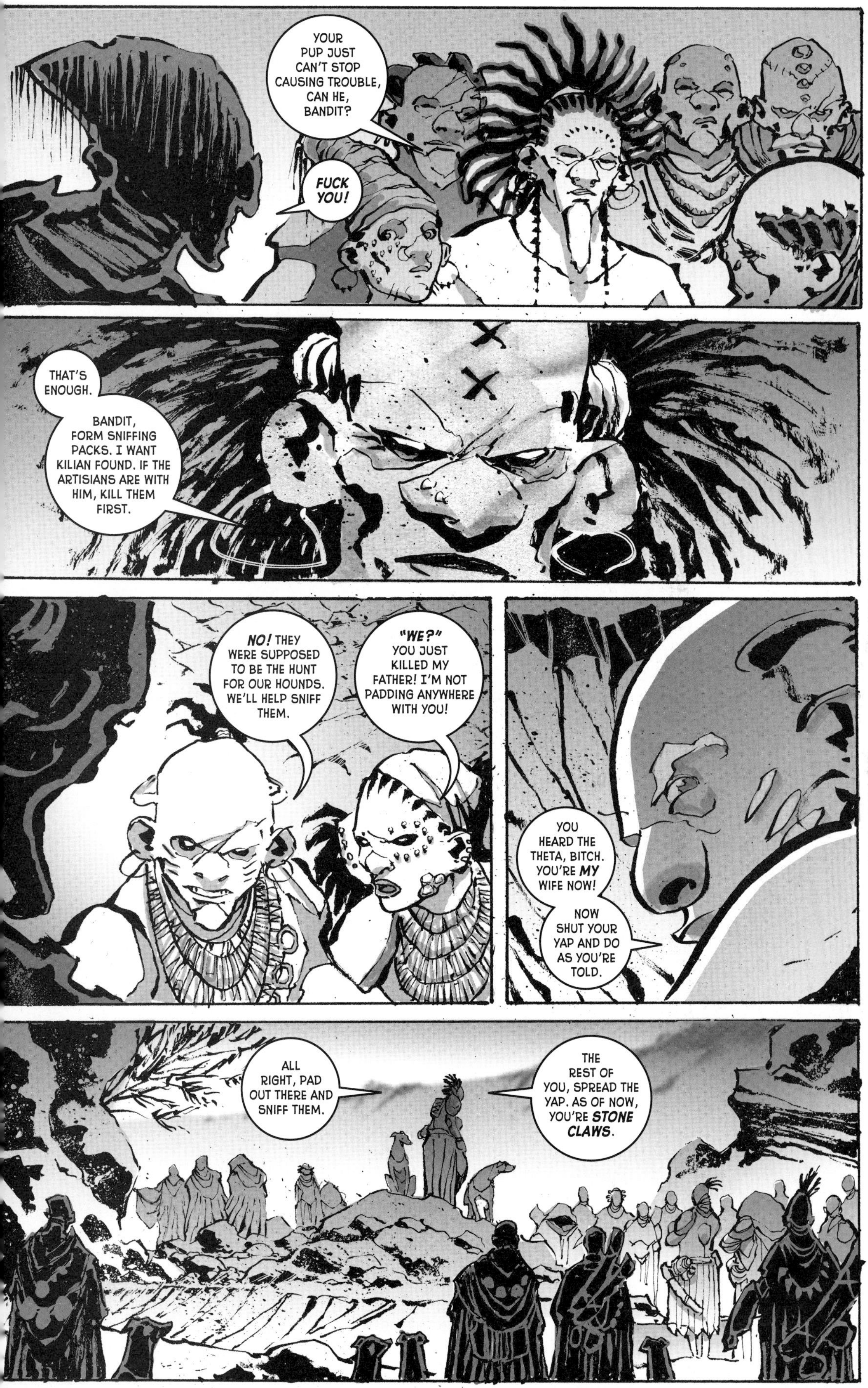

YOUR PUP JUST CAN'T STOP CAUSING TROUBLE, CAN HE, BANDIT?
FUCK YOU!
THAT'S ENOUGH.
BANDIT, FORM SNIFFING PACKS. I WANT KILIAN FOUND. IF THE ARTISIANS ARE WITH HIM, KILL THEM FIRST.
NO! THEY WERE SUPPOSED TO BE THE HUNT FOR OUR HOUNDS. WE'LL HELP SNIFF THEM.
"WE?" YOU JUST KILLED MY FATHER! I'M NOT PADDING ANYWHERE WITH YOU!
YOU HEARD THE THETA, BITCH. YOU'RE MY WIFE NOW!
NOW SHUT YOUR YAP AND DO AS YOU'RE TOLD.
ALL RIGHT, PAD OUT THERE AND SNIFF THEM.
THE REST OF YOU, SPREAD THE YAP. AS OF NOW, YOU'RE STONE CLAWS.

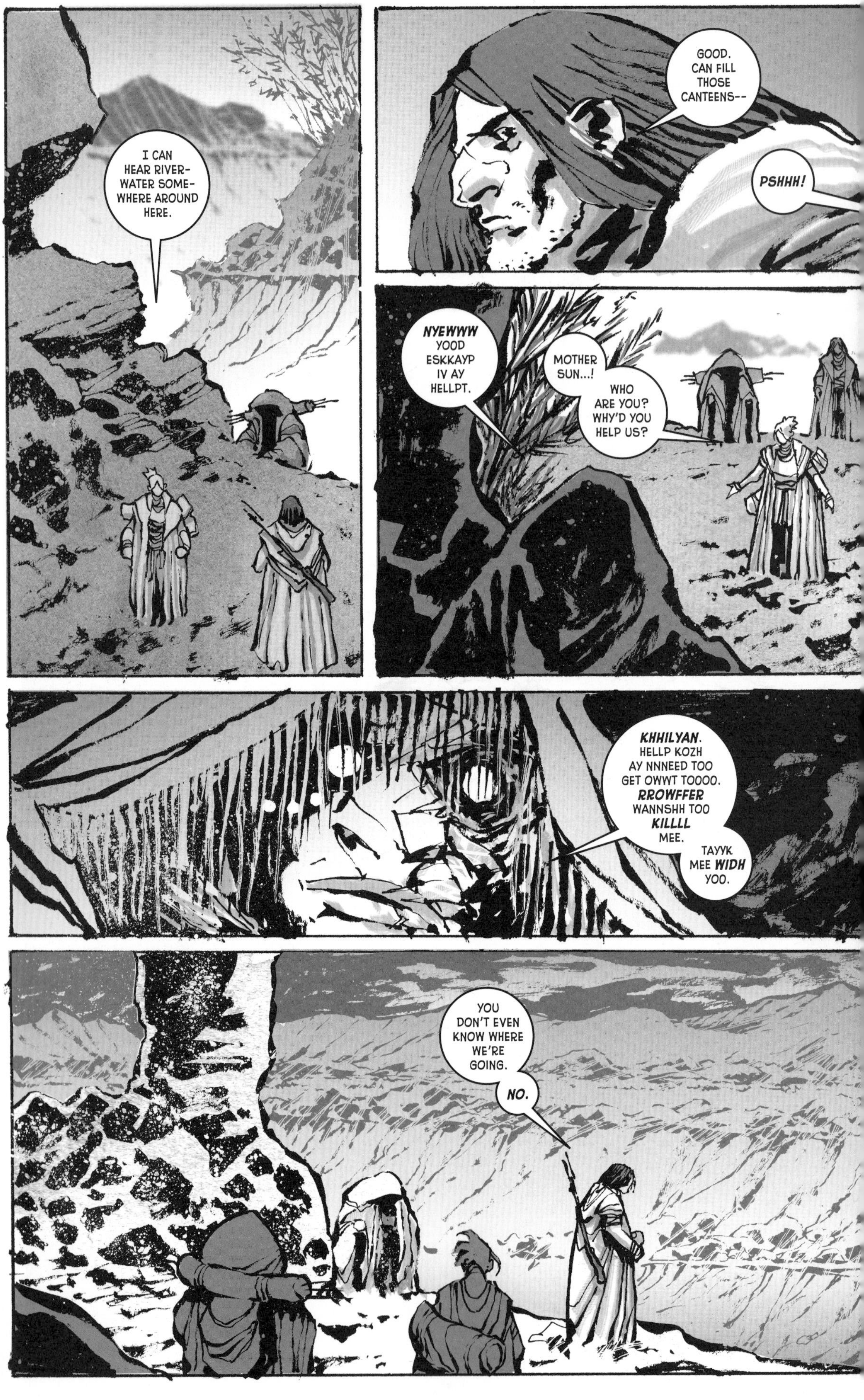
I CAN HEAR RIVER-WATER SOME-WHERE AROUND HERE.
GOOD. CAN FILL THOSE CANTEENS--
PSHHH!
NYEWWW YOOD ESKKAYP IV AY HELLPT.
MOTHER SUN...!
WHO ARE YOU? WHY'D YOU HELP US?
KHHILYAN. HELLP KOZH AY NNNEED TOO GET OWWT TOOOO. RROWFFER WANNSHH TOO KILLLL MEE.
TAYYK MEE WIDH YOO.
YOU DON'T EVEN KNOW WHERE WE'RE GOING.
NO.

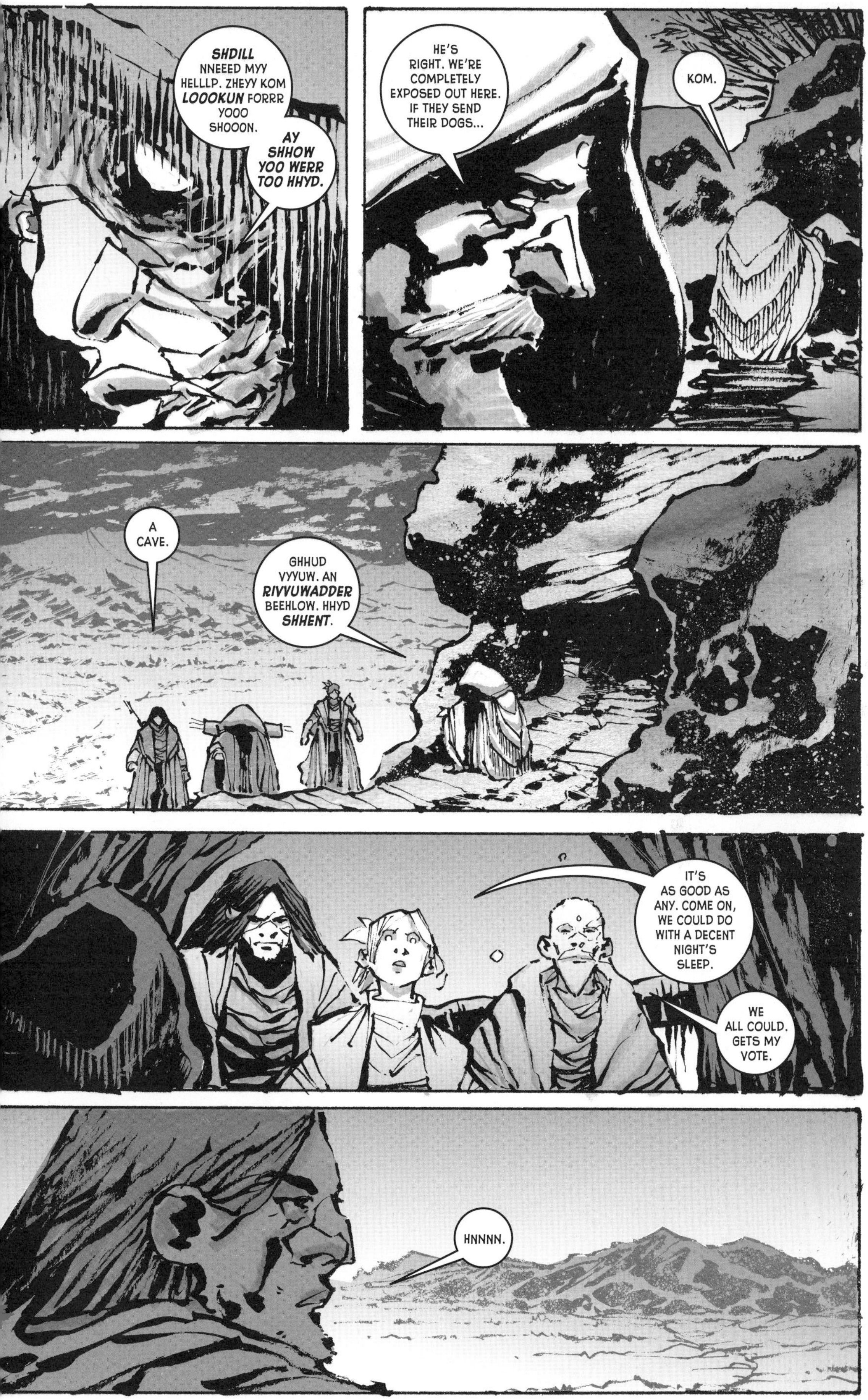
SHDILL NNEEED MYY HELLLP. ZHEYY KOM LOOOKUN FORRR YOOO SHOOON.
AY SHHOW YOO WERR TOO HHYD.
HE'S RIGHT. WE'RE COMPLETELY EXPOSED OUT HERE. IF THEY SEND THEIR DOGS...
KOM.
A CAVE.
GHHUD VYYUW. AN RIVVUWADDER BEEHLOW. HHYD SHHENT.
IT'S AS GOOD AS ANY. COME ON, WE COULD DO WITH A DECENT NIGHT'S SLEEP.
WE ALL COULD. GETS MY VOTE.
HNNNN.

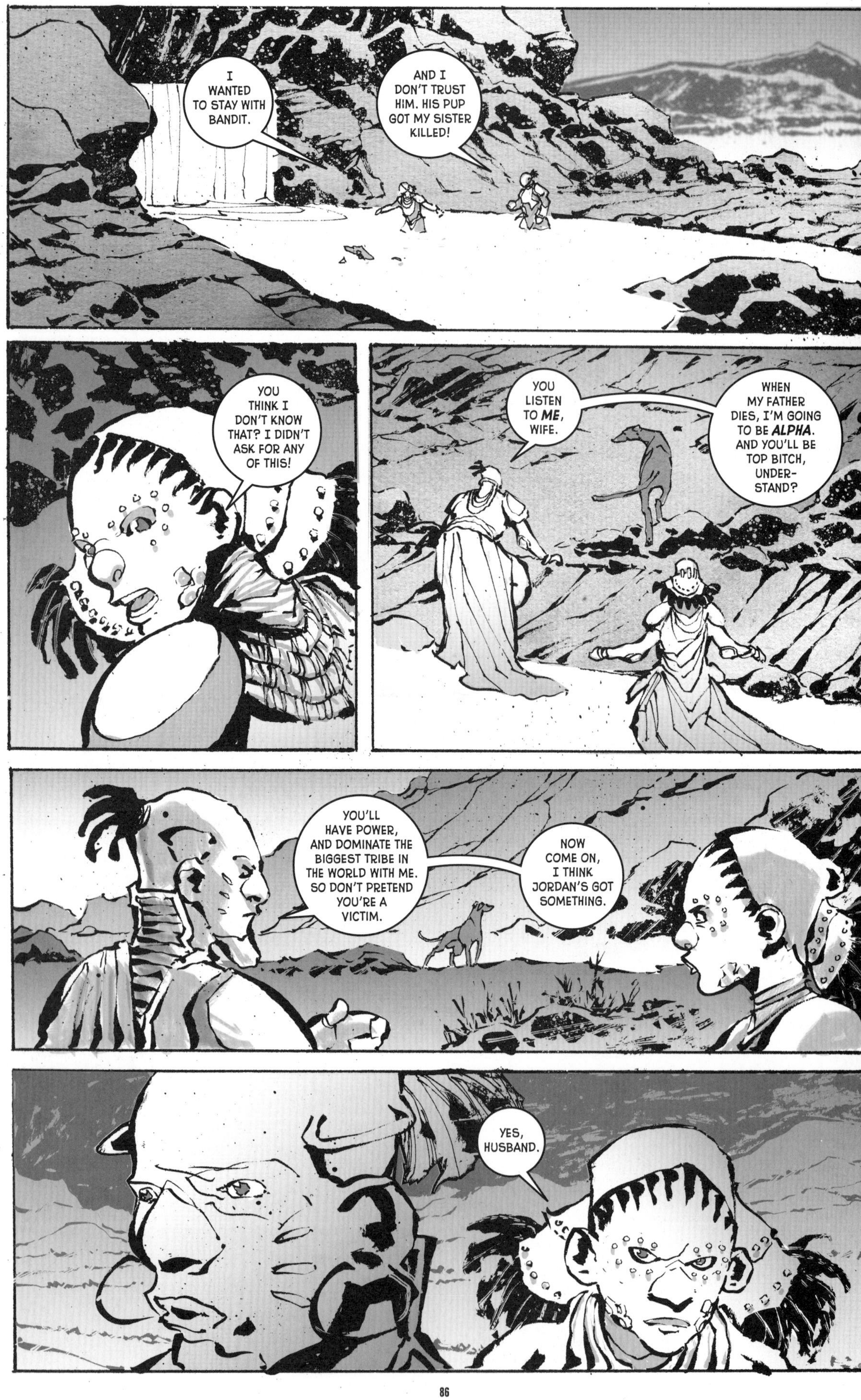
I WANTED TO STAY WITH BANDIT.
AND I DON'T TRUST HIM. HIS PUP GOT MY SISTER KILLED!
YOU THINK I DON'T KNOW THAT? I DIDN'T ASK FOR ANY OF THIS!
YOU LISTEN TO *ME*, WIFE.
WHEN MY FATHER DIES, I'M GOING TO BE *ALPHA*. AND YOU'LL BE TOP BITCH, UNDER-STAND?
YOU'LL HAVE POWER, AND DOMINATE THE BIGGEST TRIBE IN THE WORLD WITH ME. SO DON'T PRETEND YOU'RE A VICTIM.
NOW COME ON, I THINK JORDAN'S GOT SOMETHING.
YES, HUSBAND.

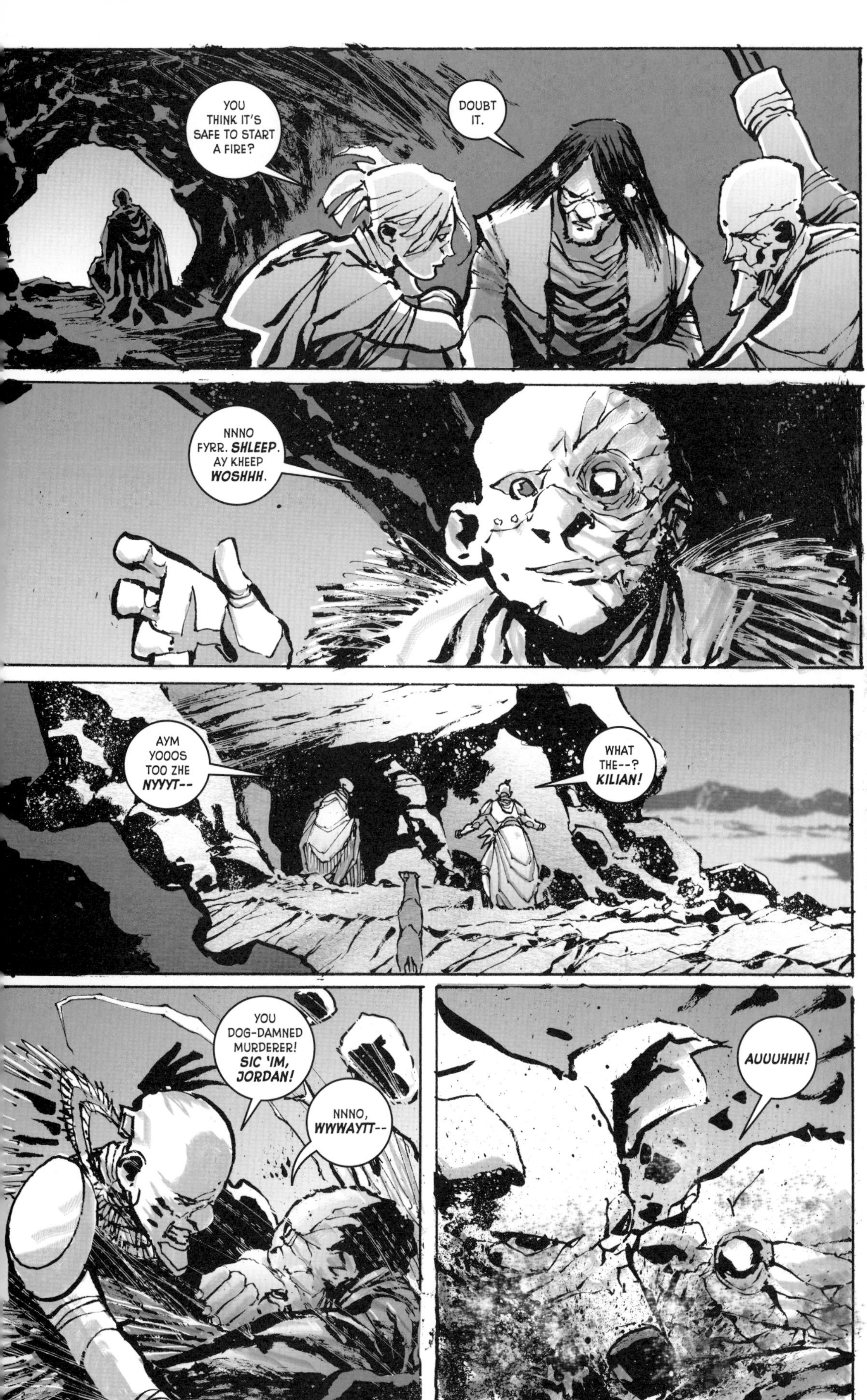
YOU THINK IT'S SAFE TO START A FIRE?
DOUBT IT.
NNNO FYRR. **SHLEEP**. AY KHEEP **WOSHHH**.
AYM YOOOS TOO ZHE **NYYYT--**
WHAT THE--? **KILIAN!**
YOU DOG-DAMNED MURDERER! **SIC 'IM, JORDAN!**
NNNO, **WWWAYTT--**
AUUUHHH!

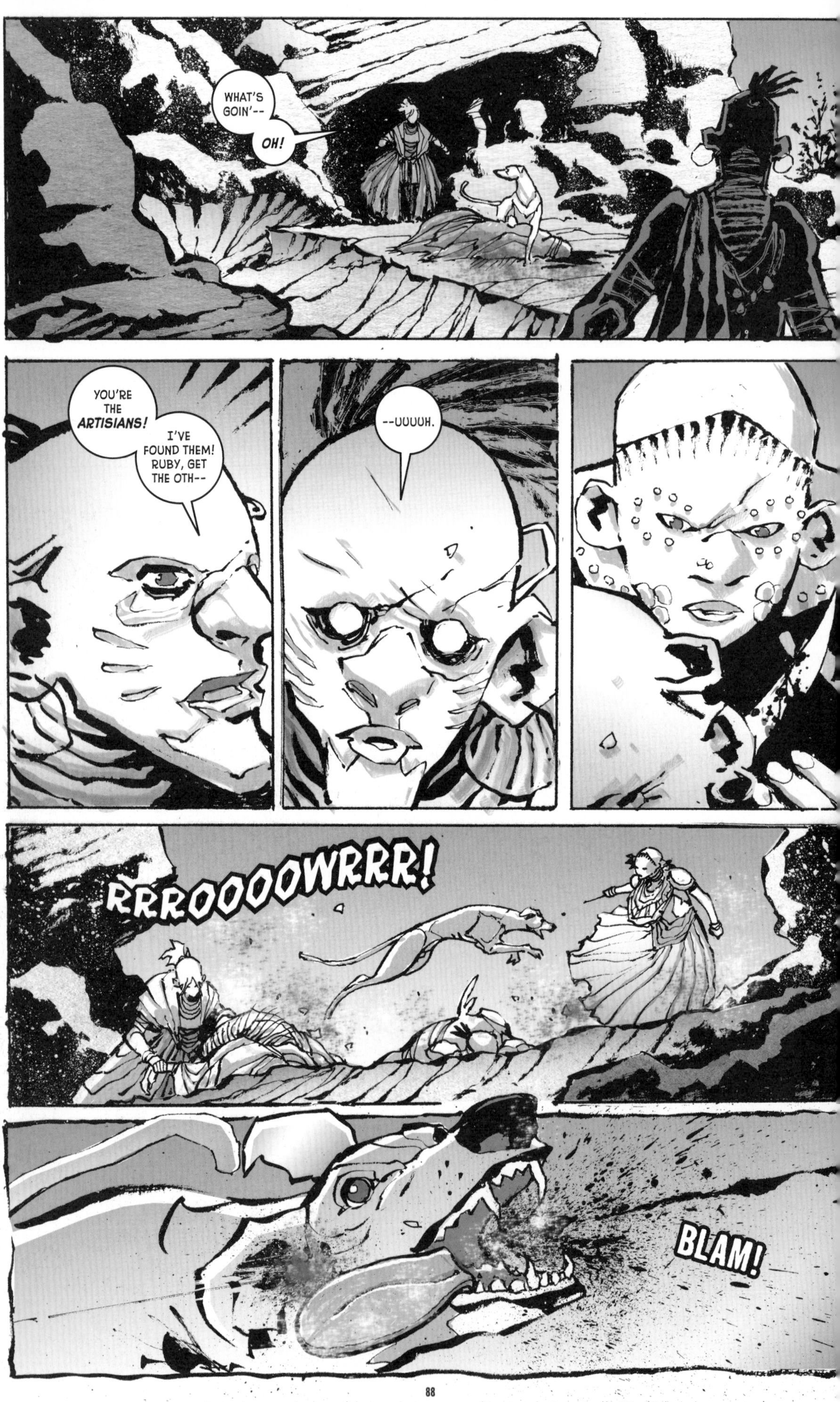

WHAT'S GOIN'--
OH!
YOU'RE THE ARTISIANS!
I'VE FOUND THEM! RUBY, GET THE OTH--
--UUUUH.
RRROOOOWRRR!
BLAM!

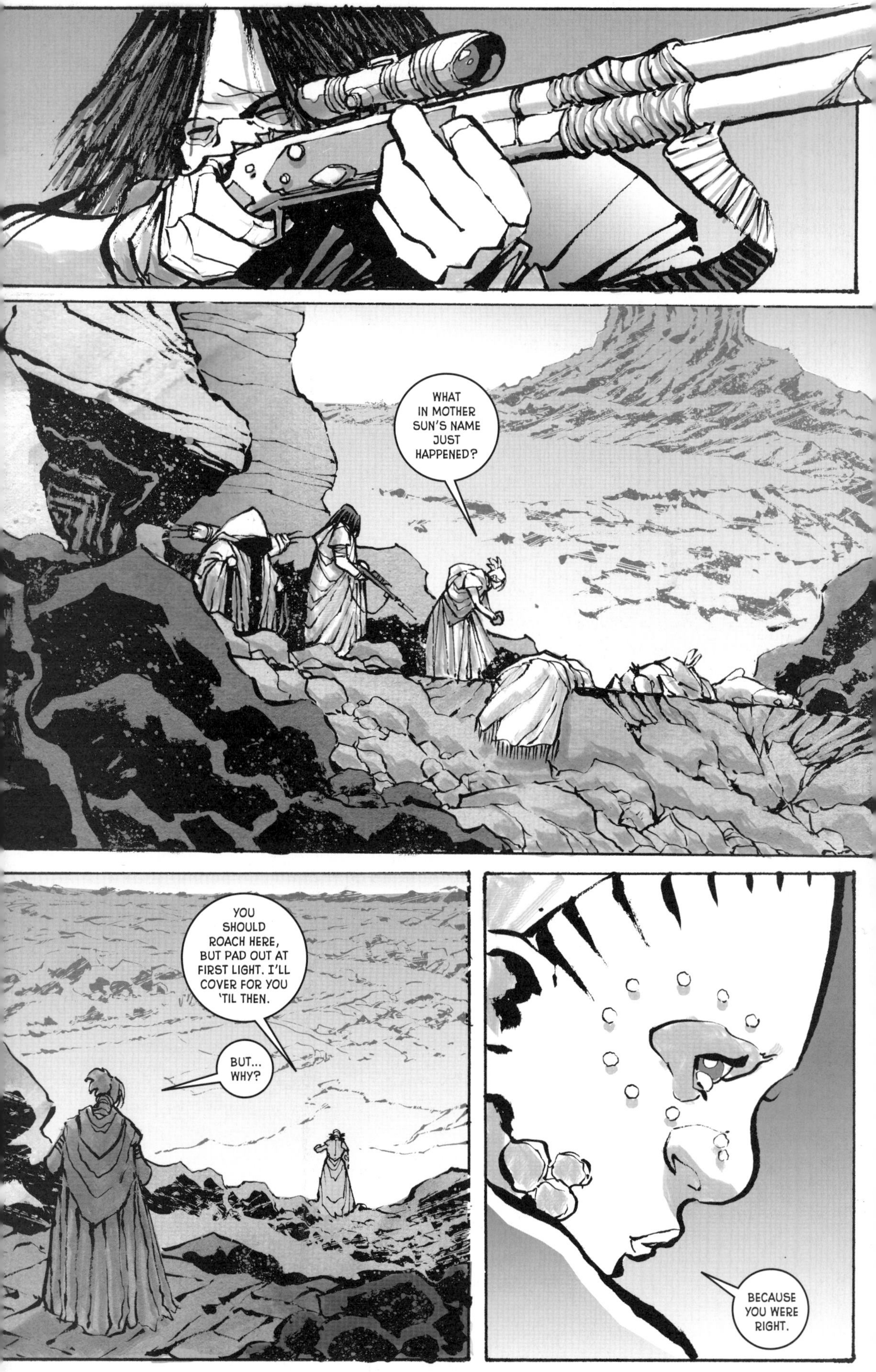
WHAT IN MOTHER SUN'S NAME JUST HAPPENED?
YOU SHOULD ROACH HERE, BUT PAD OUT AT FIRST LIGHT. I'LL COVER FOR YOU 'TIL THEN.
BUT... WHY?
BECAUSE YOU WERE RIGHT.

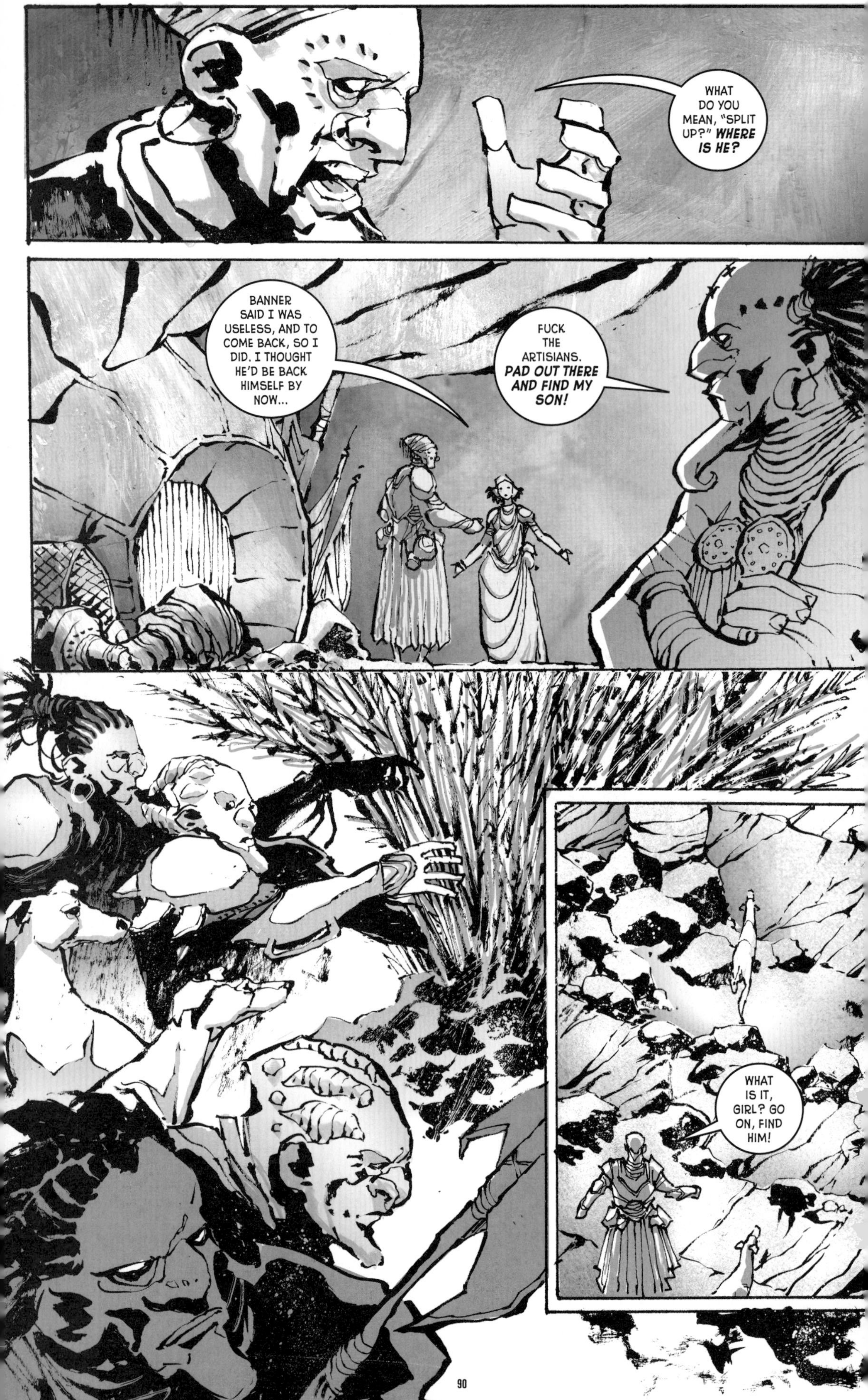
WHAT DO YOU MEAN, "SPLIT UP?" ***WHERE IS HE?***
BANNER SAID I WAS USELESS, AND TO COME BACK, SO I DID. I THOUGHT HE'D BE BACK HIMSELF BY NOW...
FUCK THE ARTISIANS. ***PAD OUT THERE AND FIND MY SON!***
WHAT IS IT, GIRL? GO ON, FIND HIM!

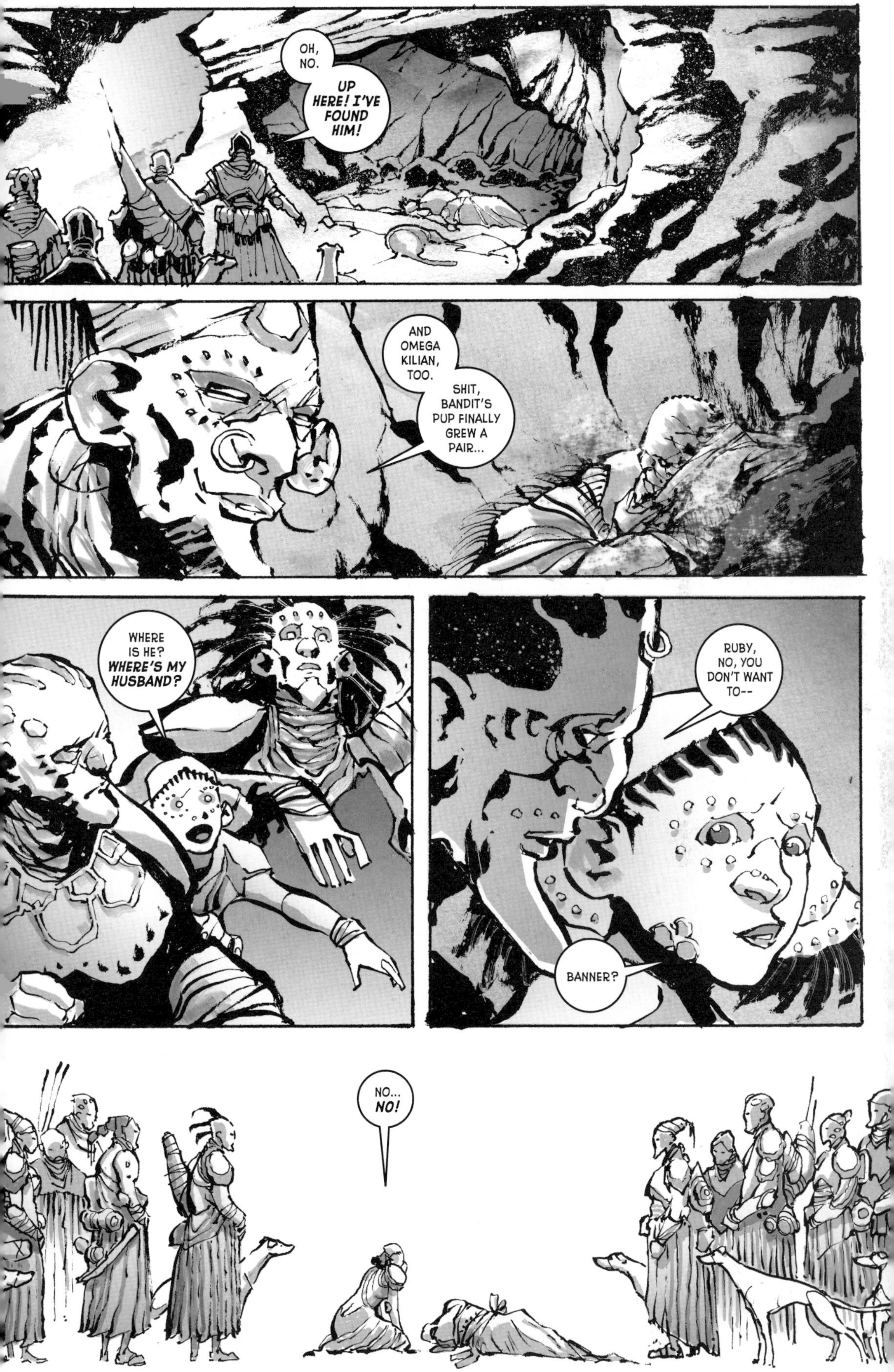
OH, NO.
UP HERE! I'VE FOUND HIM!
AND OMEGA KILIAN, TOO.
SHIT, BANDIT'S PUP FINALLY GREW A PAIR...
WHERE IS HE? WHERE'S MY HUSBAND?
RUBY, NO, YOU DON'T WANT TO--
BANNER?
NO... NO!

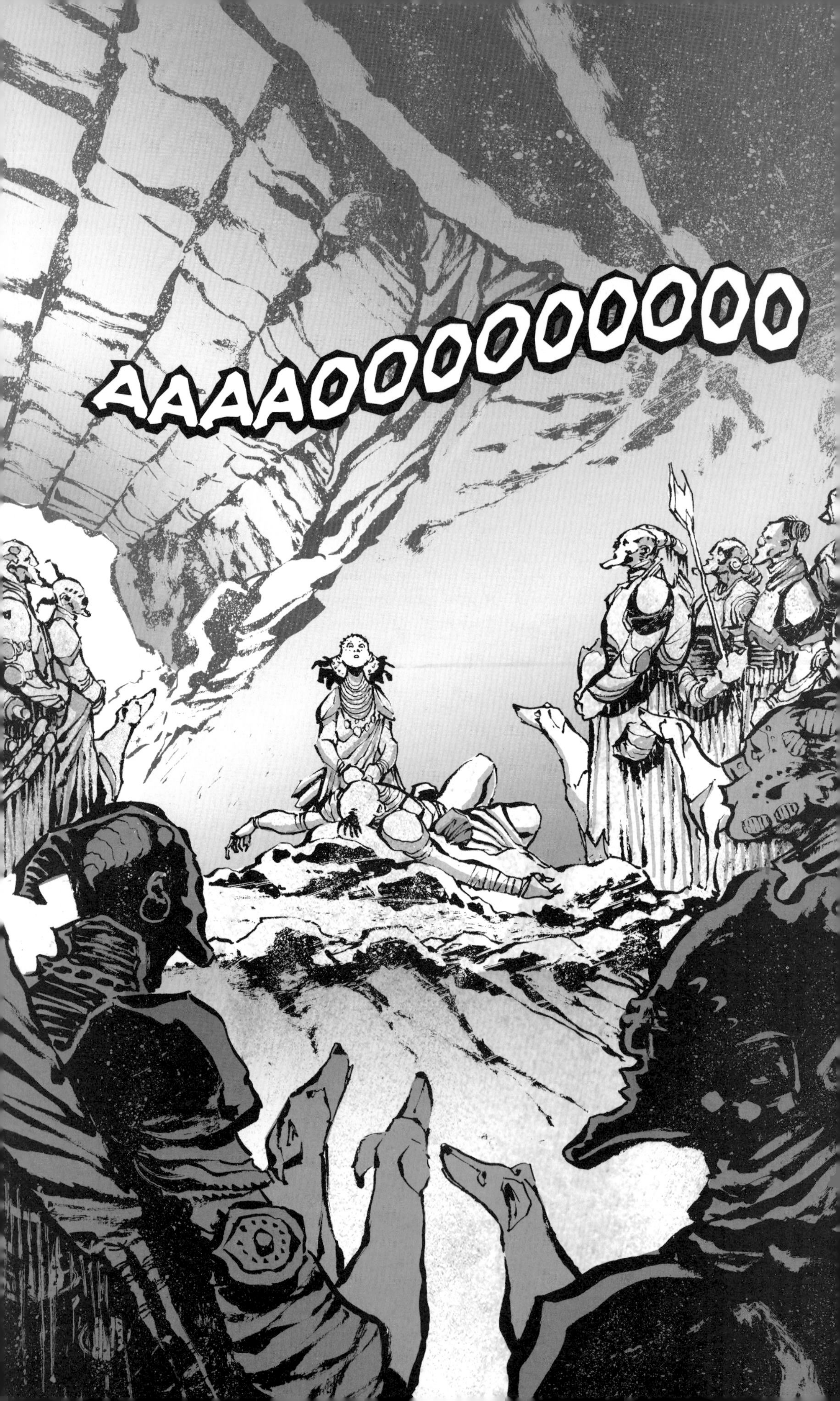
AAAAOOOOOOOOO

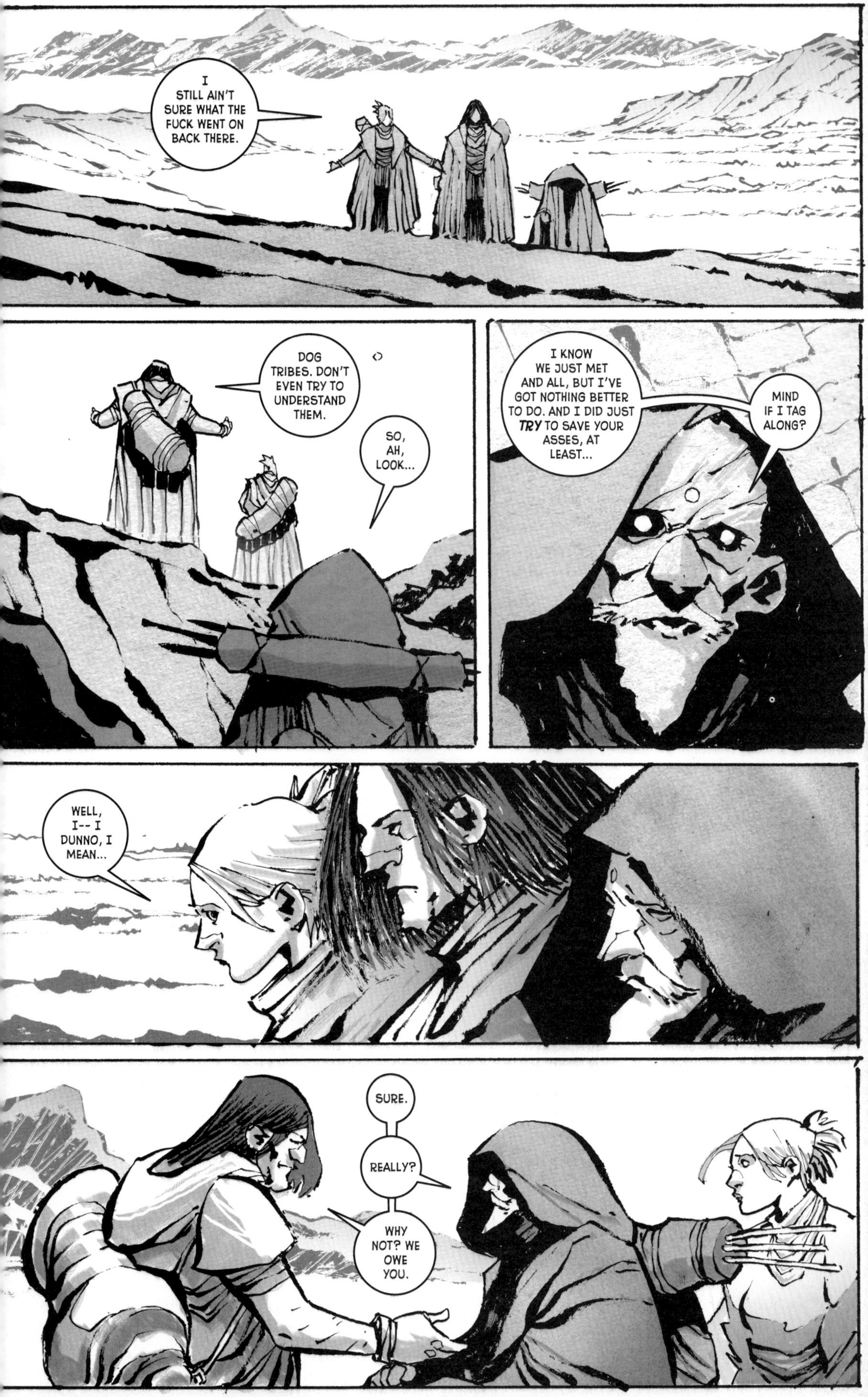
I STILL AIN'T SURE WHAT THE FUCK WENT ON BACK THERE.
DOG TRIBES. DON'T EVEN TRY TO UNDERSTAND THEM.
SO, AH, LOOK...
I KNOW WE JUST MET AND ALL, BUT I'VE GOT NOTHING BETTER TO DO. AND I DID JUST TRY TO SAVE YOUR ASSES, AT LEAST...
MIND IF I TAG ALONG?
WELL, I-- I DUNNO, I MEAN...
SURE.
REALLY?
WHY NOT? WE OWE YOU.

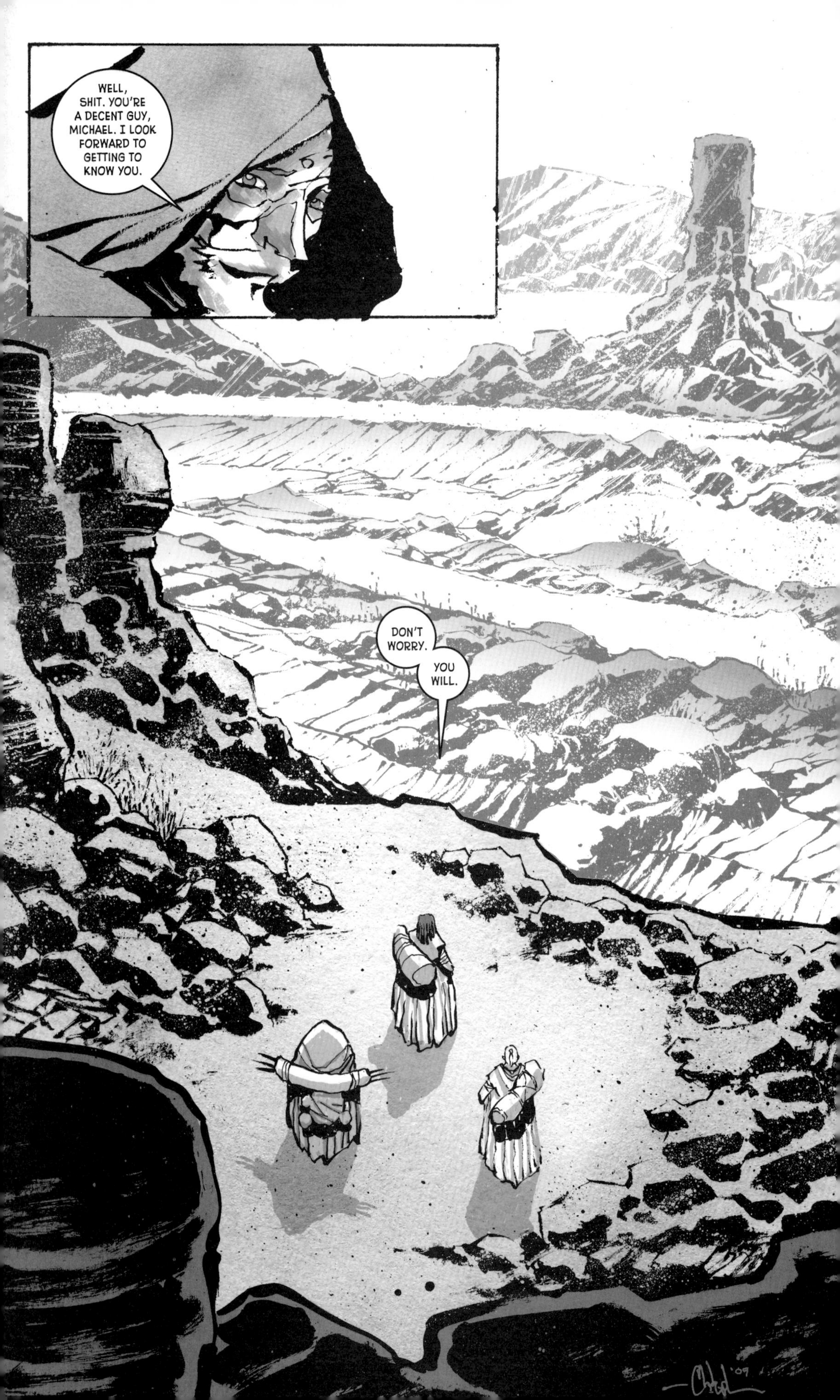
WELL, SHIT. YOU'RE A DECENT GUY, MICHAEL. I LOOK FORWARD TO GETTING TO KNOW YOU.
DON'T WORRY.
YOU WILL.

TO BE CONTINUED

CREATION OF A
DOG TRIBE

When designing any new culture for a story, it's not unusual to write pages and pages of notes and research that never make it "onto the page". But all that work isn't wasted. It helps to give a consistency and grounding to the writing of the culture that's vital if they're to feel real to the reader. The Dog Tribes were no exception — though, being a hound lover myself, they were a little easier than some of the cultures I've created for this book!

Here, then, is the culmination of all that research, summarised in a letter I sent to **Christopher Mitten** along with the first script of this story arc, and some of Christopher's sketches and pencils showing his design work for the Tribes. — **Antony Johnston**

Chris--

Most of the following aspects will be expanded on during the course of the story, but I figured you'd want as much info upfront as possible.

Dog tribes are built around human interpretations of hound behavior. They are loyal to the pack, follow a very strict hierarchy, have a unique code of honor (which has little to do with what other humans might regard as honor), regard lying and cheating as the worst of crimes, and will regularly test each other and vie for a better position in the hierarchy. Trying to improve your standing, and place yourself above another in the rankings, is normal and expected.

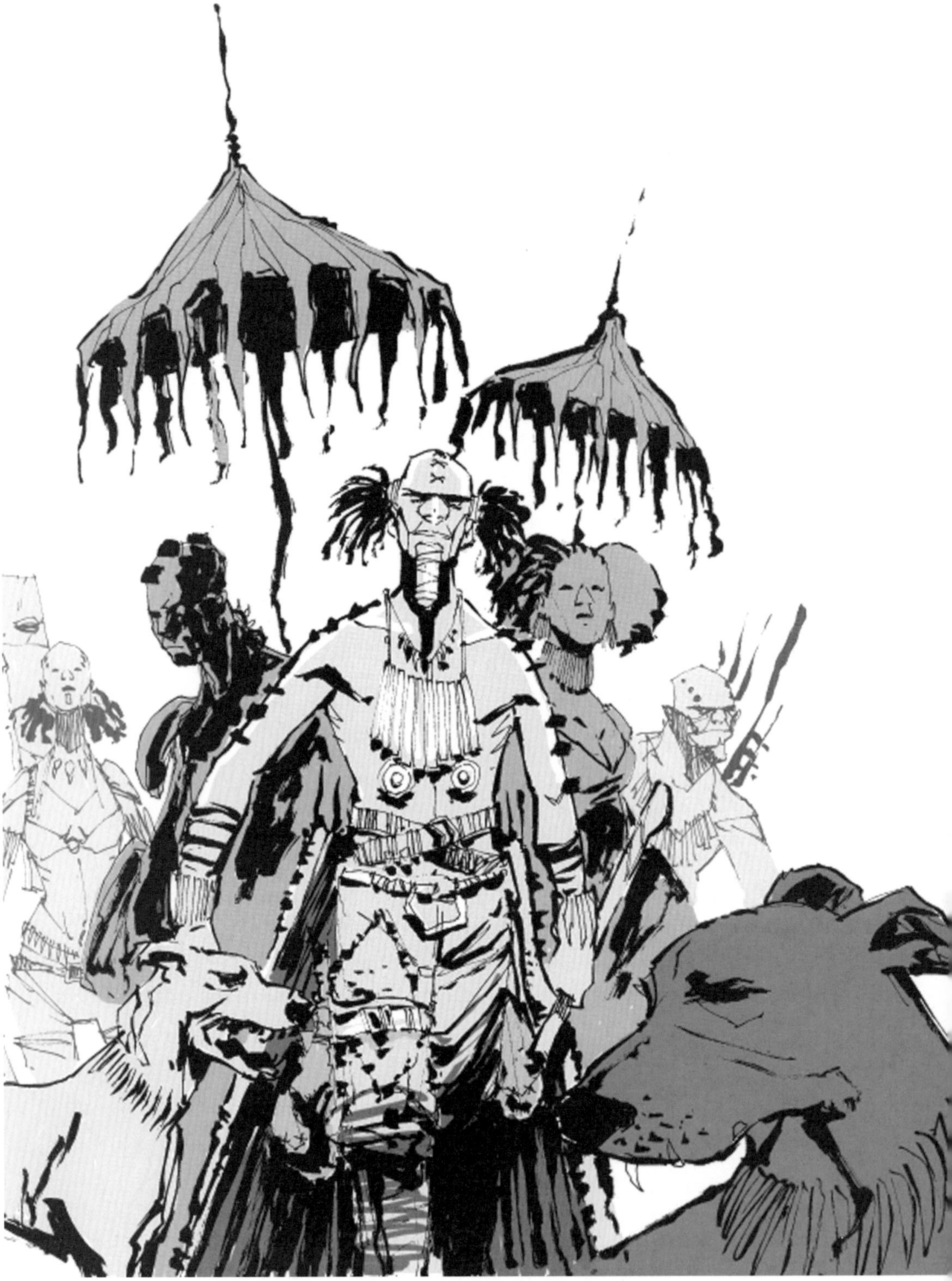

So we have a sort of counterpoint to the Newbegin council, here -- plenty of powerplay and politics, but without the backstabbing.

Normal human/hound ratio is about 2:1. Every adult man in a tribe has two hounds. Every adult woman, whether married or not, has one. Every child also has one. Any 'surplus' hounds the tribe has beyond this number belong to the tribal leader, whose title is

"Alpha". If someone loses a hound, they are gifted one from this 'pool' of dogs in a ceremony.

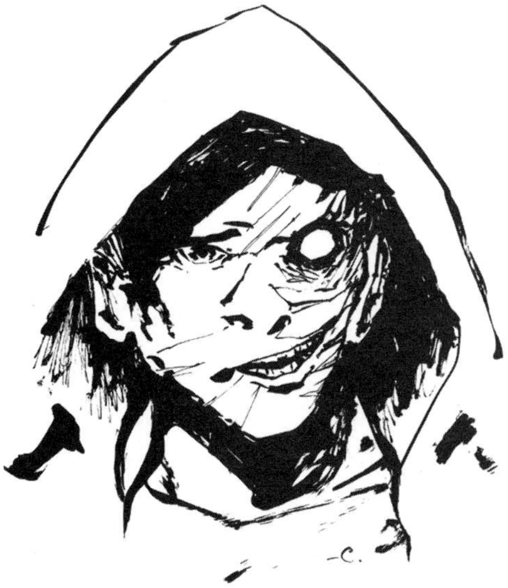

When making a journey, The dogs either walk alongside their masters, or will walk loose around the tribal group, like a guard perimeter. None of the dogs will stray more than 50-100 yards from the nearest human member, though.

NOTE that all Tribe hounds are controlled without leashes, harnesses or any other kind of restraint. They do not wear collars, or any other kind of decoration. The dogs do have 'ceremonial outfits', which we'll get to see later in this story arc, but for normal purposes they're unadorned. The main reason for this is so they can hunt without giving themselves away.

Also, these are the best-trained and most loyal dogs you'll ever meet. It's a catch-22: they need to be silent to hunt, therefore they need to be extremely well-trained, therefore collars aren't necessary.

Their most common prey are stray goats and desert rats, by the way.

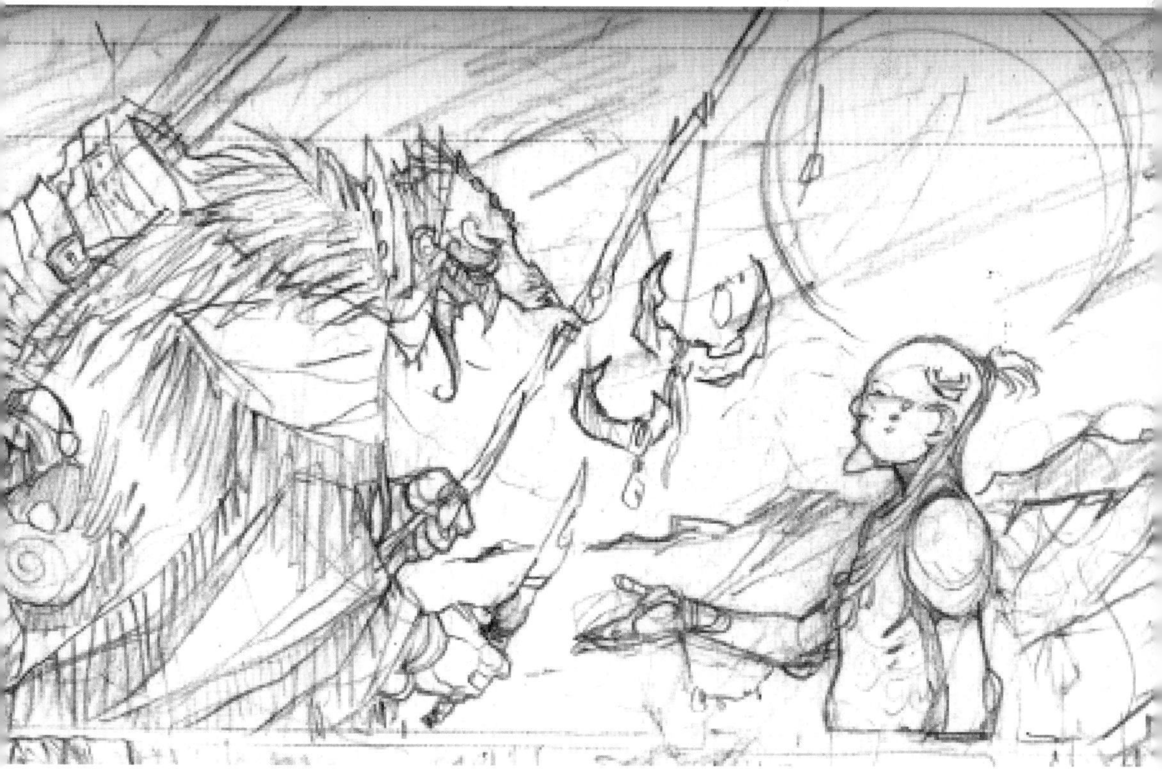

One exception is pups. Pups -- which includes any hound up to the age of 3 -- do wear collars, because they're still in training. The removal of a hound's collar, signifying its maturity into adulthood, is an important ceremony for the tribe.

The normal resting state of the hounds -- that is, when not required to walk or eat -- is to sleep. This is an evolutionary trait of all running dogs. When required to run they can reach speeds up to 40 mph in a matter of seconds, and maintain it for up to three or four miles... after which they'll be completely exhausted.

Consequently, when not required to run, they sleep to conserve as much energy as possible. This is no exaggeration -- sighthounds will normally sleep for up to 18 hours a day! Now you know why the pic ref I sent you features a lot of shots of dogs lying down.

-- Antony
May 2008, England

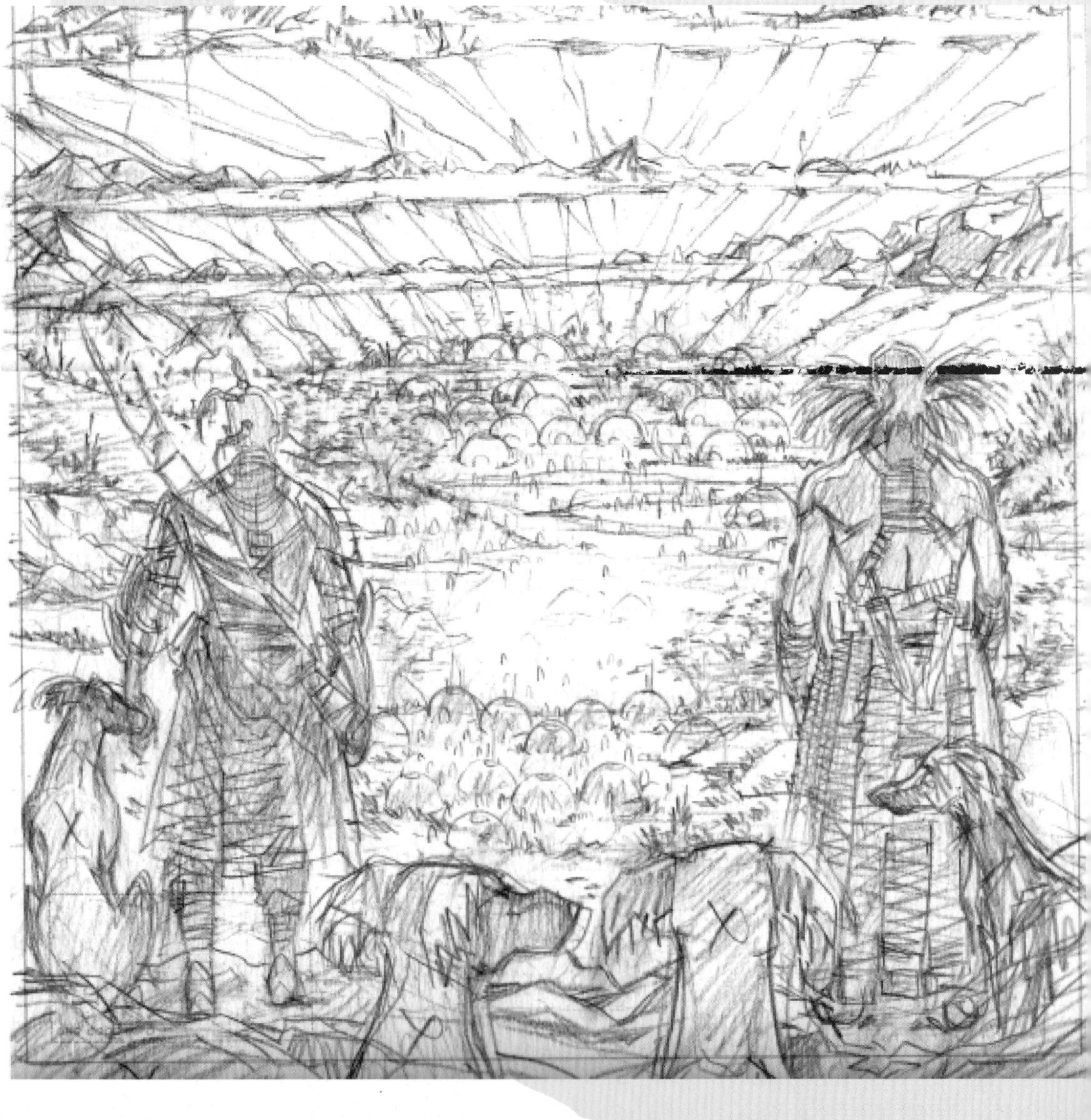

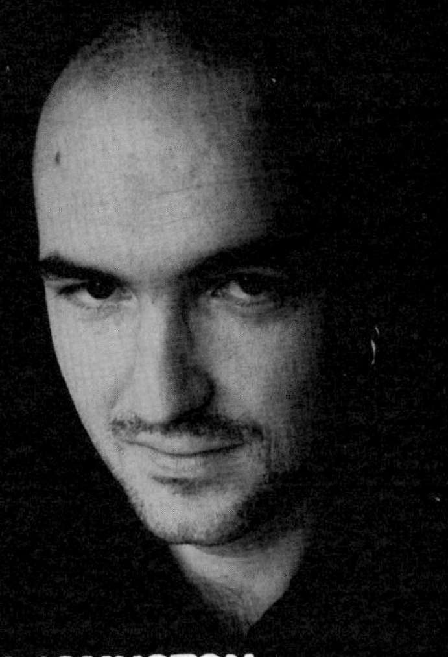

Born and raised in central England, Antony is an award-winning writer in a wide range of genres and media, including graphic novels, comic series, books, videogames and animation. He lives in Northern England and wears a lot of black.
ANTONYJOHNSTON.COM

ANTONY JOHNSTON

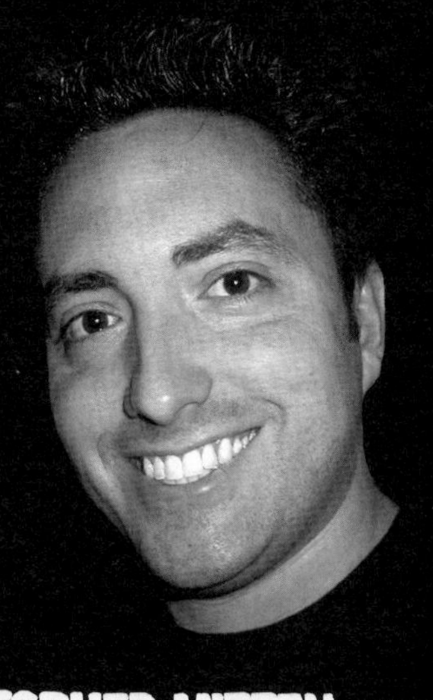

Originally from the cow-dappled expanse of southern Wisconsin, Christopher now roams the misty wilds of suburban Chicago, drawing little people in little boxes. In addition to WASTELAND, he's illustrated graphic novels such as PAST LIES and LAST EXIT BEFORE TOLL (also from Oni Press), and contributed to the COMIC BOOK TATTOO anthology from Image Comics.
CHRISTOPHERMITTEN.COM

CHRISTOPHER MITTEN

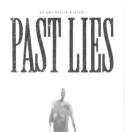

AND CHRISTOPHER MITTEN

THE
TOMB

THE TOMB
CHRIS MITTEN,
NUNZIO DEFILIPPIS
& CHRISTINA WEIR

160 PAGES • $14.95 US
ISBN 978-1-929998-95-1

ANTONY JOHNSTON & BRETT WELDELE
JULIUS

JULIUS
ANTONY JOHNSTON
& BRETT WELDELE

160 PAGES • $14.95 US
ISBN 978-1-929998-80-7

NEAL SHAFFER • CHRISTOPHER MITTEN • DAWN PIETRUSKO
LAST EXIT BEFORE TOLL
TRUCK STOP
CAFE

LAST EXIT BEFORE TOLL
NEAL SHAFFER,
CHRISTOPHER MITTEN
& DAWN PIETRUSKO

96 PAGES • $9.95 US
ISBN 978-1-929998-70-8

SPOOKED
ANTONY JOHNSTON
ROSS CAMPBELL

SPOOKED
ANTONY JOHNSTON
& ROSS CAMPBELL

168 PAGES • $14.95 US
ISBN 978-1-929998-79-1

ANTONY JOHNSTON
MIKE NORTON
CLOSER
LEANNE BUCKLEY

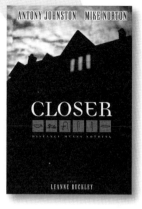

CLOSER
ANTONY JOHNSTON,
MIKE NORTON
& LEANNE BUCKLEY

160 PAGES • $14.95 US
ISBN 978-1-929998-81-4

THREE DAYS IN EUROPE
by
ANTONY JOHNSTON
&
MIKE HAWTHORNE

THREE DAYS IN EUROPE
ANTONY JOHNSTON
& MIKE HAWTHORNE

144 PAGES • $14.95 US
ISBN 978-1-929998-72-2

HRISTOPHERMITTEN.COM